THE BOOK OF ROTTERS

THE BOOK OF ROTTERS

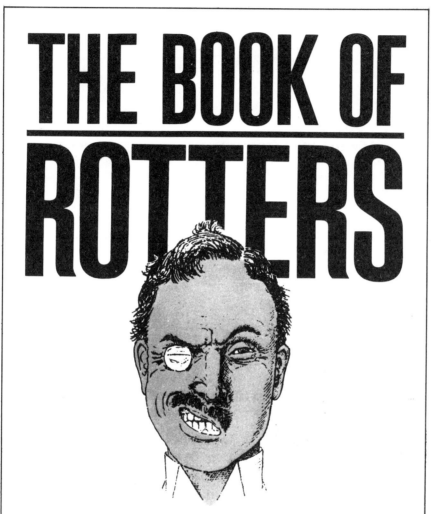

ALAN BOLD & ROBERT GIDDINGS

MAINSTREAM
PUBLISHING

First published in 1985 by
MAINSTREAM PUBLISHING COMPANY
(EDINBURGH) LTD.
7 Albany Street
Edinburgh EH1 3UG

The publishers are grateful to Alice Bold for her help and co-operation
for many of the illustrations reproduced in this volume.

ISBN 0 906391 72 5

Typeset in 11/12 Times by Studioscope in conjunction with Mainstream Publishing.
Printed by Billing & Sons, Ltd. Worcester.

CONTENTS

FOREWORD

Some of the great thinkers of the late nineteenth century perceived the individual as a creature clinging to a planet swept by vast impersonal forces. According to advanced Victorian opinion, man did not make the world in his own image but simply conformed to a predetermined economic or biological or sexual pattern. Under the influence of such determinism it became fashionable, in intellectual circles, to suspend value judgements and regard human history in schematic terms devoid of personalities.

In the popular mind, though, life remains a melodrama created by spotlessly pure heroes (or heroines) and dastardly villains — or rotters, as we prefer. Rotters do not commit involuntary acts; they are motivated. They know exactly what they are doing and it is this knowledge that makes them rotten. We do not believe, for example, that Lizzie Borden murdered her father and stepmother because she suffered from psychomotor epilepsy. We believe she acted atrociously because she decided to do so. The same goes for Ruth Ellis: rotters' crimes may be passionate but they are also planned.

In selecting the rotters on the following pages we established some principles of exclusion. We did not want to catalogue, yet again, the brutalities of an Adolf Hitler because, as the works of Hannah Arendt have pointed out, the evil of the Nazis is essentially banal. Nor did we wish to wallow in the careers of such distressingly revolting killers as the Moors murderers or the Yorkshire Ripper since the principals come across so clearly as subhuman.

We chose rotters who are recognisably human and apparently responsible for their actions. Our murderers are, invariably, characters who were accepted by contemporaries as an integral part of the social environment. What they did, therefore, genuinely roused the public to moral indignation. Admittedly, Al Capone (for instance) seems an odd entry, in this context, but we admitted his sort because a part of the American establishment not only co-operated with gangsters but supported them. Capone did not seem out of place in the Chicago that sustained him. He (and Genghis Khan, for that matter) had, of course, more opportunity for rottery than most.

Eric Partridge's *Dictionary of Slang* defines the rotter as 'an objectionable person'. We have objected to murderers, literary thieves, forgers, mobsters, spies, swindlers and the like. Strangely enough, the compilation of the book has been an edifying experience for we have identified the enemy in our midst in all his and her variety. Reader, you have been warned!

ALAN BOLD
ROBERT GIDDINGS

EUGENE ARAM

1704-59

EUGENE ARAM was a man of brilliant academic ability and outstanding
linguistic skills who committed a base crime from very selfish motives. It is
hard, when contemplating the evidence, to believe that one man could kill
another for so little. It is even harder to credit that Aram, a scholar of Latin,
Greek, Hebrew and the Celtic languages, a budding philologist of outstanding
potential, could murder a fellow human being, and live with the deed on his
conscience for so long. His victim met his end on 7 February 1745, and Aram
was not brought to justice until 1759.

Aram's birth was lowly and his parents had not the income to develop his
intellectual gifts by providing him with the right kind of schooling. When he
was sixteen he left Ramsgill, the village where he was born, and travelled from
Yorkshire to London, where he became book-keeper in a counting house. He
was taken ill with smallpox after a year and sent home.

In some ways illness was a blessing in disguise as it gave him the time to
further his studies. He immersed himself in the classics. He then tried a career
rather more congenial to his temperament — teaching. He married and in 1734
he moved to Knaresborough. His learning became a local legend, and it was
said he had an unrivalled knowledge of Chaldean, Hebrew and heraldry as
well as Latin and Greek. He was a most gentle teacher and seemed a mild and

retiring person. But there were other aspects to his character which none guessed at.

He made several friends in the town. He was very close with one Richard Houseman, a flax-dresser, and with Daniel Clark, a shoemaker. In 1744 Clark married a young lady who had a dowry of £200. This gave Aram and his friends an idea by means of which they hoped to heave themselves out of the financial rut for good.

It was very simple. Clark had become a man of substance. He could now obtain some valuable goods on credit. They could then dispose of these goods for ready money and share the loot. Clark was especially taken with the plot and acted his role superbly. Among the items he collected from various shopkeepers in February 1744 were to be found linen and woollen goods, leather of various kinds, a silver milkpot, items of jewelry, several expensive volumes, including Pope's *Homer* and Chambers *Dictionary*. Over and above this he went to several public houses and, on the strength of holding a wedding party soon, borrowed much silver plate and drinking vessels. On 8 February he disappeared.

The tradesmen looked to Eugene Aram and Richard Houseman for the return of their goods. When their households were searched some of the property was discovered, but the silver and jewelry had gone. However suspicious the authorities were, nothing could be proved. A means for detaining Richard Houseman was discovered — he was arrested for debt. Aram paid off the sum. Houseman had to be released. Aram then paid up what was still owing on his own house and left the area. The gossip died down, and the disappearance of Clark and the strange behaviour of Aram was forgotten. Then in August 1758 a workman employed at a lime-kiln at Thistlehill found some human bones. Word went round that this must be all that was left of Clark. Then Eugene Aram's wife, whom he had left behind him when he quit the area so suddenly, made an amazing statement. She deposed that Clark had been murdered, and that Houseman and her husband were the guilty parties. Her story was a startling one.

At the inquest she said that on 7 February 1744 she had been doing housework when Eugene came home. She was told to bank the fire up and to light a fire in the bedroom upstairs. She went to bed and at two o'clock in the morning Clark and Houseman arrived. She could hear the three of them talking. About an hour later her husband asked for one of her kerchiefs for Richard Houseman to tie round his head. She noticed that Clark was carrying a sack laden with objects of some weight. The three went out. At five in the morning she heard Houseman and Eugene come back. They did not seem to have Clark with them. She pretended to go to sleep but listened to the conversation between Houseman and her husband. They had obviously been up to something. Houseman was concerned in case she knew what was going on. 'Don't worry,' she heard her husband say, 'if she interferes we can shoot her.' When she heard them leave the house again, she raked through the ashes and found the remains of the scarf they had taken. It was stained with blood. She accused Houseman and Eugene of killing Clark, but they pretended not to know what she was talking about. Richard Houseman was now obviously shaken by this evidence, but he insisted that the bones which had been discovered, though they might have led Mrs Aram to have made this statement, were not actually the bones of the late Clark.

Richard Houseman then made a statement, in which he admitted being present when Clark was murdered by Aram. The body was laid to rest in St Robert's Cave. The cave was subsequently searched and the remains of Clark's body found exactly in the position that Houseman had described. Aram was traced to King's Lynn in Norfolk, where he was employed as an assistant master in a school. He was brought to trial on 3 August 1759 at York Assizes.

Richard Houseman testified against Eugene Aram, who denied everything that he deposed. Aram's defence of himself was brilliant. He concentrated not so much on demonstrating his innocence, as on discrediting the evidence against him. The body had been discovered near an old hermitage — he made great play of this: 'of all places in the world, none could have mentioned any place wherein there was a greater certainty of finding bones than a hermitage, except (he should point out) a graveyard. It has scarce or never been heard of but that every cell contains or contained these relics of humanity, some mutilated, some entire.'

It was only to be expected, he went on to suggest, that in such caves solitary bodies would be found, as they were the remains of anchoresses and hermits. Skeletons were frequently to be found in this area: 'Now it seems another skeleton has been discovered by some labourer which was fully as confidently averred to be Clark's as this . . . must some of the living, if it be promised some interest, be made answerable for all the bones that the earth has concealed and chance exposed?' He also did his best, and a very good best it was, to discredit the other circumstantial evidence against him, citing examples where people had been accused and convicted of murdering victims who were then later seen alive and well.

He was found guilty and sentenced to be hanged. While in custody he attempted suicide. He was hanged at Knaresborough and his body hung in chains. As it fell to pieces his widow collected the bones and gave them decent burial. Such was the end of Eugene Aram, who had gifts that might have contributed to the genius of his country, but who murdered a fellow citizen for material gain.

GIUSEPPE BALSAMO,
COUNT ALESSANDRO DI GAGLIOSTRO

1743-95

GIUSEPPE BALSAMO, one of the greatest of all charlatans, was born in Palermo. His mother and father were poor, and he ran away from school when he was barely thirteen. He was later sent to the monastery at Caltagirone. As a novice monk there, he gained a scanty knowledge of medicines and chemistry which he was to exploit as his stock in trade. He was thrown out of the monastery when he was twenty, and returned to Palermo.

Cagliostro's rituals and ceremonies.

He began a life of riot and petty crime. His uncle had placed him in the monastery in the hope that this might set Giuseppe up for life, and the grateful lad repaid his charity by robbing him and by forging his will. There is interesting evidence of his ability, shown very early in life, of duping otherwise quite sensible and intelligent people, by playing upon their hopes and ambitions — usually for material gain or the fulfilment of personal vanities. These abilities the young Balsamo was later to develop to the height of genius, but the latent skill in these arts showed itself very early in his career, in the episode of the goldsmith of Palermo. This unfortunate fellow allowed himself to be persuaded by Balsamo to accompany him to a large store of treasure secretly hidden in a cavern. Of course, Balsamo was the only one who knew where the treasure was situated, and the treasure could only be unearthed under cover of darkness. The generous Giuseppe led the goldsmith to the site at midnight, and there, lo and behold, he was set upon and robbed by a gang of Balsamo's young associates who were lying in wait for them.

This was a successful episode as far as Balsamo was concerned, but it made things too hot for him and he feared his life at the hands of the enraged goldsmith. He gained sufficiently out of the venture to be able to travel, and he left his native city with fifty ounces of gold. This was the beginning of his career as a travelling charlatan. He went first to Messina, where he fell in with a well-known alchemist, Althotas.

Althotas was a skilled operator and backed up his claims of being able to change base metals into gold by a genuine knowledge of oriental languages (impressive evidence of his learning and ability) and of occult sciences. He claimed to be able to weave silk from flax, and travelled to Alexandria with a store of this material which he sold at considerable profit. They were now a partnership and travelled through Egypt. They returned by way of Turkey, buying up a store of drugs, potions and trinkets of all kinds. Balsamo also soaked up the atmosphere which he was later to exploit so brilliantly, colouring his pretences with a convincing aura of the exotic, at a time when Egypt and the Middle East were being opened up not only to European trade, but also to the European imagination during the early stages of Romanticism.

Balsamo later claimed in his memoirs that they travelled to Mecca and Medina, for which there is little evidence, but they certainly were welcomed by the Grand Master of the Knights of Malta, who established the cunning pair in a laboratory where they could practice the art they claimed to have mastered — the conversion of pewter into gold. Althotas died in Malta, and Balsamo returned to Italy. He turned up in Rome, where he made a living of sorts by selling fake engravings. He resolved to grant himself a more imposing name, finally satisfying himself with Count Alessandro Cagliostro.

The Grand Master in Malta had given him written introductions to the leading figures in society, and Count Cagliostro used these to mix with the Establishment in Rome. His act was now really complete — he was aristocratic, sophisticated, bold and charming; to this he could add the claims that he was a mystic, an alchemist and purveyor of an elixir of life. He even claimed that he could render himself invisible (a gift which had he genuinely possessed it, would have prevented his being apprehended by the authorities at a later date). He now teamed up with the Roman beauty, Lorenza Feliciani, and, in 1771, the pair set out to fleece Europe, visiting Germany, London, Paris, Spain, Warsaw and other centres, posing as practitioners of the various arts of necromancy, alchemy, medicine and philosophy. A considerable measure of their success in these impostures must be attributed to the lavish display with which they travelled, with carriages, equerries and couriers in splendid liveries, and always putting up at the most splendid accommodation. Cagliostro hit on the idea of marketing his own brand of Freemasonry, and claimed to have rediscovered a branch of the brotherhood even more ancient than that which traced its origins to

Solomon's temple — the Grand Egyptian Lodge, which included females. The luscious Feliciani was naturally a Grand Priestess of the order. The ceremonies were terrifying but impressive, including as they did rituals with skulls, crossbones and other emblems of death and mortality. There is also evidence that sexual orgies played a large part in the activities of the Order. Nevertheless, he seems to have hit upon a winning formula, as the cult earned him a fortune. He was now at the height of his career. He added spiritualism to his repertory and held seances in which he gave displays of table-rapping.

He next became involved in the affair of the Queen's necklace, a scandal in which another of the participants was the wealthy and foolish Prince de Rohan, Cardinal Archbishop of Strasburg, whom Cagliostro had relieved of considerable wealth some time previously. The basis of the plot was simplicity itself. In 1783 Jeanne de Valois, Comtesse de la Motte, an adventuress who had caught the roving eye of Louis XVI, resolved to steal a diamond necklace from a jeweller by acting as if on behalf of Marie Antoinette. Cardinal de Rohan was at this time desirous of gaining the Queen's favour and was thus quite easily persuaded by Jeanne de Valois that the Queen wished him to act as her intermediary in the transaction. Jeanne even provided a woman who impersonated Marie Antoinette and granted — as he supposed — the Cardinal a personal interview, explaining the whole matter. Cagliostro was implicated in the plot, which involved forged documents as well as impersonation and — finally — the theft and breaking up of the valuable necklace. The culprits were traced and arrested. The Comtesse was branded and imprisoned, but de Rohan was released. When Cagliostro appeared before his accusers he astounded the court by his eloquent defence, and wild claims of second sight and mystic powers. He was spared imprisonment but discharged as a beggar, after serving a spell in the Bastille in 1785.

His brilliant career was now over, and, totally discredited, he passed through one capital city after another. In 1789 he was taken by the Inquisition and accused of Freemasonry, condemned to death, then pardoned, his sentence commuted to life imprisonment in the fortress of San Leone, near Urbino. Lorenza Feliciani ended her days in a nunnery. Thomas Carlyle, in his *Miscellanies*, accords him these words: 'Count Alessandro Cagliostro, pupil of the sage Althotas, foster-child of the Sheriff of Mecca, probable son of the last King of Trebizond; names also Acharat, and unfortunate child of nature; by profession healer of diseases, abolisher of wrinkles, Grand Master of the Egyptian Mason Lodge of High Science, spirit-summoner, gold-cook, Grand Coptha, prophet, priest, and thaumaturgic moralist and swindler; really a liar of the first magnitude, thorough-paced in all the provisions of lying, what one may call the *king of liars*.'

ELIZABETH BATHORI

1561-1615

THE TERRIBLE story of Countess Elizabeth Bathori was first made familiar to English readers by its inclusion in Sabine Baring-Gould's *Book of Werewolves* (1865) where she is made to seem a prototype of Stoker's Count Dracula. Her reputation has considerable historical justification. She was the wife of the Hungarian Count Nadasdy, whom she married when she was fifteen. Her marriage made her mistress of the castle of Csejthe in Transylvania. Her husband fought in the wars against the Turks, where he acquired an interest in torture and the implements of torture. The Count died in 1604 and his wife became obsessed with the retention of her own, once considerable, beauty.

The legend is that one day while administering what she regarded as well-earned discipline upon a servant-girl, the unfortunate girl's beating caused blood to splash upon Countess Bathori's face. When she cleansed her face of its stain she became convinced that it enhanced her beauty, and an insatiable appetite was born.

She bathed in virgins' blood each morning at dawn. Her assistants scoured the countryside for victims to supply her sanguine tub. A further refinement was her announcement that peasant blood was no longer good enough. It had to be aristocratic virgins' blood. She opened what was in effect a finishing school for the daughters of the nobility. Eventually her crimes overtook her and four corpses were discovered outside her castle. An investigation was carried out and the dreadful secrets of Csejthe castle were totally revealed. She was an aristocrat and therefore beyond the normal laws but an act of the Hungarian parliament was passed to deal with the matter. Her assistants were burnt alive but the Countess Elizabeth Bathori herself was bricked up in a small apartment at the back of her own castle where she died four years later. It was estimated that she had caused the deaths of six hundred and fifty young girls.

SAWNEY BEANE

15th century

THE STORY of Sawney Beane is buried deep in the folk memory of Scotland and first materialised in print in Captain Alexander Smith's *Complete History of the Lives and Robberies of the most Notorious Highwaymen, Robbers, etc.* (1719). In 1734 Charles Johnson elaborated on the tale in his *Complete History of the Lives and Actions of the Most Famous Highwaymen, Murderers, Street Robbers, etc.* All subsequent details about the Beanes are derived from Smith and Johnson.

Alexander (thus Sandy or Sawney) Beane was born, during the reign of James VI, near Edinburgh. Disinclined to work for a living, he left the Edinburgh area in the company of a like-minded young woman. Soon the couple set up home in a cave in the cliffs at Bennane Head, three miles north of Ballantrae. There they lived on the flesh of those they murdered and robbed. According to Smith and Johnson they carried the corpses to their lair, quartered them, salted and pickled the limbs and dried them for food.

The family expanded incestuously until it comprised of Sawney, his lady, eight sons, six daughters, eighteen grandsons and four granddaughters. It was a formidable force, a small army that had a ready supply of food.

Apparently the Beane tribe would attack passers-by *en masse* then prepare their bodies for human consumption. As outsiders who saw the Beanes never lived to tell the tale, the people of Ballantrae lived in a state of terror. People went missing and the only traces of them were the bits and pieces of human bodies that were washed up by the sea. For Sawney and his brood could not cope with all the flesh they had stored, so sometimes they threw the legs and arms of dried human bodies into the sea.

Because the entrance to the Beanes' cave was difficult to discover, the mystery was unsolved for more than two decades. Then, after a local fair, the Beanes lurked by the West Road and attacked a man and his wife riding home from the merriment. As Charles Johnson says: 'The man, to save himself as well as he could, fought very bravely against them with sword and pistol, riding some of them down by main force of his horse . . . In the conflict the poor woman fell from behind him and was instantly murdered before her husband's face; for the female cannibals cut her throat and fell sucking her blood with as great a lust as it had been wine. This done, they ript up her belly and pulled out her entrails.'

Still the man kept up his struggle and was rescued when some thirty folk, also returning from the fair, came to his assistance. The Beanes withdrew and retreated to their lair. None of them was captured in the skirmish but now the locals knew that the ogre of Ballantrae was actually a collection of murderous creatures.

A band of some four hundred horsemen was assembled, with bloodhounds to sniff out the lair of the Beanes. When the cave was discovered, the armed men who entered it were appalled at the spectacle they saw. Beane and his brood crouched together in a rock chamber which contained the gory evidence of their cannibalism. Johnson explains: 'Limbs, arms, thighs, hands and feet of men, women and children were hung up in rows like dried beef. A great many limbs lay in pickle; and a great mass of money, both gold and silver, with watches, rings, swords, pistols and a large quantity of clothes which they had taken from those whom they had murdered were thrown together in heaps, or hung up against the sides of the den.'

The human remains were buried on the sea-shore and the Beanes were taken to Leith where they were executed without trial. The penises of the men were cut off and thrown into fires, while the women watched; then the hands and legs of the men were cut off and they were left to bleed to death. When the men died the Beane women were thrown onto three separate fires and burned to death.

Sawney Beane: his incestuous brood robbed, killed, dismembered, smoked and ate their victims. Their fate was suitably gruesome, and all forty-eight died in agony.

CHARLES BECKER

1869-1915

CHARLES BECKER was the quintessential bent copper. He was a murderer and extortionist who ran a corrupt police department in New York and died in the electric chair. He was born in New York City, did not excel at school and rose through the ranks in the New York City Police Department to become Lieutenant. When Rhinelander Waldo became Police Commissioner he made Becker his aide. Waldo was impressed with Becker and next made him head of Special Squad Number One. This squad had an interesting and, for Becker, a very useful brief, to curtail the corruption, bribery, graft and prostitution which was then an open scandal in New York City. To do this Becker claimed (with justification) that he needed a special team of exceptionally strong-armed cops. What he really created was a criminal special patrol group.

Using his tough guys in uniform he developed a perfect protection racket. He raked 25% of the takings from gambling and prostitution in the Tenderloin and Broadway strips. Racketeers who refused to co-operate in Becker's arrangement found their premises received a visit from his boys. When they left these places they were wrecked. If clients continued to be uncooperative Lieutenant Becker brought evidence against them in court and they finished up inside. It was all so simple. The lesson was soon learned — it was far easier in the long run to pay up and shut up. Becker also stage-managed the means of collecting, employing some of the wierdest characters he could find to pick up the hush money. These men emphasised the power of Becker's message, as they conveyed their own sense of fear. There was 'Billiard Ball' Jack Rose, who was completely bald, the mad killer 'Big Jack' Zelig and Dracula look-alike Harry Vallon.

One man whom Becker had fleeced for years was the owner of a gambling joint named Herman 'Beansie' Rosenthal. Becker called at his club, The Hesper, once a week. From time to time, Becker used to take a dislike to his customers and this usually showed itself in his accusing them of disloyalty. He claimed that 'Beansie' was talking too much, and he demanded more of the club's income. 'Beansie' protested and so Becker had his terrorists wreck the place. He closed The Hesper down, put a patrolman on duty outside, and stationed policemen in Rosenthal's flat. Mrs Rosenthal had a breakdown.

Becker had now driven Rosenthal to breaking point. His business was shut down and his wife was ill. He decided to strike back. He went to the District Attorney, Charles S Whitman and spilled the beans. Whitman had wanted to nail something on Becker for a long time and what Rosenthal told him was music to his ears. He revealed the names of all of Becker's associates, the places, the amounts of money paid to Becker — enough to make an indictment of considerable substance. The District Attorney convened the grand jury to move the indictment.

Rosenthal was shot down in the street outside the Café Metropole on West 43rd Street on the night of 21 July 1911. The assassination was done on the orders of Becker. Although witnessed by numerous people, the killers believed that Becker's control of the Police Department would protect them. Lieutenant Becker had issued orders to ensure that if any witnesses turned in the number of the getaway vehicle the evidence would never be processed.

Eventually, the District Attorney found out that Becker's clan were hiding a witness to the killing in the cells where he would be unable to give evidence. He went to visit the witness and even though an officer loyally attempted to prevent his talking to him, Whitman was able to get the number of the vehicle. It was traced to 'Billiard Ball' Jack Rose.

Rose believed that Becker would save him and he stalled as long as he could, but in the end he thought that if he was going to sink, then he was not going to go down alone. He gave the names of the other killers Becker had briefed for the job. They all agreed in their story that they had been specifically employed by Becker.

Charles Becker was tried for Rosenthal's murder and convicted and executed in the electric chair on 7 July 1915. He was a man of heavy build and a large frame — well over six feet tall — and it horrifically required several jolts to kill him. Whitman became Governor of New York by the time Charles Becker was executed. Becker's wife had the following epitaph placed on her husband's tombstone: 'Charles Becker. Murdered July 7 1915. By Governor Whitman.'

COLONEL THOMAS BLOOD

1618-80

THE LIFE and career of Thomas Blood, full of violence and intrigue as it was, seems like a determined effort to justify the validity of his surname. Not a great deal is known about his early life. He was believed to have been born in Ireland, the son either of a blacksmith or an ironmaster. During the Civil War he fought on the Parliamentarian side and attained the rank of colonel. In a good war for him, he managed to gain possession of estates and property forfeited by supporters of Charles I and earned a goodly annual income from them. He was embittered by the Restoration, doubly so by the fact that he was deprived of his estates. This served to intensify his anti-royalist feeling and turned him into a harder Presbyterian.

He developed into a full-time conspirator. In 1663 he was involved in a plot to seize Dublin Castle and lay hands on the Duke of Ormonde, the Lord Lieutenant of Ireland, who had been one of the leaders of the group which intrigued for the return of Charles II. This was an attempt to overthrow royal power in Ireland. Its failure caused Blood to lie low, first in Ireland and then later in Holland. There is some evidence that he next conspired with the Fifth Monarchy Men in London. This strange religious sect drew most of its membership from Cromwell's army. They believed in the imminence of the millennium, the 'fifth monarchy' when Christ would return and rule the earth. Their moral code was based on that of Moses. The failure of their hopes caused them to turn against Cromwell, and their leaders were punished. But in the early years of the Restoration the sect again caused trouble. Their leader, Thomas Venner, and ten others were put to death. Blood escaped harm and then intrigued with the Covenanters in Scotland.

The Covenanters were a running sore in Charles II's attempts to maintain well-being in the north. The term Covenanter was used to describe all those who subscribed to the undertakings to defend the Reformed Church in Scotland. The Scottish Presbyterians supported the English Puritans in suppressing episcopacy. They were later persecuted by Cromwell and the Independents. Because Charles II needed Scottish support he signed the covenant in 1650, and again in 1651. In 1662 the covenant was declared unlawful. The nobility in Scotland supported the sovereign, but thousands of the Scottish population stood by the solemn league and covenant which they

19

had undertaken. Years of terrible persecution followed, and the movement was finally crushed at the battle of Bothwell Bridge in 1679. Many then took the Oath of Allegiance, but thousands whose conscience would not allow them to renege were sent to the American plantations. Thomas Blood was in his element in this kind of activity and is several times heard of during the crisis with the Covenanters. He was certainly present at the battle of Pentland Hills in 1666.

He escaped totally unscathed from his involvement in the Fifth Monarchy conspiracy, and the Covenanters. It was rumoured that he must have come to some arrangement with the government which had included his betrayal of comrades to the authorities. A man who had led military adventures in Ireland, worked as a spy for the Dutch in the Dutch Wars, conspired in Scotland and London against the government was now hardly likely to settle down to enjoy a quiet life — nor did he. In 1670 he was in Romford, calling himself Ayloffe and practising as a doctor of medicine. But he was planning to get his own back on the Duke of Ormonde, who was currently living in London.

Thomas Blood intended to rob Ormonde as he drove to a banquet at the Guildhall on 28 May 1670. Ormonde's coach was attacked by Blood and his ruffians, and Ormonde's life was certainly in danger. Thomas Blood fired his pistol at the former Lord Lieutenant of Ireland, but missed him. As help arrived, Blood dashed off in the failing light. He returned to hiding and plotted his greatest escapade, the robbery of the crown jewels.

The crown jewels were held in the Tower of London. Their Keeper was one Talbot Edwards, who was getting on in years. They were kept in a strong room, but from time to time Edwards allowed visitors to see them. The strong room was, in fact, part of Edwards' official residence. This fact was central in Blood's audacious scheme. In the early part of 1671 a country vicar and his good lady came to London. They were, of course, Thomas Blood and an accomplice. The parson asked permission to see the crown jewels, and this was granted. While viewing these precious objects, the parson's wife was taken ill and fainted. Talbot Edwards' wife was very resourceful in the help she administered to the parson's wife, and a friendship was deliberately cultivated by Blood and his partner in crime.

Mrs Edwards was the proud mother of a beautiful daughter, and anxious to secure a good match for her. She was very glad to learn from the parson's wife that her husband had a prosperous nephew who was looking for a wife. It was arranged informally to discuss the matter on 9 May and on that day the parson and a couple of friends arrived at Talbot Ewards' residence. They explained that the marriageable nephew would be arriving shortly. While they were waiting they asked Edwards if they could have a view of the famous crown jewels.

Totally duped, the kindly old man led them to the strong room. Here they immediately set upon him and beat him severely. Thomas Blood ran him through with his sword. This did not kill him, however. The immediate task was for the conspirators to stow the precious objects into the bag they had brought with them and escape with the booty. Blood flattened the crown so it could be stuffed in the bag. Some of the gems fell out, and he unceremoniously scooped them up and pocketed them. The sceptre would not go in the bag. One of Blood's partners was attempting to file through it when the alarm was raised. At that very moment they were interrupted. Talbot Edwards had a son who was serving in the army in Flanders. Unexpectedly he was on leave and called to visit his parents. He caught them red-handed.

This extraordinary piece of villainy had very nearly succeeded. In fact, Thomas Blood might well have escaped, but his horse slipped and he was arrested. He refused to be questioned by anyone but the king himself and was eventually interviewed by Charles II, in company with his brother James, Duke of York (later James II) and Prince Rupert. Blood explained to His Majesty that he was not altogether sorry the plot had misfired. He was disappointed to learn the real value of the property. 'I had thought the Crown itself to be worth £100,000, yet it seems the whole Regalia is valued only at a beggarly £6,000!' was his comment. The king was impressed with Blood's arrogance and bearing, and Rupert testified that he was a stout good fellow, even though at a certain stage in his military career he had deserted the royalist cause and gone over to Cromwell. Charles II asked him what he would do if he was to spare his life and Blood answered, 'I would endeavour to deserve it, Sire!' He was taken back to the Tower.

Not knowing what his fate was to be, Thomas Blood waited nearly a week. Charles II knew a second Dutch war was imminent, and he realised Blood would be useful to him. But he could not simply spare his life without first consulting Ormonde. He answered Charles II, 'If the King can forgive an attempt upon his Crown, I can easily pardon an attempt on my life!' Charles pardoned him, gave him a pension of £500 a year in Irish lands and a place at court. He was often to be seen swaggering about the town, over-dressed and over-loquacious. John Evelyn, the diarist, observed him at this stage of his career and recorded, 'I noted Mr Blood in a fine new perriwig. Exceeding pleasant and jocose. He is a tall, rough-boned man with small legs, a pock-marked face, and little hollow, blue eyes.'

Blood had always got on well with George, Duke of Buckingham, but in 1679 they seem to have fallen out, for he brought a charge against him of gross immorality. Buckingham sued Blood for £10,000, on the basis that he had sworn to a false statement. Blood lost his case but died on 24 August 1680 in the midst of these legal proceedings.

ANTHONY BLUNT

1907-83

ANTHONY BLUNT was one of the smoothest agents ever to be unmasked in Britain. Before Andrew Boyle's investigative classic, *The Climate of Treason* (London, 1979), exposed him as the Fourth Man in the spy-ring containing Burgess, Maclean and Philby, he was greatly respected as a powerful intellectual force in the English Establishment. In 1945 he succeeded Sir

Kenneth Clark as Surveyor of the Royal Pictures, in 1947 he was appointed Director of the Courtauld Institute and Professor of History of Art, and in 1956 he was knighted. He was also made Slade Professor of Fine Art at Oxford and Cambridge, given honorary degrees from Bristol, Durham, Paris and Oxford and became an honorary Fellow of Trinity College, Cambridge.

He got on famously with the Queen, was celebrated for his scholarly work on Poussin, and was recalled with affection, even awe, by contemporaries as distinguished as Louis MacNeice who in *The Strings Are False* (London, 1965) wrote, 'In my own house (at Marlborough College) the dominant intellectual was Anthony Blunt, who had a precocious knowledge of art and an habitual contempt for conservative authorities. He was very tall and very thin and drooping, with deadly sharp elbows and the ribs of a famished saint; he had cold blue eyes, a cutaway mouth and a wave of soft brown hair falling over his forehead . . . He truculently admitted that he preferred things to people. He considered it very low to talk of politics.'

After Marlborough, Blunt continued his education at Cambridge where he read, first, mathematics then modern languages. He graduated with a double first in 1930 and, as a result of a dissertation on Poussin, became a Fellow of Trinity in 1932. His clear, calculating mind — so incisive on aesthetic matters — attracted him to the theory of Marxism and the person of Guy Burgess, a younger Cambridge man. Blunt and Burgess were both members of 'The Apostles' who, in the words of Andrew Boyle, 'affected the graces of experts, though they were more adept at splitting literary and metaphysical hairs, and should have stuck to that'.

Though Blunt claimed that Burgess had recruited him to the service of Soviet intelligence it was probably the other way round. Blunt had a special status as a precocious don and he was equipped with a dominant personality. He was a talent spotter for the Soviet Union, while at Cambridge, and spread the Marxist word with skill. In 1979 Blunt insisted that his motives were ideologically impeccable and that he wanted to use Marxism as a weapon against Hitler. However, there is no doubt that he enjoyed duplicity and relished the role of talent spotter for Stalin. As well as recruiting Burgess he cultivated the friendship of Harold 'Kim' Philby.

On the outbreak of World War II, Blunt volunteered and was taken into the Intelligence Corps as a field security officer. In 1940 he joined MI5 where his duties included the checking of diplomatic bags passing between neutral countries. 'Here,' writes Boyle, 'Blunt's linguistic gifts and consummate cunning proved of value to his unsuspecting British superiors and of greater value to his Soviet control. Long before the German invasion of Russia in June 1941, he had established his reputation for reliability with his masters in London and Moscow.' Boyle also suggests that Blunt's activities had a deadly aspect for it is 'at least probable that information he handed over to the Russians during this . . . period may well have led to the deaths of Poles, Czechs and even German Communists'.

When Burgess and Maclean fled to Russia in 1951 Blunt was, understandably, alarmed. He was advised to follow his friend Burgess to Moscow but refused, dreading a dreary life in the Soviet Union. In 1955 both Blunt and Philby were contacted by their Soviet superiors and reactivated,

Blunt as a message-boy for his masters. By the time that Philby was exposed as a spy, in 1963, Blunt was extremely concerned for his own safety. Indeed, there was always the possibility that the unpredictable Burgess might betray him in return for a possible pardon. As a known friend of Burgess, Blunt had been interrogated several times by MI5 and had easily outwitted his interlocutors. When he was questioned for the twelfth time, on 23 April 1964, Blunt agreed to confess only after he had secured a guarantee of immunity against prosecution and disclosure. Even after this development, Blunt kept his academic cool. Though he retired as Surveyor of the Royal Pictures in 1972 he agreed to continue as Adviser of the Queen's Pictures and Drawings. He seemed to be safe until Andrew Boyle appeared on the scene.

When *The Climate of Treason* came out in 1979 Sir Anthony Blunt was codenamed 'Maurice' in it. Though there was always a risk of libel, *Private Eye* magazine drew its own conclusions from Boyle's book and named Blunt as 'Maurice'. With the circulation of the story in the country's leading satirical magazine there were questions in the House of Commons. On 15 November 1979 Prime Minister Margaret Thatcher made a statement naming Blunt as a man who had talent-spotted for the Russians in the 1930s and passed information to them during World War II. She also noted, 'Successive Attorneys General in 1972, in June 1974, and in June 1979, have agreed that, having regard to the immunity granted in order to obtain the confession, which has always been and still is the only firm evidence against Blunt, there are no grounds on which criminal proceedings could be instituted.'

Blunt was, however, stripped of his knighthood and savaged by the popular press who felt that his upper-class credentials had saved him from prosecution. James Callaghan, Leader of the Opposition, endorsed this view when he said, 'there has been a tendency to treat Mr Blunt with kid gloves'. Blunt himself, at his press conference of 20 November, expressed few regrets. He felt that his career as a Soviet agent 'was a case of political conscience against loyalty to country — I chose conscience'. Andrew Boyle, on the other hand, said in the expanded edition of his important book, 'I am happy to have contributed my part by writing the book which led to Blunt's public exposure'.

LIZZIE BORDEN

1860-1927

IN THE WORDS of the immortal jingle:

> Lizzie Borden took an axe
> And gave her mother forty whacks;
> And when she saw what she had done,
> She gave her father forty-one.

Well, not quite. Sometime, early on Thursday morning, 4 August 1892, Mrs Abby Borden, Lizzie's stepmother, was struck down in the upstairs guest room of the family house at 92 Second Street, Fall River, Massachusetts. The back of her head had been shattered by nineteen axe wounds; there was another wound at the back of the neck and yet another had sliced off part of her scalp. She was sixty-three years old.

Andrew Borden, Lizzie's father, was seventy years old on 4 August 1892. Probably the most powerful man in Fall River, a town dominated by the Bordens, he was president of the Union Savings Bank, director of the First National Bank, director of the Durfee Safe Deposit and Trust Company, director of the Globe Yarn Mill Company, director of Troy Cotton and Woollen Manufacturing Company, director of the Merchants Manufacturing Company.

On the morning of the murder Andrew Borden left the house to attend to his financial affairs. Around 10.40 am he returned to 92 Second Street. When he entered the house Lizzie was standing at the top of the stairway, having come from the guest room. Lizzie told her father, 'Mrs Borden has gone out — she had a note from somebody who is sick'. At 10.50 am Bridget Sullivan, the Bordens' maid, heard Lizzie shouting to her to come quickly from her third floor room. 'Father's dead!' said Lizzie. 'Somebody's come in and killed him!' Eleven axe blows had been hammered on the top of his skull as he slept. An eye had been cut in half, his nose had been severed. A variant on the famous jingle states:

> Lizzie Borden took an axe
> And gave her mother forty whacks.
> Then she stood behind the door
> And gave her father forty more.

That murderer had, indeed, stood behind the dining-room door which was in line with the head of the couch on which Borden rested.

As Lizzie's sister Emma was away from the house at the time of the murder and as the maid Bridget Sullivan had absolutely no motive, suspicion naturally focused on Lizzie. At the inquest, on 9-11 August 1892, Lizzie claimed to have no doubts about her own innocence, though she was evasive. Her inquest testimony was published in the Providence *Journal*. 'I decline to say,' Lizzie stated, 'whether relations between [Abby Borden] and myself were those of mother and daughter or not . . . So far as I know, I was alone in the house the larger part of the time while my father was away. I was eating a pear when my father came in. I had put a stick of wood into the fire to see if I could start it. I did no more ironing after my father came in . . . I don't know what time my father came in. When I went out to the barn I left him on the sofa. The last thing I said was to ask him if he wanted the window left that way . . . I knew there was an old axe downstairs and last time I saw it, it was on the old chopping block. I don't know whether my father owned a hatchet or not.'

Lizzie was thirty-two at the time of the killing and was known to be hostile to Abby Borden. She addressed her stepmother as 'Mrs Borden', not mother, and deeply resented the fact that her father — a man notoriously mean with money — had made a financial gift to Abby's half-sister. According to a story, told in Robert Sullivan's definitive *Goodbye Lizzie Borden* (London, 1975), Lizzie once decapitated a tabby cat belonging to Abby Borden. Lizzie avoided her stepmother as often as possible, even at meal-times. Mrs Hannah Gifford, a Fall River dressmaker, recalled that Lizzie had referred to her stepmother as 'a mean good-for-nothing'.

Lizzie's behaviour before and after the murders was highly suspicious. The day before the killings, as a Fall River pharmacist told the Fall River *Globe*, Lizzie had unsuccessfully attempted to buy prussic acid. On the Sunday morning, three days after the murder, Lizzie burned one of her dresses in the kitchen stove. There was therefore no blood (except for one, possibly menstrual, spot) on any other dress, presumably because she changed and washed after slaughtering Abby Borden and because she attacked her father from behind the dining-room door, which prevented the blood spattering on the clothes she was then wearing.

The evidence strongly suggests that the double murder was an inside job perpetrated by someone who knew all about the Borden home. In the cellar police found a hatchet head which had been washed then dusted with ashes; the blade of this handleless hatchet fitted the wounds on both Bordens.

At her trial Lizzie was defended on the grounds that there was no blood on her clothing and the fact that she had burned a dress was largely ignored. Further, the defence pointed out that Lizzie was a respectable spinster. George D Robinson, the counsel for Lizzie's defence, made an emotional plea to the jury. 'To find her guilty,' he said, 'you must believe her to be a fiend! Does she look it?' The prosecution did not effectively press the powerful case against Lizzie: that the note she mentioned, in the hearing of Bridget Sullivan, failed to materialise; that she was alone in the house when Abby Borden was killed (Bridget being outside washing windows); that she alone was in a position to commit the murders and cover her tracks; that she had burned a relatively new dress; that she had attempted to buy prussic acid, a poison, the day before the murders; that she had a motive in her hatred of Abby Borden.

Lizzie never testified. When Chief Justice Mason asked her if she wished to speak she said, 'I am innocent. I leave it to my counsel to speak for me.' On 21 June 1893 she was found not guilty. Judge Dewey, who heard the trial, told the Boston *Globe*, 'I am perfectly satisfied with the verdict . . . I was satisfied when I made my charge to the jury that the verdict would be not guilty, although one cannot always tell what a jury will do.' The London *Daily Telegraph* of 22 June summed up the popular feeling towards Lizzie: 'the self-possession of the prisoner was such as to excite universal comment . . . She refused to say one word either in acknowledgement or denial of the charges brought against her, declined to make any statement, and rested her defence solely upon the inability of the State to prove its case.'

Lizzie was well placed to get off with the murder. It was not easy for the people of Fall River to believe that its most prominent citizen, Andrew Borden, had been killed by his daughter. It was difficult for the jury to accept that the self-assured woman before them was capable of an atrociously violent crime. Lizzie was championed by women's groups and by the two local ministers, W Walter Jubb and E A Buck. Lizzie, after all, was a member of the Central Congregational Church, and was a familiar figure in the Christian Endeavor Society, the missionary committee, the Sunday school and the Woman's Christian Temperance Union. Lizzie simply did not conform to the popular idea of a homicidal maniac, which is what she was on 4 August 1892.

As Robert Sullivan says, 'Lizzie Borden, an unpleasant spinster, had, in the most barbarous manner, savagely butchered her elderly father and her docile stepmother. Now — by orchestrating guile, stubborness, complete unflappability and incredible luck — she had become a heroine, even an idol, to a large segment of the American people . . . For two days the nation's press reflected the rejoicing of Lizzie's supporters as they hailed the jury's verdict; congratulatory messages inundated her; exultation reigned; and Lizzie was the focal point of attention.'

After the trial Lizzie left 92 Second Street and settled in 'Maplecroft', a big house on French Street, Fall River. She lived quietly though sometimes made trips to Boston and other cities. When she died, on 1 June 1927, she left $1 million of which $30,000 went to the Animal Rescue League of Fall River. 'I have been fond of animals,' Lizzie said, 'and their need is great, and there are so few who care for them.' She was buried in the plot that contains the remains of her victims. Lizzie's grave is marked with a stone stating 'Lizbeth', a name she came to prefer to the infamous Lizzie.

HORATIO WILLIAM BOTTOMLEY

1860-1933

BOTTOMLEY WAS a popular journalist and editor of considerable flair. His genius for public fraud on a large scale surpassed his abilities with the pen and the typewriter. Even the matter of his parentage he managed fraudulently to convert to something he considered more appropriate to his place in life. He was the son of a tailor who married the sister of a famous secularist, Jacob Holyoake. Horatio reconstructed the matter of his creation by claiming he was in fact the son of Charles Bradlaugh (1833-91), the famous social reformer, secularist, iconoclast and radical MP. There was no truth in this, although many claimed to see a resemblance. He was orphaned when he was five and educated at the Sir Joseph Mason Orphanage, Edgbaston, which he left when he was fourteen. He then tried a variety of jobs, including clerk, errand boy and shorthand court reporter. Speaking at the Oxford Union in 1921, a year before his trial at the Old Bailey, he said, 'I have not had your advantages, gentlemen, what poor education I have received has been gained in the University of Life.' These were formative years for him, and he was to put their lessons to very good use. His knowledge of the instincts, frustrations, anxieties and ambitions of the ordinary man in the street, combined with a knowledge of the legal system and a smattering of insights into financial matters, he was later to turn to monumental use.

In the mid 1880s he was a moderately successful provincial journalist. As founder of the *Hackney Hansard* he attempted to do for local politics what Hansard had done for Parliament. His success egged him on to other ventures in printing, publishing and journalism which were put to the public as mergers and conglomerates of various enterprises. But even at this stage his hand was in the till. Much of the capital invested went into his bank account. In 1893 these companies were in the hands of the receiver and Bottomley was tried for conspiracy to defraud. His spirited, eloquent, convincing and wholly successful defence of himself was one of the earliest displays of the genuine Bottomley talent.

He then set about making a fortune in earnest, mainly by crafty investments and buying and selling at the right time. West Australian gold shares were a very good yield to him. His personal charm and overwhelming plausibility charmed investors wherever he went. Lawsuits brought against him failed miserably. He was a natural lawyer and handled things brilliantly in court. He also had no scruples about bribing witnesses. These attributes were to serve him well throughout his extraordinary career.

Triumph followed triumph and Bottomley became a household name. As Liberal MP for South Hackney, a whole new world of useful contacts in the business and financial sphere was open to him, and as editor and founder of the notorious *John Bull*, he gained an additional powerful weapon. *John Bull* not only provided him a platform to spread the news of his sundry dubious companies, it also raked in a fortune. He blackmailed companies into buying advertising space in *John Bull* by threatening to expose their business practices.

The first signs of cracks in the edifice appeared in 1908. He was tried for conspiracy to defraud in connection with one of his companies. The complex confusion of his book-keeping and his ability at legal flannel saved him this time, but in 1911 an additional lawsuit led to his bankcruptcy and resignation from Parliament.

The 1914 war re-made him. He went on the stump up and down the country making patriotic speeches for money. He continued to run *John Bull* which became even more tub-thumpingly nationalist. The money rolled in and he freed himself from bankcruptcy. In 1918 he became an MP again. Using personal appearances and the tremendous publicity offered in the pages of *John Bull* he launched his biggest and most dastardly swindle, Victory Loans. This was a lottery — supposedly — but its real purpose was to enrich him. The government had issued War Bonds with a face value of £5, available to the buyer at a reduced price of £4.5s. Bottomley rightly perceived that this was a huge sum for the ordinary man in the street, whom he believed he knew so well. Bottomley founded the Victory Bond Club. The basis of the swindle was simple — people would put in what they could, no matter how little, it was all acceptable. Horatio Bottomley would put in large investments on their behalf. It was estimated in 1919 that Joe Public had coughed up some £500,000 to the funds. A sum was handed over to the Treasury but Bottomley himself pocketed £150,000. The news leaked out and the Chancery Court ordered his affairs to be fully investigated. One of his partners spilled the beans. Although Horatio Bottomley made a brilliant impression in court and was as flamboyant and colourful as ever, he lost his case and was sentenced to seven years penal servitude.

A pantomime lyric during the 1914 war shows how deep his appeal was to ordinary people:

A wire I'll send to a gentleman friend
I'll call him Horatio B
He's noted today for seeing fair play,
In a country that claims to be free.
If you feel in a plight, to his journal you write
And you'll get reparation in full.
So you'll say with me, Good Luck to HB.
And continued success to *John Bull*.

But Bottomley's career was now in ruins. He was released in 1926 and attempted to start again. He founded a new journal, which failed to take off. He sold his life-story to the press and made pathetic appearances in public, once on the boards of the Windmill Theatre. Bankrupted again in 1930, he died penniless in 1933. A J P Taylor records in *English History 1914-1945* that a friend of his visited him in prison and found him stitching mailbags. He asked, 'Ah, Bottomley, sewing?' and Bottomley replied, 'No. Reaping.'

THOMAS BROCK, JOHN PELMAN and MICHAEL POWER

19th century

THERE IS something unwholesome in giving evidence which leads to the conviction of one's fellows. Nevertheless, in its ceaseless endeavours to stem the tide of human criminality, society has often seen fit to spare or reward those who provide information about the activities of their partners. Between the reigns of William and Mary and George II statutes had been passed which gave rewards to informers. This reward system became an essential part of the economic infrastructure of criminal society. Keeping a gang of criminals on one's books and living on the income they provided from their activities, and from time to time handing them over for reward from the authorities of law and order, was a profitable business (see *JONATHAN WILD*). The rewards were on a scale from £10 for information leading to the conviction of a sheep-stealer, to £40 for cases of treason, robbery and counterfeiting.

By a pitiless logic it then seems reasonable deliberately to set up criminal activities simply in order to expose luckless persons to the forces of law and order. This was obviously part of the criminal justice system and its allied industries during the eighteenth century and the early nineteenth century. One shameful example is the case of Thomas Brock, John Pelman and Michael Power — a disreputable trio of rotters who attempted to earn income from duping simple, needy and unemployed Irishmen in London in 1816. The one person who emerges with human warmth and credit from this sordid tale is Sir Matthew Wood (1768-1843) who was then Lord Mayor of London.

Three Irishmen were on trial for coining. They were accused of fabricating base shillings and bank tokens. During the course of their trial, in which they were convicted, the Lord Mayor became suspicious of some of the evidence presented against them. He came to the conclusion that the three men who brought the prosecution, Thomas Brock, John Pelman and Michael Power, were somehow so well acquainted with the accused, that such an understanding existed between them, that their knowledge of the accused — Quin, Riorton and Connolly — was so complete and so pat that they themselves must in some way be very closely connected with those activities for which the three were on trial. An investigation was launched into the affair.

Quin, Riorton and Connolly, the three convicted men, were brought face to face with their accusers in the course of the investigation, but they refused to say anything at all against Brock, Pelham or Power. When pressed on the matter, they asserted that they were all 'under an oath'. They were all Irishmen and all Roman Catholics, and believed they had been bound under a solemn oath not to say anything about their activities which might embarrass their accusers, who had clearly taken advantage of their poverty, simplicity and social vulnerability. A priest was called in and after some debate with the accused men he was able to convince them that they were not in fact bound by such an oath, as it did not possess the sanctity of an oath taken in a court of law. The three men then revealed the entire nature of the plot constructed by Brock and his two partners, which had resulted in the apprehension, trial and conviction of Quin, Riorton and Connolly.

The three conspirators were then indicted for participation in the crimes for which Quin, Riorton and Connolly stood convicted. A witness named Barry appeared and gave evidence to the effect that Pelham had approached him to get some men to fabricate bad shillings. Power was to colour the coins once they had been cut. Barry advised them to go to the market at Cheapside where they would find several poor Irishmen ready and willing for such employment. The three convicted men were discovered at the corner of King Street and were engaged by Brock and his partners. The three Irishmen were told they could not be employed unless they took an oath of secrecy on a piece of paper. This they did, believing it to be solemn and binding. A room was rented, they were supplied with brass sheeting, scissors and other tools of the coiner's art. When the operation was in full swing, the word was given, officers entered the premises and Quin, Riorton and Connolly were arrested, tried and convicted.

In the course of the investigation of Brock, Pelham and Power, some quite damning evidence came to light. Pelham's landlady deposed that the actual scissors used by the Irishmen in their 'crime' had been procured by her at the direct request of Pelham himself. A shopkeeper gave evidence that Brock and Pelham had purchased the hammer and files in her shop. The conspirators exerted their energies to discrediting the witnesses, but the jury returned a verdict of guilty and all three were transported. The story has a happy ending — the three unfortunate Irishmen were pardoned and the Lord Mayor raised a fund for them. Subscriptions came in generously, and the three 'convicts' were able to return to their native land with enough capital to set up as farmers.

DEACON BRODIE

1741-88

BURGHER BY DAY, burglar by night: Deacon William Brodie has been scrutinised as a classic case of the Scottish split personality. Robert Louis Stevenson collaborated with W E Henley on a play, *Deacon Brodie*, which was privately printed in 1880 and produced (without success) in 1882. More sensationally, Stevenson had a nightmare, in 1885, about a man 'being pressed into a cabinet when he swallowed a drug and changed into another'. On the advice of his wife Fanny, Stevenson expressed the nightmare in allegorical form and *The Strange Case of Dr Jekyll and Mr Hyde* (1886) was unleashed upon the world. Stevenson, himself drawn to both the rewards of work and the delights of play, was fascinated by Brodie as an egregious example of the divided self.

Stevenson was not the only Scottish writer to utilise the Brodie story. Muriel Spark's *The Prime of Miss Jean Brodie* (1961) portrays an Edinburgh spinster psychologically disfigured by duality since she is narrowly self-righteous as well as expansively romantic. Jean tells two girls in the Brodie set, 'I am a descendant, do not forget, of Willie Brodie, a man of substance, a cabinet-maker and designer of gibbets, a member of the Town Council of Edinburgh and a keeper of two mistresses who bore him five children between them. Blood tells.'

The personality who thus inspired Stevenson and Spark was born in the Old Town of Edinburgh where his father, Francis, was a wright (cabinet-maker) who rose to the rank of Deacon (leader) of the Wrights. An adventurous youth, William was attracted to the Theatre Royal in the North Bridge and loved to watch performances of his favourite play, John Gay's *The Beggar's Opera*. Already his nightlife was given over to excitement. Apart from the histrionic delights of the Theatre Royal, there was the cockpit and the Cape Club — a fraternity of men fond of conversation and conviviality.

William eventually succeeded his father as Deacon of the Wrights (from 1781-3 and from 1786-7). He also obtained a seat on the Town Council.

Part of his work as Deacon was to fit new doors and locks to shops in the city and this put him in a special position of trust.

Despite his prominence as a leading citizen, Deacon Brodie attracted dark rumour. Of course, it was known that he kept two mistresses, Anne Grant and Jeannie Watt, but that was understandable. What was really deplorable was the low level of the company he kept in the cockpit in the Grassmarket. It was thought that a man of Brodie's standing, with his grand home in Brodie's Close in the Grassmarket, should avoid rubbing shoulders with his social inferiors.

In August 1786 Edinburgh was alarmed by the news that the bank of Messrs Johnston and Smith had been robbed. In October the goldsmith James Wemyss, of Parliament Close, was relieved of a substantial amount of jewelry. Throughout 1787 the burglaries continued and the gang responsible seemed to have an almost supernatural ability to open locked doors.

Early in 1788 Deacon Brodie found himself in trouble when he was caught using loaded dice at a gaming-table in Clark's Tavern, Fleshmarket Close. James Hamilton, furious at being cheated out of money in this way, petitioned the Town Council against the Deacon. No action was taken but the incident confirmed official opinion that a highly respectable citizen should not spend his evenings gambling in drinking dens.

On Wednesday, 8 March 1788, there was an audacious attempt to break into the General Excise Office in Chessel's Court, by the Canongate. Although the burglars did not manage to take much, their willingness to mount a robbery on such a scale caused consternation. On the Friday evening John Brown, an Irishman, came to see the Sheriff-Clerk about the Secretary of State's offer of a free pardon to anyone giving information leading to the arrest of the notorious gang who were undermining the security of Edinburgh. Brown persuaded an official to come with him to the King's Park and showed him a collection of counterfeit keys hidden under a stone at the Salisbury Crags.

Brown named some of the members of the gang and George Smith, a Cowgate grocer, and Andrew Ainslie, a High Street shoemaker, were arrested and confined in the Tolbooth. Brown also hinted that the leader of the gang was a well-known man in a privileged position.

When he heard that Brown was talking and Smith and Ainslie were in prison, Brodie got out of Edinburgh. Realising that the Deacon had abandoned him, Smith made a full confession that implicated Brodie as the mastermind behind the burglaries. Brodie, Smith explained, had made copies of keys he himself had fitted to shops. For the break-in at the General Excise Office he had sent Smith to make a putty impression of a key, then made a duplicate.

The Sheriff-Clerk's office reacted to this information by issuing an advertisement:

> Whereas William Brodie, a considerable House-Carpenter and Burgess of the City of Edinburgh, has been charged with being concerned in breaking into the General Excise Office for Scotland, and stealing from the Cashier's Office there a sum of money — and as the said William Brodie has either made his escape from Edinburgh, or is still concealed about that place — A REWARD OF ONE HUNDRED AND FIFTY POUNDS STERLING is hereby offered to any person who will produce him alive at the Sheriff Clerk's Office, Edinburgh, or will secure him, so as he may be brought there within a month from this date.

The Deacon had escaped to Holland but before leaving he sent some letters to Edinburgh where they were examined by Harry Erskine, Dean of the Faculty of Advocates, then passed to the Sheriff. In a letter to his friend Michael Henderson, Brodie wrote, 'Were I to write to you all that has happened to me and the hairbreadth escapes I made from a well-scented pack of bloodhounds, it would make a small volume.'

Brodie was arrested in Amsterdam and brought back to Edinburgh to stand trial, in August, before Lord Braxfield. At the trial Brodie was accused of 'breaking into a house used or kept as an Excise Office, or other public office, under cloud of night, and from thence abstracting and stealing money'. He was found guilty and sentenced to death. Braxfield told Brodie: 'It's much to be lamented that those vices, which are called gentlemanly vices, are so favourably looked upon in the present age. They have been the source of your ruin; and, whatever may be thought of them, they are such as assuredly lead to ruin. I hope you will improve the short time which you have now to live by reflecting upon your past conduct, and endeavouring to procure, by a sincere repentance, forgiveness for your many crimes.'

On 1 October 1788 Brodie went to the gallows. Apparently he tried to outwit death by wearing a steel collar under his neckerchief and bribing the hangman to make a short drop. However, the rope was adjusted and Brodie duly dropped to his death. His bizarre personality is perhaps best conveyed by the will he made before he died: 'And lastly my neck being now about to be embraced by a halter I recommend to all Rogues, Sharpers, Thieves and Gamblers, as well in high as in low stations to take care of theirs by leaving of all wicked practices and becoming good members of society.'

ELIZABETH BROWNRIGG

died 1767

ELIZABETH BROWNRIGG spent the early part of her life in private service. She then married James Brownrigg, a plumber and house-painter, and lived at

Flower-de-Luce Court, Fleet Street, and at a small house in Islington. The couple had sixteen children. She obtained the post of midwife at the workhouse in St Dunstan's parish where she seemed to discharge her duties quite satisfactorily. She began to take on apprentices from the workhouse, among them Mary Mitchell and Mary Jones in 1765. The intention was that these girls should take the place of servants and save the Brownriggs money while Mrs Brownrigg continued as a midwife. These orphan girls were initially treated quite well but things soon changed.

It transpired at a later date when enquiries were made that Elizabeth Brownrigg beat Mary Jones until she could raise the whip no longer from sheer exhaustion. This happened frequently. She would revive the girl with cold water and then continue the treatment. Mary resolved to escape and in fact succeeded by stealing the house door-key which she noticed hanging on the wall. She returned to the Foundling Hospital. She told the authorities at the Hospital what had happened to her at the Brownriggs' house and her condition was examined by the surgeon. The governors ordered their solicitors to write to the Brownriggs, requesting under the penalty of prosecution that the reasons for these 'severities' be properly explained. No answer was received, and the governors, not wishing to continue the matter, dropped the line of enquiry. Mary Jones was discharged. She was lucky to escape, as subsequent events testified.

Meanwhile Mary Mitchell was experiencing the tortures of the damned, being whipped from morning until night, forced to live on food scarcely fit for human consumption, and made to sleep on a mat in the coal-hole. Miraculously she, too, managed to escape, but was unfortunate enough to bump into the Brownriggs' younger son in the street. He forced her to return with him. The reward of her attempted escape was an increase of the severity of her daily regimen. She was stripped naked, tied up and beaten with a hearth broom, horse-whip or cane, whatever came readily to Mrs Brownrigg's hands. She was even chained to the yard door like an animal. Other girls apprenticed to the family at the same time received similar treatment and were frequently so badly beaten that, according to the *Newgate Calendar*, 'their heads and shoulders appeared as one general sore; and when a plaister was applied to their wounds, the skin used to peel away with it'. The barbarity became even more systematic, with the girls being tied to a water-pipe that ran across the kitchen ceiling, and, when this bent under the strain, to a hook in the beam which Mr Brownrigg had affixed for the very purpose.

Another of the Brownriggs' victims was Mary Clifford. Fortunately, Mary had an aunt in the country, who came to London to see how she was getting on. Being informed that she was at the Brownriggs' household, her aunt called but was refused admittance. Mr Brownrigg even went so far as to threaten her with proceedings if she continued to make a disturbance. The lady was leaving when Mr Deacon, a baker, who lived next door, called her in and told her that he and his wife had been concerned for some time at the moans and groans they heard issuing from the Brownriggs' household. Mrs Deacon said that she 'suspected the apprentices were treated with unwarrantable severity'. She promised that she would try and find out what was going on.

Soon after this James Brownrigg purchased a pig at Hampstead market and brought it home where it was installed in a covered yard. The yard was ventilated with a sky-light which was frequently open to give the animal air. Mr Deacon told his servants to keep a watch out and to look in every time they noticed that the sky-light was removed. The real nature of the Brownriggs' household now began to emerge. The servants saw some of the girls kept inside and observed the terrible conditions they were in. Mrs Deacon wrote to Mary Clifford's aunt and this good lady then reported to the overseers of St Dunstan's, imploring them that something be done. A Mr Grundy of St Dunstan's, together with several of the female overseers of the workhouse, then went to call on the Brownriggs and demanded to see Mary Clifford. James Brownrigg denied all knowledge of the unfortunate girl, but offered to produce Mary Mitchell. This was not the girl they wanted to see, and Mr Grundy then sent for a constable to search the house. At this stage, incredibly, nothing untoward was found.

Mr Brownrigg was in a threatening mood but the determined Mr Grundy took Mary Mitchell with him. When her clothes were removed at the workhouse the evidence of the weeks of physical ill-treatment clearly showed themselves. The unfortunate girl was assured that she would not be sent back to the Brownriggs' household, and she then gave an account of the treatment she and the other girls had sustained. Mr Grundy went back to make a strict search of the premises, and the Brownriggs on their part threatened legal proceedings. It was at this stage that poor Mary Clifford was discovered hidden in a cupboard. She died a few days later at St Bartholemew's Hospital.

James Brownrigg was confined but his wife and son made their escape. They shifted from one address to another, bought clothes in a rag-fair so as to disguise themselves, and took lodgings finally with a chandler named Dunbar in Wandsworth.

Mr Dunbar happened to read a newspaper in which the fugitives were described. He went to London where he sought out Mr Deacon, who was able to recognise the couple as the wanted persons. The father, mother and son were tried at the Old Bailey. Elizabeth was found guilty of murder and ordered to be executed, but the father and son were acquitted of the higher charge, although detained to be tried for 'a misdemeanour' for which they were convicted and sentenced to six months confinement.

After her sentence Mrs Brownrigg confessed her guilt to the prison chaplain and acknowledged that her sentence was a just one. Accounts of the time record that the parting between her and her husband and son 'was affecting beyond description. The son falling on his knees, she bent herself over and embraced him; while the husband was kneeling on the other side.' Elizabeth Brownrigg was hissed and booed most vehemently on her way to Tyburn. The spectators were quite used to spectacles of this kind, but it was reported that seldom had a condemned prisoner been so assailed by curses and cries of abhorrence, and that these public demonstrations continued for some considerable time after she was clearly dead. Her body was dissected and anatomised at Surgeon's Hall, where her skeleton was hung up for some years as a curious relic of a most barbarous creature.

William Burke *William Hare*

WILLIAM BURKE

1792-1829

Up the close an' doon the stair,
Roon' the toun wi' Burke an' Hare:
Burke's the butcher, Hare's the thief,
Knox the boy that buys the beef.

THAT JINGLE is still in oral circulation in Edinburgh where Burke and
Hare, between them, murdered sixteen unfortunates whose bodies were
destined to further the study of anatomy as practised by the brilliant Dr
Robert Knox, the most popular teacher at the Medical School.

Burke's name has passed into the English language. It is preserved, in the
Oxford English Dictionary, as a verb meaning 'To murder, in the same manner
or for the same purpose as Burke did; to kill secretly by suffocation or
strangulation, or for the purpose of selling the victim's body for dissection ...
To smother, "hush up", suppress quietly'. Burke, Hare and Knox have
featured as characters in a play, *The Anatomist* (1930) by James Bridie, and in a
filmscript, *The Doctor and the Devils* by Dylan Thomas. Burke and Hare
continue to haunt the imagination of Edinburgh.

William Burke came to Scotland from Ulster and worked as a navvy on the
Union Canal. With his mistress Helen McDougal he moved to Edinburgh
where, in 1827, he met his fellow-Ulsterman William Hare. Burke and Hare
were clearly two of a kind so Burke, with Helen McDougal, settled in Log's
lodging house in Tanner's Close — a seedy establishment in the West Port run
by Hare's wife Margaret.

On 29 December 1827 one of Margaret Hare's lodgers died. As this man,
Donald, owed Margaret Hare £4 Burke and Hare decided to sell his dead

body. After removing the corpse from its coffin, they made up the weight with a bag of tanner's bark. They took Donald's corpse to 10 Surgeon Square where it was inspected by Dr Robert Knox who gave them £7.10s for it. As Burke recalled, Knox asked no questions as to how the body had been obtained. Hare took £4 to cover Donald's debt, plus a 5 shilling commission. Burke pocketed the rest and realised that, by the law of supply and demand, as Knox needed a constant source of anatomical material for his research and lectures, there was a lot of money to be made from dead bodies.

An old miller called Joseph was evidently dying of fever in Log's lodging house; Burke decided to put him out of his misery. He took 'a small pillow and laid it across Joseph's mouth, and Hare lay across the body to keep down the arms and legs'. They collected £10 for Joseph's corpse. When another lodger, a young Englishman, displayed signs of jaundice Burke decided to act again but this time no pillow was used. The murderer's thumb was placed under the victim's chin and two fingers blocked the passage of air to his nostrils. The Englishman was the first to be 'burked' and his corpse also brought in £10, courtesy of Dr Knox.

On 12 February 1828 Burke and Hare murdered Abigail Simpson, an old woman who had arrived in Edinburgh to collect a pension. Burke and Hare took her to the lodging house, got her drunk and burked her the following morning. When Knox saw the corpse he 'approved of it being so fresh, but did not ask any questions', according to Burke's confession.

Burke and Hare were now running a profitable enterprise and were always on the lookout for fresh supplies. In April 1828 they burked Mary Paterson, a beautiful young prostitute. Unfortunately for them, Mary's body was well known to some of the students and one of them identified her. Burke, however, explained that he had bought the corpse in the Canongate and that Mary had drunk herself to death. As he had provided her with whisky before killing her, it was a plausible story and Burke and Hare were free to go about their business.

Burke's confession, as published in the Edinburgh *Courant*, gives details of their methods: 'When they first began this murdering system they always took them to Knox's after dark; but being so successful, they went in the day-time, and grew more bold . . . They often said to one another that no person could find them out, no one being present at the murders but themselves two; and that they might as well be hanged for a sheep as a lamb. They made it their business to look out for persons to decoy into their houses to murder them. Burke declares, when they kept the mouth and nose shut a very few minutes, they could make no resistance, but would convulse and make a rumbling noise in their bellies for some time; after they ceased crying and making resistance, they left them to die of themselves: but their bodies would often move afterwards, and for some time they would have long breathings before life went away.'

As a consequence of their success, Burke and Hare became over-confident and murdered a citizen even more familiar than Mary Paterson. Daft Jamie was one of Edinburgh's colourful characters: a figure of fun whose idiotic appearance was greatly appreciated by the children who baited him. In October 1828, Daft Jamie was invited to Log's lodging house where he was offered drink, which he did not like, and snuff, which he did. Jamie was then taken to a bedroom where, in the words of Burke's official confession, 'Hare suddenly turned on him, and put his hands on his mouth and nose; and Jamie, who had got drink, but was not drunk, made a terrible resistance, and he and Hare fell from the bed together, Hare still keeping hold of Jamie's mouth and nose; and as they lay on the floor together, [Burke] lay across Jamie, to prevent him from resisting, and they held him in that state till he was dead.'

When the body had been sold, for the usual £10, to Dr Knox some of his students recognised it but Knox denied that it was the corpse of Daft Jamie and, without further ado, got on with the job of dissecting it.

About a week after the burking of Daft Jamie, Burke and Hare murdered Mrs Docherty, a pauper woman who came to Log's lodging house. But this time Mrs Gray, a visitor to the lodging house, became suspicious when she discovered that the woman was missing. Eventually she discovered the body of Mrs Docherty under a bed and the police were called in to arrest Burke, Hare and Helen McDougal. It was 1 November 1828.

As the Crown had problems in making a convincing case against the murderers, Hare was promised his freedom if he turned King's evidence and testified against Burke. He did so and Burke was found guilty while the case against Helen McDougal was not proven. What happened to Hare, after this legal melodrama, is not known for certain. When he was released he left Edinburgh to escape from the fury of the mob.

As Burke told the Edinburgh *Courant*, his guilt was equally shared by Hare. He seemed to be relieved, though, that the nightmare was over: 'Burke declares that it was God's providence that put a stop to their murdering career, for he does not know how far they might have gone with it, "even to attack people on the streets", as they were so successful, and always met with a ready market; that when they delivered a body they were always told to get more. Hare was always with him when he went with a subject, and also when he got the money.'

Hare was a man without conscience but Burke, in the opinion of Lord Cockburn who met him, had some recognisably human qualities: 'Except that he murdered, Burke was a sensible, and what might be called a respectable man; not at all ferocious in his general manner, sober, correct in all his other habits, and kind to his relations.'

Nevertheless Hare got his freedom while Burke was hanged before a crowd of some 25,000 spectators in Edinburgh. Sir Walter Scott wrote, in his Journal, for 28 January 1829, 'Burke the murderer hanged this morning. The mob, which was immense, demanded Knox and Hare, but though greedy for more victims, received with shouts the solitary wretch who found his way to the gallows out of five or six who seem not less guilty than he.' On 7 March 1829 Scott, out of sorts, 'felt like one of the victims of the wretch Burke, struggling against a smothering weight on my bosom, till nature could endure it no longer.'

Ironically, Scott was to endure the image of Burke until the end of his life. On 18 May 1831 he put in an appearance at Jedburgh on behalf of the Tory candidate for Roxburghshire. As Scott's carriage passed a group of radical Hawick weavers it was stoned and his attempt to make a speech was drowned out in abuse. The Tory candidate was, predictably, elected and Scott left

Jedburgh to a hail of stones and cries of 'Burke Sir Walter'. This hostility had a profoundly disturbing effect on Scott who, on his deathbed in 1832, several times reiterated the phrase, 'Burke Sir Walter'.

As for Dr Robert Knox, his reputation never recovered from the Burke and Hare scandal. He remained in Edinburgh until 1841 but was widely regarded with contempt. He died in 1862, spending the last twenty years of his life in London where he supported himself by writing and lecturing.

SIR CYRIL BURT

1883-1971

IN HIS LIFETIME Sir Cyril Burt was regarded as the major force in British psychology, an authority on the subject of intelligence which he pursued from 1909 onwards. As a result of his persuasive advocacy of mental testing, generations of British children were subjected to intelligence tests that determined the quality of their secondary schooling. Burt worked with the Education Department of the London County Council from 1913 to 1932 and was professor of education (1924-31) and psychology (1931-50) at London University.

His influence was enormous and it was widely accepted that he had put mental testing on a rigorously scientific basis. He believed that intelligence was genetically inherited, insisted that innate intelligence could be accurately measured by IQ tests, argued (for example in his 1943 paper on *Ability and Income*) that intelligence and occupational status are correlated.

Burt's great prestige was derived from his apparently impeccable scientific credentials. The son of a doctor, he was academically brilliant. As a child he met Sir Francis Galton, one of his father's patients, and was influenced by the anthropologist's account of eugenics, as expressed in such works as *Hereditary Genius* (1869) and *Natural Inheritance* (1889). Burt came to believe that poverty was a sign of the inferior intelligence of the working class and that society as a whole suffered because the poor produced large families and thus reduced the national level of intelligence.

Over the years Burt published several papers detailing his research into separated monozygotic twins. Obviously, if the twins scored equally well (or otherwise) in intelligence tests then this result established the genetic basis of intelligence and destroyed the environmentalist argument. Burt claimed to have tested fifty-three pairs of twins with the help of his assistants Margaret Howard and J A Conway. The results always endorsed the hereditary case. It is now recognised, however, that Burt fabricated his data since the statistical scores were impossibly consistent. Moreover, he invented his two assistants as no trace has ever been found of Howard and Conway. Rather than admitting that his views amounted to emotionally-based assertions Burt expressed himself in a scientific jargon that overwhelmed his contemporaries and colleagues.

AL CAPONE

1899-1947

THE NAME AL CAPONE is synonymous with violent crime; his nickname 'Scarface' is cinematic shorthand for mayhem. How this ham-fisted killer made such an impression on the consciousness of the Western world is a tale of two American cities — New York and Chicago.

In 1893 Gabriel and Teresa Caponi emigrated, from Naples to the USA, where they slightly altered their surname to Capone. Alphonse was the fourth of their nine children; he was heavily built and heavy-handed and rapidly established himself as the toughest kid on the block in Williamsburg, Brooklyn. He became a member of one of Brooklyn's most vicious outfits, the Five Points Gang, and from a very early age idolised its leader Johnny Torrio.

The young Capone was well suited to his work as a bouncer in the Harvard Inn, a brothel in Brooklyn. He enjoyed his bonecrushing duties and liked to intimidate those around him. When he insulted a girl drinking at the bar of the

Harvard Inn, however, her brother Frank Galluccio came at Capone with his stiletto. He made three deep slashes on the left side of Capone's face, a permanent disfigurement that led to the name 'Scarface'. When Capone made it big in the criminal underworld, he retained Galluccio as a bodyguard, thus demonstrating, or so he hoped, that he had a forgiving nature.

In 1910 Torrio had gone to Chicago to help Big Jim Colosimo with his network of brothels. To add more muscle to the organisation, Torrio brought Capone to Chicago in 1919. Capone flourished in the violent atmosphere and graduated from being one of Colosimo's bouncers to become a collector earning $2,000 a week. He put on airs and graces, promoting himself as a businessman and enjoying nights at the opera to hear the music of his favourite composer, Verdi.

When Prohibition came, in 1920, Johnny Torrio urged Colosimo to become a bootlegger. Big Jim wanted nothing to do with that racket and told Torrio, 'We stay out. That's final.' Torrio asked Al Capone to do him a favour. Obligingly, Capone shot Big Jim dead, in his nightclub, on 11 May 1920. Torrio was now in charge of Big Jim's empire, Capone was his second-in-command.

By bribing police chiefs and threatening witnesses, Capone found he could literally get away with murder in Chicago. On 8 May 1924 he heard that Ragtime Joe Howard had added injury to a previous insult. Not only was Joe saying how easy it was to hijack Torrio's beer trucks but he kicked one of Capone's men to make the point that Italians were cowardly. Capone confronted Joe and shot him six times in the head.

Capone was arrested but the state attorney, W H McSwiggin, could find no witnesses to testify against 'Scarface'. Capone held a grudge against the attorney and personally murdered him in due course.

Torrio and Capone ran the South Side of Chicago while the North Side was controlled by Dion O'Bannion and his gang of 'Irish bastards' (to quote Capone). Frontiers were generally observed by both sides but Capone lusted after O'Bannion's territory. He ridiculed O'Bannion's refusal to run a prostitution racket in the North Side and exploited this situation by infiltrating his own whores into the area. O'Bannion already despised Capone for killing 'like a beast in the jungle'. Hymie Weiss, O'Bannion's number two, now informed one of Capone's associates, 'You can tell Capone this for me. If he ever pulls anything . . . on us, I'm going to get him if I have to kill everybody in front of him to do it.'

On 8 November 1924 three of Capone's killers strolled into O'Bannion's flower shop on North State Street and shot him down. Hymie Weiss led O'Bannion's men in a brutal drive for revenge and they gunned down Johnny Torrio. He somehow survived his wounds, but left Chicago to Capone: 'It's all yours, Al.' It was almost true. With $5 million a year, Capone was fabulously wealthy. From his headquarters in the Hawthorn Hotel, in the Chicago suburb of Cicero, he lorded it over his criminal colleagues.

Still, O'Bannion's men were determined to kill Capone. On 20 September 1926 they shot at him in the restaurant of the Hawthorn. It was just a warning and soon they were back with eight carloads of machine-gunners. Capone's headquarters were sprayed with bullets but nobody was killed. Capone's pride was hurt, though: 'Those bastards are dead,' he prophesied. The marked men were Hymie Wiess, Vincent Drucci and George 'Bugs' Moran, O'Bannion's chief enforcer.

Weiss was shot by John Scalise and Albert Anselmi — Capone's top gunmen — and Drucci was conveniently killed by a cop. Only 'Bugs' Moran had still to be taken care of and Capone was planning something special for him.

On St Valentine's Day, 14 February 1929, five men walked into a garage at 2122 North Clark Street, the headquarters of Moran's bootlegging operation. Three of the men were dressed as policemen, two were not. They ordered seven of Moran's Irish gangsters to line up facing the wall, then machine-gunned them down. When Moran heard details of the massacre he said, 'Only Capone kills like that', then made himself scarce.

On 7 May 1929 Capone held a dinner at which he produced a baseball bat and smashed in the heads of John Scalise and Albert Anselmi. Only a couple of months before, those same men had carried out the St Valentine's Day Massacre for him. That night in May, though, they were out of favour and so were horrifically done to death by 'Scarface' himself.

Capone was eventually arrested, by federal agents, for failure to pay income tax. At his trial he claimed, 'All I ever did was to sell beer and whisky to our best people'. But he was sentenced, on 24 October 1931, to eleven years in prison — first in Leavenworth, then in Alcatraz. He was released in 1939 because of his good behaviour and bad condition. Capone's health had collapsed in prison and though he was as demented as ever he was no longer in a position to harm anyone. He retired to his Florida estate and lived as a recluse with memories, perhaps, of the hundreds of men whose deaths he had caused.

ELIZABETH CHUDLEIGH,

COUNTESS OF BRISTOL, DUCHESS OF KINGSTON

1720-88

THE TRIAL OF Elizabeth Chudleigh was almost the sole topic of conversation in high society England in 1776. The *Gentleman's Magazine* held over an account of the rebellion in the American colonies: 'The importance of this trial, and our desire to gratify our readers with the substance of it at once, has obliged us to postpone the account of American Affairs.' She was tried for bigamy, before the House of Lords in April 1776. The offence was described by the Lord High Steward as 'destructive to the peace and well-being of Society, hateful in the sight of God, and a heavy criminal charge'.

Elizabeth Chudleigh was one of the most celebrated women of the age. She was extremely beautiful. One of her contemporaries said of her, 'She has a ravishing smirk'. She was fully aware of the best ways to display her charms.

She once went to a public ball in a completely transparent gauze dress. She always had a weather eye on the main social chance: her marriages were her investments, her loveliness her capital. She had a penchant for two of everything — husbands, lovers, estates and titles, bottles of wine (this bibular capacity impressed Frederick the Great). When a two-headed cow was born in Essex Horace Walpole said that it must be hers.

She was born in 1720, the daughter of one Colonel Thomas Chudleigh. She was by no means well-educated — some biographers claim that she was in fact illiterate — but Elizabeth was soon to find her ample seductive charms an adequate compensation for her inability to manage the ablative absolute. By her mid-twenties she had been 'befriended' by Sir William Pulteney, a brilliant and wealthy statesman, later Earl of Bath.

As a result of her association with Pulteney, Elizabeth was appointed Maid of Honour to Augusta, Princess of Wales, at Leicester House. She now came to the attention, as they say, of James, Duke of Hamilton, who was a minor. He fell passionately in love with her, and devoted most of his energies in 1744 to the task of wooing her. During this year Elizabeth also met Augustus John Hervey, younger brother of the second Earl of Bristol. Augustus was a lieutenant in the Royal Navy. A brief whirlwind romance culminated in their marriage. For political reasons the marriage had to be kept a secret. Hervey had no more than his pay, and the disclosure of Elizabeth's marriage would have lost her the position of Maid of Honour to the Princess of Wales. At dead of night, early in August 1744 they were married in the little village of Laineston in Hampshire. This obscure parish had been wisely chosen as it lay at the foot of the garden of a house belonging to a relative of Miss Chudleigh's. The bridal party was able to enter the churchyard by the back gate.

Four days (and nights) later, Lieutenant Hervey sailed for the West Indies and Elizabeth 'Hervey' (née Chudleigh) returned to Leicester House, nominally a Maid of Honour. Hervey was away for two years, and Elizabeth lived — a spinster as far as the rest of the world was aware — in Conduit Street. When the Lieutenant returned he stayed with his wife for just one month. He sailed and returned once more before they finally parted, after a whole series of disagreements, in 1747. In the same year Hervey's little son, born to Elizabeth after their separation, lived only a few months. Those at Leicester House still had no idea that she had ever been married.

According to English law in the eighteenth century a spinster could buy and sell property and enter into contracts, but a married woman could not. Elizabeth, accepted everywhere as Elizabeth Chudleigh, spinster, did all these things. But in 1759 it seemed that it might be politic for her to reveal her marriage to Augustus John Hervey, because his father, then Earl of Bristol, was dying. A disclosure of her marriage to Hervey — heir to the Earldom — would make her Countess of Bristol, an acknowledged heiress of one hundred thousand pounds. She sought out the priest who had married them, the Reverend Amis. Sadly he was at death's door himself, but the intrepid Elizabeth pursued him even here, and under pressure from her and her lawyer the waning cleric summoned his energies, swallowed his scruples and altered the parish records to include the marriage on '4th. August A.D. 1744, of Augustus John Hervey, Lieutenant, to Elizabeth Chudleigh, spinster.'

Unfortunately the Earl of Bristol recovered, and lived for another ten years. But in that time Elizabeth was not idle. She made an impression on George II, with whom she had a flirtation. Bearing in mind George's reputation for a distinct lack of personal generosity, the gift to her of a gold watch costing thirty-five guineas, bought with his own money, 'and not charged on the Civil List', assumes considerable significance.

She also caught the eye of Sir Evelyn Pierrepoint, Duke of Kingston, and became his mistress. Prizing the role of Duchess more than that of Countess, she now decided that she wanted a divorce from Hervey — a course which at this period could only be achieved by private Act of Parliament. Hervey's advice to Elizabeth was that the Duke of Kingston had money and influence enough to get Parliament to dissolve the marriage. But she was in a difficult position. At one time she had wanted to marry Hervey because she hoped to become Countess of Bristol. The marriage had to be secret for the sake of her situation at Leicester House. Then when the old Earl of Bristol seemed about to die, she had had the marriage written up. But she now wanted to be Duchess of Kingston. Divorce would reveal the fact that she had been married and had illegally gained properties. She would lose her pension.

Fortunately she had an able lawyer. She presented a suit against Hervey for jactitation of marriage — that is the offence of falsely claiming to be a person's spouse. If successful it would mean Hervey could never again claim that he'd been married to her. He had no proof, as she had not told him that the parish records at Laineston had been altered. In February 1769 she was granted the decree she wanted.

A few months later she married the Duke of Kingston. He died in 1773, leaving her everything. She had a life estate in everything he possessed, and the rest of the Duke's family received nothing. But the Duke's daughter and her husband did not let matters rest there. Their researches revealed her former marriage to Hervey and they charged her with bigamy. Returning from Italy, the new Duchess claimed the right to be tried by her Peers.

Bigamy was a felony and could be punished by death or branding. Her trial in the House of Lords opened on 15 April 1776 and lasted a week. After all due deliberations their Lordships found her guilty. Only the second Duke of Newcastle (a noted sportsman) qualified his verdict, by saying that she was 'erroneously, but not intentionally guilty'. Elizabeth now claimed benefit of clergy. This plea had originally meant that clerics were exempt from the authority of secular magistrates respecting crimes and misdemeanours. This privilege was extended to the laity: at one time anyone who could read could claim benefit of clergy. Based on the tenet of Chronicles XVI 22: 'Touch not my anointed, nor do my prophets no harm', it applied to all who, being able to read and write, were capable of entering into Holy Orders. But here was something Elizabeth Chudleigh could not have two of. Benefit of clergy could be claimed but once.

The Lord High Steward addressed her: 'Madam, you are admitted to your clergy in the form and manner in which you have claimed . . . I am now therefore to tell you, that if you should ever be guilty of a similar offence, or of any crime amounting to felony, that no such claim can again be allowed, but you will thereby incur a capital punishment.' He rose and broke his white staff, and proclamation was made ordering every person to depart, and repair quietly home in God's peace and the King's peace.

Elizabeth's marriage to Hervey was declared valid in 1777 (he had become third Earl of Bristol two years previously). She travelled on the continent and visited Russia, where she got on well with Catherine the Great. She bought a valuable estate in Russia and died in Paris in 1788. She never needed benefit of clergy a second time.

ARCHBISHOP HIERONYMUS COLLEREDO

18th century

WOLFGANG AMADEUS MOZART, arguably the greatest musical genius the world has witnessed, began his career in a blaze of glory as a performing prodigy. He could play the clavier at the age of four, the violin at the age of seven. His astonishing gifts made him an international celebrity and when he returned to his native Salzburg in 1771 he was determined to assert his artistic independence. Unfortunately for Mozart, Salzburg was about to be controlled by a man who felt that musicians should accept the inferior status accorded to them at the time.

Archbishop Hieronymus Colloredo was forty-years old when he was elected ruler of Salzburg on 14 March 1772. To welcome the newly elected Colloredo into Salzburg, Mozart was commissioned to compose a dramatic serenade *Il Sogno di Scipione* (K.126). Colloredo was alarmed by Mozart's fluency and anxious to assert his power over him. On the fifth anniversary of Colloredo's election — 14 March 1777 — Leopold Mozart asked the Archbishop if he and his son could leave Salzburg for a while. There was no direct reply but in June, Colloredo instructed his musicians to prepare for Joseph II's visit to Salzburg. After the visit Leopold repeated his request and this time Wolfgang was allowed leave of absence.

The composer longed to establish himself in the wider musical world. On 1 August 1777 Mozart, depressed by the petty conditions at the Salzburg court, wrote to the Archbishop asking for his complete release: 'Your Grace will therefore be so good as to allow me to ask you most humbly for my discharge, of which I should like to take advantage before the autumn, so that I may not be obliged to face the bad weather of the ensuing months of winter. Your Grace will not misunderstand this petition, seeing that when I asked you for permission to travel to Vienna three years ago, you graciously declared that I had nothing to hope for in Salzburg and would do better to seek my fortune elsewhere.' The Archbishop replied that Mozart was free to leave. He took advantage of this to go to Munich, with his mother, while an apprehensive Leopold remained in the Archbishop's service.

On 3 July 1778 Mozart's mother died and, having failed to find the success he needed in Paris, the composer returned to Salzburg early in 1779. Colloredo took him back as an organist and continued to treat him as a nonentity with some talent as an entertainer whose duty was to do as he was told.

At the end of 1780 Mozart was allowed, by the Archbishop, to take a leave of absence in Munich in connection with a performance of *Idomeneo*. In March 1781 the Archbishop summoned him to his temporary residence in Vienna to rebuke him for prolonging his leave of absence without permission. To further humiliate Mozart, Colloredo refused to allow him to organise his own concert. The situation was becoming unbearable for Mozart and came to a climax on Wednesday, 9 May, when he arrived at the Archbishop's to ask for travelling expenses.

As Mozart was a humble servant, in the opinion of the Archbishop, he was asked to go back to Salzburg with a parcel. Mozart explained that he could not return until the Saturday which prompted a valet to suggest that he should explain this delay personally to Colloredo. What happened next is described vividly in a letter Mozart wrote to his father on 9 May 1781: 'I am still seething with rage! . . . Twice already that — I don't know what to call him — has said to my face the greatest *sottises* and *impertinences*, which I have not repeated to you, as I wished to spare your feelings, and for which I only refrained from taking my revenge on the spot because you, my most beloved father, were ever before my eyes.' Mozart then cited the request that he should take charge of the Archbishop's parcel.

When Mozart entered the room, Colloredo's first words were, 'Well, young fellow, when are you going off?' Mozart said that he could not leave the same day as the seats on the coach were all taken. Colloredo exploded with indignation: 'Then he rushed full steam ahead, without pausing for breath — I was the most dissolute fellow he knew — no one served him so badly as I did — I had better leave to-day or else he would write home and have my salary stopped. I couldn't get a word in edgeways, for he blazed away like a fire. I listened to it all very calmly. He lied to my face that my salary was five hundred *gulden*, called me a scoundrel, a rascal, a vagabond. Oh, I really cannot tell you all he said. At last my blood began to boil, I could no longer contain myself, and I said, "So Your Grace is not satisfied with me?" "What, you dare to threaten me — you scoundrel? There is the door! Look out, for I will have nothing more to do with such a miserable wretch." At last I said: "Nor I with you!" "Well, be off!" When leaving the room, I said, "This is final. You shall have it to-morrow in writing." . . . I had twice played the coward and I could not do so a third time.'

A month later, when Mozart attempted to present a petition on the subject of his resignation to the Archbishop, Count Arco — the high steward — 'hurls me out of the room and gives me a kick on my behind'. Mozart was free, at last, and had to face a future that would combine brilliant artistic success and economic misery.

Reflecting on the kick on his backside, in a letter of 13 June 1781 to his father, Mozart said, 'Salzburg is no longer the place for me, except to give me a favourable opportunity of returning the Count's kick, even if it should have to be in the public street'. In fact, Mozart never paid either the Archbishop or the Count back in kind. Mozart's revenge was in making the offensive character Osmin, in *Die Entführung aus dem Serail*, a combined caricature of Colloredo and Arco.

47

WILLIAM CORDER

1804-28

WILLIAM CORDER must be Suffolk's most famous murderer, and he must rank among the nation's most celebrated rotters. He was born the son of a well-to-do farmer in Polstead, Suffolk. He was one of eight children, but two of his brothers died in infancy. He was a bright boy at school and it was expected that he would follow his thrifty and able yeoman father and make his living from the land. He was rather sharp-featured and short-sighted, and his habit of holding a page close to his face to facilitate reading earned him the nickname 'Foxy'. He was to prove vulpine in later life in rather more sinister ways. He always seemed to have been attracted by the idea of having a good time and was a rowdy young jackanapes, often mixed up in tricks and mild examples of dishonesty, such as thieving. He was not inclined to the work ethic, but had an eye for the main chance and the easy way. As a teenager he was soon in poor company, but always seemed able to bluff his way out of serious trouble. His father had his doubts about him, but his mother's opinion was that boys will be boys, and to a considerable extent she indulged him. The death of his father and his elder brothers left William in charge of the farm at Polstead, and he began to live fast and loose. He developed expensive tastes — for the turf and fine clothes — as well as drink and a wide variety of young female company.

Social mythology has done its work on young Maria Marten, the girl who was so tragically to tangle with William Corder, though to call her an 'experienced' young woman in no way reduces the horror of Corder's terrible crime. Maria was born in 1801. She was the daughter of the local mole-catcher. Her parents saw to it that she had a good schooling and she affected some rather genteel airs. She was a beautiful young woman and was never short of male company. She had had a couple of serious affairs, one of which resulted in a child who was aged three at the time of her association with William Corder. The couple met in 1826. It was rumoured in the village that the father of her previous child, who had died in infancy, was none other than William's elder brother, Thomas Corder. She was receiving financial support for her surviving daughter from its wealthy father, who was a neighbouring farmer. Corder found this income useful to finance some of his sporting activities.

William Corder began to court Maria in earnest and went out of his way to make a good impression on her family. The Martens lived in a cottage at the end of a row just a few hundred yards from the infamous red barn which has made this case so famous. They saw in William the answer to a rather difficult problem. He was very interested in Maria and showed all the signs of being very fond of her. He was well off, it seemed to them, and it might not otherwise be easy to marry off their daughter quite so well. She did already have an illegitimate child, which might have been an obstacle to a good marriage. Her friendship with William Corder soon produced another child. He was considerate enough to arrange for her to be delivered of this encumbrance away from the village. The child died within a month. Suspiciously enough, as it was to seem later, in the light of subsequent events, Corder took the body away at night and buried it in an unmarked, secret grave. Although William Corder had promised the woman marriage, and had always led her parents to believe in his honourable intentions, there now followed a period when William and Maria were known frequently to quarrel.

Their disagreements were invariably about money, and Maria's mother got the definite impression that what was happening was that William Corder was spending the allowance which Maria was receiving from the father of her young daughter. The child's father was adamant in his assertions that her allowance had been dispatched. William Corder claimed that he had seen a copy of a writ which was to be served on Maria for burdening the parish with her pauper children. The sordid fact is that Corder had intercepted the letter and pocketed the money himself. The story of the writ made no sense to Maria, which is hardly surprising, as it was an invention of William Corder's. Nevertheless, at this stage, he was still claiming that he intended to marry her. Maria waited to see reliable evidence of the arrangements.

Currently, he was making arrangements for her, but these were not of the kind which she had in mind. In May 1827 he told her that they were to be married on the 14th of that month at Ipswich. He took her away but brought her back without marrying her. On Wednesday and Thursday of the same week the couple went out but came back again, still with no marriage service having been read over them. Then on that Friday, 18 May, he came to her again and explained a plan. In spite of the writ and the fact that the village constable might be out looking for her — which Maria believed to be the case — he had a scheme worked out which would enable them to get married that very day. She was to dress as a man, in trousers, striped waistcoat, top coat and a hat which hid her long hair. William would collect her in the gig and, taking her clothes with her in a bundle, she could change in the red barn before they went off to church. She took with her a petticoat, stockings, white stays, a black cambric skirt and a reticule. Her mother packed these items in a brown holland bag. Mrs Marten also clearly remembered a green neck scarf.

The account in the *Newgate Calendar* reports that: 'In the course of a conversation which took place between Corder and the mother of the girl, before their going away, the former repeatedly declared his intention to make the girl his lawful wife, and he urged as a reason why she should go with him immediately, that he knew that a warrant had been issued against her, for her bastard children. Within a few minutes after Corder had quitted the house, he was seen by the brother of the girl walking towards the Red Barn, with a pickaxe over his shoulder.'

William Corder came back from the 'wedding' and lived with his mother in Polstead. He explained Maria's absence was only temporary, saying that she was staying with friends of his while he squared things with his family and friends. Maria was not seen even as late as that September, in which month William Corder announced that he was going to the continent. He took £400 with him and before he left he was most insistent that the red barn be filled with stock. His mother subsequently had several letters from him, saying the happy couple were living in the Isle of Wight. Curiously enough, these letters were posted in London.

Mrs Marten began to grow very apprehensive about her daughter. She was troubled by terrible dreams in March 1828. On three consecutive nights she dreamed that Maria had been murdered and buried in the red barn. She worked on her husband's fears and eventually he obtained permission to search the barn, on the face of it to look for Maria's clothes. The grain which Corder had arranged to have stored there was now gone, and a dreadful discovery was made — after digging for only a few moments he found a piece of his daughter's shawl. Further excavations revealed that human remains had been buried at a depth of about eighteen inches. It was his daughter's body, by now seriously decomposed, but recognisable from her dress and certain marks on her teeth. A coroner's inquest found that Maria had died by violent means, a bullet had passed through her right eye and there was a wound in her throat as if from some sharp implement. The body was clothed in a shift, petticoat, stays, stockings and shoes. It had been thrust in a sack. Corder was now under suspicion and attempts were made to track him down in London. He was found, married to another woman, whom he had encountered five months previously through a matrimonial agency. Corder was running a school for young ladies in Brentford. The officer who arrested him gained easy access by posing as a father who wished to place his child in Corder's educational establishment.

Corder initially denied that he ever knew anybody called Maria Marten. When his house in Ealing Lane was searched, a pair of pistols, a powder flask, balls and a dagger were found. These items were later identified as having been in Corder's possession while at Polstead. Mrs Marten recognised the bag the firearms were kept in and a cutler recognised the knife as one he had specially sharpened for Corder a few days before Maria Marten disappeared. The accused was taken back to Polstead to be examined by the coroner and, the case now having become much talked about, many people turned up to see him brought back to town. Vast crowds attended the court. Corder was clearly much agitated as the depositions of the various witnesses began to tell against him. A verdict of 'Wilful Murder' was brought against him, and he was sent to the county jail to await his trial at the Shire Hall, Bury St Edmunds. Again numerous onlookers arrived to watch the scene and his passage to court was the occasion of shouts and groans.

Corder's defence was that he had taken Maria to the barn as arranged and that he intended to go through the marriage with her, but that they had a quarrel and she shot herself with his pistol in a fit of depression. He was the only person who could tell how she met her end, but as suspicion would light on him, he had concealed the body. His subsequent acts were arranged to support the belief that he and Maria had gone away together. The other marks on her body he explained as the results of its being disinterred. He was found guilty and sentenced to death. His wife had believed initially that he had been arrested for bigamy, but throughout his trial for murder she had clearly been under a terrible strain.

Before his execution he admitted his guilt in a full confession: 'I acknowledge being guilty of the death of poor Maria Marten, by shooting her with a pistol. The particulars are as follows. When we left her father's house we began to quarrel about the burial of the child, she apprehending that the place wherein it was deposited would be found out. The quarrel continued for about three quarters of an hour upon this and about other subjects. A scuffle ensued, and during the scuffle, and at the time I think that she had hold of me, I took the pistol from the side-pocket of my velveteen jacket and fired. She fell, and died in an instant. I never saw even a struggle. I was overwhelmed with agitation and dismay — the body fell near the doors on the floor of the barn. A vast quantity of blood issued from the wound and ran on to the floor and through the crevices. Having determined to bury the body in the barn (about two hours after she was dead), I went and borrowed the spade off Mrs Stowe; but before I went there, I dragged the body from the barn into the chaff-house, and locked up the barn. I returned again to the barn, and began to dig the hole, but the spade being a bad one, and the earth firm and hard, I was obliged to go home for a pickaxe and a better spade, with which I dug the hole, and then buried the body. I think I dragged the body by the handkerhief that was tied round her neck. It was dark when I finished covering up the body. I went the next day and washed the blood from off the barn floor. I declare to Almighty God I had no sharp instrument about me, and that no other wound but the one made by the pistol was inflicted by me. I have been guilty of great idleness, and at times led a dissolute life, but I hope through the mercy of God to be forgiven.' He was hanged on 11 August 1828 before a crowd of at least seven thousand.

The 'Murder in the Red Barn' was one of the most sensational and celebrated crimes of the day. While the trial of William Corder was proceeding, a camera obscura in the streets was exhibiting the crime, and hardly had Corder been hanged than the first production of *Murder in the Red Barn* took place at the Royal Pavilion Theatre, Mile End. The rope with which Corder had been hanged was sold off for a guinea an inch. A section of his skin, suitably tanned to preserve it, was exhibited for years at the shop of a leather-seller in Oxford Street.

The terrible crime of William Corder was further implanted in popular consciousness by street-shows, puppet-plays, ballads and melodramas. The indefatigable J Catnach, printer of street literature in Seven Dials, London, published a set of verses supposedly by William Corder:

Come all you thoughtless young men, a warning take by me,
And think upon my unhappy fate to be hanged upon a tree;
My name is William Corder, to you I do declare,
I courted Maria Marten, most beautiful and fair.

I promised I would marry her upon a certain day,
Instead of that, I was resolved to take her life away.
I went into her father's house the 18th day of May,
Saying, my dear Maria, we will fix the wedding day.

If you will meet me at the Red-barn, as sure as I have life,
I will take you to Ipswich town, and there make you my wife;
I then went home and fetched my gun, my pickaxe and my spade,
I went into the Red-barn, and there I dug her grave.

With heart so light, she thought no harm, to meet him she did go
He murdered her all in the barn, and laid her body low:
After the horrible deed was done, she lay weltering in her gore,
Her bleeding mangled body he buried beneath the Red-barn floor.

Now all things being silent, her spirit could not rest,
She appeared unto her mother, who suckled her at her breast;
For many a long month or more, her mind being sore oppress'd,
Neither night or day she could not take any rest.

Her mother's mind being so disturbed, she dreamt three nights o'er,
Her daughter she lay murdered beneath the Red-barn floor;
She sent the father to the barn, when he the ground did thrust,
And there he found his daughter mingling with the dust.

My trial is hard, I could not stand, most woeful was the sight,
When her jaw-bone was brought to prove, which pierced my heart quite;
Her aged father standing by, likewise his loving wife,
And in her grief her hair she tore, she scarcely could keep life.

Adieu, adieu, my loving friends, my glass is almost run,
On Monday next will be my last, when I am to be hang'd;
So you, young men, who do pass by, with pity look on me,
For murdering Maria Marten, I was hang'd upon the tree.

WILLIAM HENRY CRANSTOUN

1714-52

and *MARY BLANDY*

executed 1752

WILLIAM HENRY CRANSTOUN was the son of the 5th Lord Cranstoun, who met and married Anne Murray of Leith. He was a captain in the British army and came to London on recruiting service, where he met Mary, the daughter of a solicitor of some prosperity at Henley-on-Thames. Mary was a handsome young woman and had many suitors, but Cranstoun took her heart by storm. It is difficult to work out why. He was not good looking and was not a man of great intellect, sophistication or charm. It is true he had aristocratic connections, he was brother to a Scottish lord, and nephew of Lord Mark Ker, who had in fact got him his commission.

When he pressed his attentions on Mary Blandy and asked her father for her hand in marriage Mr Blandy began to resist, as he was by no means taken with the young gallant. Mary's father was informed by a disappointed suitor that Cranstoun had a wife and children in Scotland. Mr Blandy told Mary what he had learned and was surprised to realise that she knew already and did not consider this an obstacle to her marriage to Cranstoun. The young officer had told her that this Scottish 'connection' was not in fact a real marriage, and that it could be ended at any time suitable to him. Mr Blandy then refused Cranstoun access to the Blandy house and Cranstoun departed. This was a matter of some sadness not only to Mary, but to her mother, who had taken to the Scottish Lothario. Soon after Cranstoun's departure, Mrs Blandy fell ill.

Mary's mother insisted that Cranstoun return and he came to her bedside. She instructed that no one but Cranstoun, whom she called her 'dearly loved son', was to nurse her. Mrs Blandy died soon afterwards.

Cranstoun and Mary then devised a terrible plot. Cranstoun was to return to Scotland and send Mary the means to poison her father. This was to be done gradually so that it might seem a long illness. They laid a convincing path for Mr Blandy's demise, claiming they had heard strange music in the house which was a sure sign of his coming death. Cranstoun asserted that he had second sight and that he had seen Mr Blandy's spirit walking and making signs indicating that Mr Blandy was to die. Mary constantly chatted to the servants about these and other signs and portents. Meantime, from Scotland Cranstoun sent Mary certain white powders 'to clean Scotch pebbles' — the powder was in fact arsenic.

Her love for him and his supposed fortune of £10,000 caused Mary to administer this poison to her own father gradually over the course of the winter. Mr Blandy suffered terrible pains in his intestines and his teeth became loose — several of them dropping out. She called him a toothless old rogue and wished him in hell. At one time he said his tea was too bitter to drink. An old charwoman finished it off and it nearly killed her. A servant who drank a cordial prepared by Mary for her father was taken ill for three weeks. Mary now became more cautious. She administered the poison in a thin gruel where she considered it was less likely to be detected.

All this while Cranstoun was in Scotland, writing Mary letters which encouraged her to get on with the terrible deed. Mary foolishly warned the servants against tasting the food she prepared for her ailing father, actually saying that it would 'do for them' if it passed their lips. Mr Blandy lived until the following summer.

Cranstoun wrote from Scotland urging Mary to double the dose, and assuring her that Lady Cranstoun was decorating the apartments at Sennel House, the Cranstoun mansion, where the happy couple were to live once this obstacle to their marriage had been removed. He knew by now that his marriage to Anne Murray was legal and binding, but nevertheless he abetted Mary Blandy in the murder of her father. Mr Blandy's agonies increased. He told his daughter that it was like having a fireball inside him. Mary's answer was that he would never be in good health while it was there.

But Mary was an incompetent murderess. One of the maids was about to wash up Mr Blandy's dinner plates and as she went to rinse it she saw the white powder glittering at the bottom of the basin. Her suspicions aroused, she took it next door and showed it to the neighbour. This lady kept it and had it examined by an apothecary. Although the results were not known until poor Mr Blandy had died, the tests proved the substance to be arsenic.

Mary was observed throwing Cranstoun's letters into the fire, together with a small packet containing a white powder. A servant noticed what she was doing, pulled the remnants out of the flames and preserved them. Written in Cranstoun's handwriting on the packet were the words 'Powder to clean the pebbles'.

Towards the end she confessed to her father what she had done, and blamed Cranstoun for the whole scheme. She promised her father that she would never see her lover again if her father would only forgive her. Mr Blandy magnanimously blessed his daughter and forgave her from the bottom of his heart. Mary said: 'Every word is like a sword of fire piercing my heart.' She implored her father not to curse her. He answered: 'I curse thee? No — I bless thee, and hope God will bless thee and amend thy life.'

Mary then gave a visitor a letter to post to Cranstoun, but the person was suspicious of Mary's manner, took the letter aside and opened it. She read the contents and copied them out:

> Dear Billy — My father is so bad that I have only time to tell you that if you do not hear from me soon again, don't be frightened. I am better myself. Lest any accident should happen to your letters, take care what you write.

The person entrusted to post this letter took it and showed it to the ailing Mr Blandy. He murmered, 'Poor love-sick girl! What will not a woman do for the man she loves!' He eventually died in considerable pain and the same day Mary Blandy attempted to run away. She tried to bribe a manservant with £500 to accompany her. The same evening she asked her maidservant to summon a post-chaise to carry her to London. But she was arrested.

The evidence told heavily against her. Her lover, William Henry Cranstoun, immediately he heard that Mr Blandy had died, and that Mary, the object of his affections, had been arrested, fled from Scotland and escaped to France. While Mary was standing trial for her life, he was supported by friends at Boulogne. Some officers in France, who were related to the wife he had abandoned in Scotland, threatened to expose him, and so he fled again. He changed his name to Dunbar and lived in Flanders. Here he became seriously ill, was taken in by monks at Furnes, and died in their hands.

Mary was found guilty and sentenced to death. She was hanged at Oxford on 6 April 1752.

AMELIA ELIZABETH DYER

1839-96

A FORMER Salvation Army officer stood trial on 21 May 1896, at the Old Bailey. While held in custody she sang hymns in a tuneless voice in her cell. She stood calmly in the dock, blinking and smiling, with the Sankey and Moody hymn-book in her hands. As the proceedings continued, it was noticed that she constantly pored over its contents, silently mouthing the words to herself.

The following year the Infant Protection Act — subsequently renamed the Children Act in 1908 — was passed by parliament. Under this Act any person or persons who undertook for reward the maintainance or nursing of infants under the age of seven had to give written notice to the local authority of this fact within forty-eight hours of receiving the child. The names and addresses of all persons involved in the transaction, and the date of birth and sex of the child had to be recorded. The death or the removal of the child to another place of domicile was likewise to be notified. The local authority had the right to visit premises where children being cared for by those other than their parents were living. No insurance could be taken out by anyone adopting or fostering a child.

The trial of this strange religious-seeming woman in her late fifties, and the act of 1897 are very closely connected. The woman was Amelia Elizabeth Dyer, known to history as the Reading Baby Farmer.

Mrs Dyer had made a tolerable living for some time by taking in — for an outright fee, usually of £10 — the unwanted and invariably illegitimate young children of mothers unable to support them. She murdered the infants by strangling them, and disposed of their bodies in packages weighted with a brick in the waters of the Thames. She then sold or pawned the clothes which might have been provided with them and went on to collect her next victim. When her crimes were under investigation the police found between two and three hundredweight of undisposed clothing and fifteen pawn tickets for various collections of baby clothing at Mrs Dyer's addresses in Reading and Willesden. They also discovered over forty bodies of very young children in various stages of decomposition in the Thames. Forensic examination proved beyond doubt that these children had been murdered — none of them had been still-born — and all had been strangled with tape.

Mrs Dyer was brought to justice ultimately by some pencilled writing on a sheet of brown paper wrapped round the body of one small girl. The name and address of a Mrs Dyer could clearly be deciphered. This paper was traced to a draper's shop in Reading. The police then visited a certain house in Kensington Road, Reading. It was empty. Their enquiries revealed that the occupant had moved to lodgings in Caversham. While this address was visited and Mrs Amelia Elizabeth Dyer taken into custody, a thorough search of the address in Kensington Road was undertaken.

The findings of the police at this address constructed the most monumental case against the accused — letters which detailed offers of adoption couched in moving and sentimental terms; telegrams from mothers enquiring about the welfare of their children; pawn-tickets for babies' clothes; receipts detailing payments for advertisements in various London newspapers.

One case alone is sufficient to example the manner of this extraordinary woman's method of work. In the opening months of 1896 a young woman named Evelina Edith Marmon gave birth to a baby girl. She could not afford to keep the child; she worked behind the bar in a public house, and had neither the time nor the money to devote to motherhood. She saw an advertisement in a local newspaper, asking for a child for adoption. She wrote in reply and had a charming letter which the postmark told her came from Caversham, near Reading:

> Dear Madam:
>
> In reference to your letter of adoption of a child, I beg to say that I shall be glad to have a dear little baby girl, one that I can bring up and call my own. First, I must tell you that we are plain, homely people, in fairly good circumstances. I have a good and comfortable home. I am alone a great deal, and I don't want a child for money's sake, but for company and comfort. A child with me will have a good home, and a mother's love and care. We belong to the Church of England. I hope to hear from you again.
>
> > Yours faithfully,
> >
> > Annie Amelia Stanfield.

Evelina wrote in answer and was relieved to learn that dear, kindly Mrs Stanfield would happily look after her child at an outright price of £10. Evelina thought she would be able to scrape up this sum somehow, and wrote to say so. She added that she would like to come and visit her little Doris from time to time. Homely Mrs Stanfield answered her letter:

> I shall be only too pleased for you to come and see me sometimes. I assure you that it would be as great a treat to us as the change would be to you. I should really feel more comfortable to know the dear little soul had someone who really cared for her. I shall value her all the more, rest assured.
>
> My husband idolises children. There is a lovely orchard at the back of the house where Baby can enjoy the fresh air . . .

Evelina lived in the Midlands, but Mrs Stanfield came there to collect the child. Her mother paid up, kissed Doris goodbye and after promising to keep in touch Mrs Stanfield left. The body of poor little Doris Marmon was identified a month later after being fished out of the waters of the Thames at Reading.

The police arrested Mrs Dyer, alias Stanfield, and her son-in-law Arthur Ernest Palmer. Charges against Palmer were later dropped as Mrs Dyer wrote a confession which she handed to the matron of Reading jail. She wrote it to the Chief Superintendent of police:

> Sir:
>
> Will you kindly grant me the favour of presenting this to the magistrates on Saturday, 18th. inst. [April]. I have made the statement now for I may not have the opportunity then. I must relieve my mind. I do not know, and I feel my days are numbered, but I do feel it is an awful thing drawing innocent people into trouble. I do know I shall have to answer before my Maker in Heaven for the awful crimes I have committed, but, as God Almighty is my judge in heaven as on hearth (*sic*) neither my daughter, Mary Ann Palmer, or her husband, Arthur Ernest Palmer, I do most solemnly declare that neither of them had anything at all to do with it. They never knew I contemplated doing such a wicked thing until it was too late. I am

speaking the truth and nothing but the truth, as I hope to be forgiven. I myself and I alone must stand before my Maker in heaven to give answer for it all.

Witness my hand,

Amelia Dyer.

She wrote in similar terms to other members of her family. She was found guilty in May 1896 at Reading of the murder of Doris and another child whose body had been found at the same time, one Harry Simmons, who had been adopted by the same methods. She was then confined in Holloway pending her trial at the Old Bailey.

When she was tried on 21 May 1896 the only possible defence was insanity. It was true that she had been confined at various mental institutions at various times earlier in her life, but the prosecution was able to convince the jury that she had gone in voluntarily to escape pressing creditors or to avoid having to answer awkward enquiries from the mothers of children whom she had taken care of. The jury came to believe that her religious mania and loss of memory (another symptom she manifested while in custody) were simulated. Some of the most revealing evidence was given in court by her own daughter, Margaret Palmer. In June 1895, she deposed, she had been living in Cardiff. Her mother had joined her there and she had three babies with her. Mrs Palmer had with her an adopted daughter of ten. She was about to leave for town and had entrusted her mother with this child, whom she was never to see again. Her mother told her that a rich lady had taken a fancy to her and had begged to be allowed to take her away to live with her. When Mrs Dyer subsequently came to Reading she had only one baby with her.

The judge asked what had become of the others? Mrs Palmer said that her mother had told her that one had died and another two had been given back to their parents. The court was visibly chilled by some of her testimony:

> On one occasion my mother came to see me, bringing an infant with her. I was putting my own baby to bed. The one she had with her was crying bitterly and she said: 'I will undress this one, too. That will quiet it.' I then went into the next room to see to my own little one, and when I returned, I saw the baby lying on the couch, closely muffled in a shawl, seemingly asleep. My mother would not let me go near it. The next morning I was surprised to see no trace of the infant. But I caught a glimpse of a bundle underneath the couch. I later found some tape had vanished from my work-box. When my mother left the house, I said to her; 'What will people say if you come here with a baby and leave without one?' She replied; 'You must make some excuse or other.'

Mrs Dyer admitted to fostering and killing babies for fifteen years. Her prices ranged form £10 to as much as £70 if she thought the parents could afford such a sum to hush up a little social indiscretion. At the time of her trial she was, in fact, still receiving payments from parents who were paying her by instalments. She was unable to make a statement as to the full number she had disposed of, only saying: 'You'll recognise mine by the tape'. She was hanged at Newgate on 10 June 1896.

RUTH ELLIS

1926-55

THE LAST WOMAN to hang in Britain was born in Rhyl, North Wales. Ruth's father Arthur Neilson was a cellist who played, under the name Hornby, on ocean-liners and in cinema and theatre orchestras. In the 1930s he abandoned his musical career and went to work as a porter and telephonist in Basingstoke. Ruth left Fairfields Senior Girls' School at the age of fourteen and got a job as a waitress in Reading.

Dark-haired and vivacious, Ruth was also impulsive. When her father was injured during the Blitz she risked her own life to pull him out of the bombed building. After working in a factory near Camberwell, Ruth spent some time in hospital suffering from rheumatic fever. To aid her recovery she took up dancing as a form of therapy and gradually her passion for performing became a priority. She did a drama course at Richmond, sang with a danceband and worked as a photographer's assistant.

Attractive, and attracted, to men Ruth became pregnant by Clare, a French Canadian, but discovered that her lover had a wife and children back home in Canada. When Ruth's son was born, in 1944, she called him Clare Andrea 'Andy' Neilson and supported him by working as a photographer's model.

Gradually, Ruth drifted towards the nightlife of London. She was hired as a hostess in the Court Club, Mayfair, by the proprietor Morris Conley. The job was lucrative and more glamorous than anything Ruth had done before and she enjoyed the company of the young men who spent their evenings in the club. Ruth was especially fond of George Johnston Ellis, a divorced dentist and advanced alcoholic. 'I thought he was rather pathetic,' she admitted. 'He told such wild tales I think he really believed them. He used to spend a lot of money and was good for champagne. He seemed to have taken a liking to me.' Distressed by Ellis's drinking, Ruth persuaded him to go into hospital as a voluntary patient seeking help for his alcoholic problem. She agreed to marry Ellis only on the condition that he would continue his treatment. After the ceremony on 8 November 1950, Ellis kept his word and returned to hospital.

After taking the cure Ellis was employed as a dentist at Warsash, Hampshire. He soon fell off the wagon and was a constant source of embarrassment to Ruth. She gave, however, as good as she got. A passionate and jealous woman, she was convinced her husband was having affairs with his female patients and often turned up at their houses to check on the drunken dentist. On 2 October 1951, Ruth's daughter Georgina was born, but the marriage was clearly collapsing and a month later Ellis tried to divorce Ruth on the grounds of cruelty. His application was unsuccessful as the Ellises had been married for less than three years. Ellis could not cope with Ruth any longer and left her. She called Morris Conley who gladly gave her her old job as a hostess at the Court Club — or Carroll's as it was renamed.

While her parents looked after her children, Ruth moved — courtesy of Morris Conley — into a one-room flat in Oxford Street. As well as changing her address she changed her appearance: she became a blonde and behaved with abandon, enjoying casual affairs with Conley's customers. In 1952 she had an ectopic pregnancy and underwent an operation in the Middlesex Hospital.

In 1953 Ruth returned to Carroll's which now welcomed members of the Steering Wheel Club, including doctor's son David Blakely, a twenty-four-year-old racing driver. When Blakely was five his father had been found not guilty of murder. Divorce followed and Blakely's mother married Humphrey Wyndham Cook, a racing driver. Blakely had funds to flash around: he inherited £7,000 when his father died in 1952 and he received an allowance from his stepfather. Ruth was not particularly impressed; and after their first encounter she thought him a 'pompous little ass'.

Morris Conley admired Ruth's manner and, in 1953, appointed her manageress of the Little Club, Knightsbridge, and gave her a rent-free flat above the club. As a member of the Little Club, Blakely made much of the manageress and Ruth now liked him enough to welcome him to her flat as a lover. As J H H Gaute and Robin Odell explain, in *Lady Killers* (Bath, 1980), 'David [Blakely] was leading a double life, for on 11 November [1953] an announcement in *The Times* told the world of his engagement to the daughter of a wealthy manufacturer. David slept with Ruth Mondays to Fridays, but deserted her at weekends when he returned to his parents' home in Penn, Buckinghamshire. This was an extraordinary routine, because he had a weekday job at Penn as an engineer . . . His mother and step-father lived in a spacious house in which David had his own self-contained flat with a separate entrance from the house. His weekends were mostly taken up with his pursuit of motor-racing and wild party-going.'

Ruth became pregnant by David and in February 1954 had an abortion. Two months later she met Carole Findlater, a friend of David's. She already knew Anthony 'Ant' Findlater since Carole's husband, like Blakely, frequented the Little Club. Ant and David had joined forces to develop the 'Emperor', a new sports car, so Blakely saw a lot of Carole. In May 1954, the month that Ant and Carole Findlater had a baby girl, Ruth was once more contending with her own husband, Ellis. He had turned up at the Little Club and was again trying to divorce Ruth on the grounds of mental cruelty. She decided to defend herself by citing the subject of Ellis's outrageous drinking.

By this time Ruth had other boyfriends besides Blakely. She enjoyed provoking Blakely by ostentatiously keeping the company of one of his friends, Desmond Cussen. In June 1954 Blakely went to France to participate in the Le Mans race. He told Ruth he would be back for a birthday celebration in the Little Club but failed to materialise. This irritated Ruth who turned to Desmond Cussen for sexual consolation. When Blakely eventually came back to London, early in July, he was somewhat the worse for wear during an unfortunate evening at the Little Club. He announced that his engagement was off; Ruth sprayed Carole Findlater with a soda syphon, a joke that backfired when Carole left in a fury.

Ruth and Blakely soon got together again but she had a characteristic outburst of jealousy when she spotted evidence of his infidelity. David 'got into bed,' Ruth explained, 'and was stretching over to switch out the light when I noticed love bites all over his shoulders, neck and back. I went quite cold with shock, and I told him to get out and leave the flat.' The next day David returned to the Little Club, full of remorse. 'He was emotionally upset,' Ruth recalled, 'and he went down on his knees, crying and saying "I'm sorry, darling. I do love you. I'll prove it", and he asked me to marry him, and I said, "I don't think your mother or family will agree to this."' Blakely said that, if necessary, he would marry Ruth secretly. It was an offer enticing enough to persuade Ruth to withdraw her defence against Ellis's divorce action.

Blakely raced, in August 1954, at the International Sports Car event in the Netherlands. His car ran into trouble and he came back to England to face further problems. His dream-car, the 'Emperor', was swallowing most of his money and his stepfather was talking about stopping his allowance. Blakely took his anger out on Ruth; he threatened suicide and struck her for making overtures to her customers. As a result of Blakely's boorish behaviour Ruth lost her job. She accepted Desmond Cussen's offer to move into his Devonshire Street flat; many nights, though, were spent with Blakely at the Rodney Hotel, an arrangement Desmond had to tolerate.

Sharing Ruth with another man was not, however, good enough for Blakely. On Christmas Day, 1954, he turned up at Desmond's flat to make one of his scenes, after which he and Ruth left to spend the night at the Findlaters' flat in Hampstead. Blakely was so much restored by the experience that he drove the 'Emperor' into second place in the Kent Cup at Brands Hatch.

For some weeks Ruth and Blakely carried on their stop-go relationship, sometimes rowing and sometimes spending nights together at the Rodney Hotel. One row was particularly spectacular and Blakely phoned two friends, Ant Findlater and Clive Gunnell, to rescue him from Desmond's flat where Ruth had scratched his face. The morning after the night before Ruth sent a telegram to Blakely with the message: 'Haven't you got the guts to say goodbye to my face — Ruth'.

On 14 January 1955, shortly after Ruth's telegram had been sent, Ellis was granted a decree nisi which meant that after six weeks Ruth would be free to marry Blakely — if he so wished. On 6 February Blakely came to Desmond's flat looking for trouble and knocked Ruth about a bit. Next day Desmond drove her to Blakely's flat in Penn where she hoped to 'get an apology from that bastard'. Some words were exchanged there before Ruth returned with Desmond. Next day she and Desmond saw Blakely's Vanguard outside the Bull Hotel, Gerrards Cross. Desmond went into the pub, summoned Blakely outside and invited him to 'try beating me up instead of a woman'. Blakely backed off, apologised to Ruth and drove away. When Ruth arrived back at Desmond's, after having her bruises examined at Middlesex Hospital, she found carnations and a card with the message 'Sorry darling, I love you, David'.

At this point Ruth decided to move out of Desmond's flat so she could spare him further exhausting incidents. She found a flat at 44 Egerton Gardens, Kensington. Desmond paid the rent of six guineas a week and Blakely moved in with Ruth. As usual they fought and made up with their usual intensity; Ruth collected a fair amount of bruises which did nothing to help her attempt to resume her career as a model. To make matters worse, Ruth was pregnant again. On 25 February 1955 Ellis's decree nisi was made absolute but Blakely refused to celebrate with her. Inevitably, there was another period of enstrangement.

Ruth could not live for long without Blakely, so Desmond drove her to the Steering Wheel Club where she confronted her 'loverboy' (as she called Blakely). Convinced that Blakely was being unfaithful to her, Ruth spent a night watching a house in Penn for signs of Blakely's presence. 'I was obviously jealous of him now,' she later acknowledged. 'I mean the tables had been turned. I was jealous of him, whereas he, before, had been jealous of me. I had now given up my business — what he had wanted me to do — left all my friends behind connected with clubs and things, and it was my turn to be jealous of him.'

Blakely resented Ruth spying on him and during their next set-to at Egerton Gardens he hit her in the face, grabbed her by the throat and punched her in the stomach. Within a few days she had a miscarriage but Blakely was totally indifferent to Ruth's predicament since the 'Emperor' was being troublesome and had to be withdrawn from a race. Still suffering from her miscarriage, losing blood and feeling depressed, Ruth felt that Blakely had 'turned me into a surly, miserable woman. I was growing to hate him, and he was so conceited and said that all women bored him. He was so much in love with himself.'

On Wednesday, 6 April 1955, Blakely made an effort to be nice to Ruth. He gave her a photograph inscribed 'with all my love'. Next night he took her to see a film but on Good Friday he was away to work on the 'Emperor'. When he saw Ant and Carole Findlater he told them of the trouble Ruth was causing him and they invited him home for the weekend in their flat at Tanza Road, Hampstead.

Predictably enough, Ruth was upset when Blakely did not show up on Friday evening. She went to Tanza Road where there was no answer when she rang the doorbell. When she phoned from a callbox the receiver was replaced at the sound of her voice. She tried the doorbell a second time and was sure she could hear a woman's mocking laughter in the flat. To make her presence felt she broke three windows in Blakely's Vanguard, parked outside the Findlaters' flat. The police came and told her to go home. 'I did not sleep,' she remembered later.

On the morning of Easter Saturday, 10 April 1955, Ruth rang Tanza Road. Ant Findlater took the call and was told by Ruth, 'I hope you are having an enjoyable holiday, because you have ruined mine'. After lunch with Desmond, Ruth came back to Egerton Road and put her son Andy — staying with her over the Easter holidays — to bed. Still nursing her wrath over the conspicuous absence of Blakely she felt 'very upset and I had a peculiar idea that I wanted to kill him'. Fortuitously there was a .38 calibre 6-shot Smith and Wesson revolver in the flat (though how it got there is still a matter for conjecture) and she put it into her handbag.

Back at Tanza Road, the Findlaters and Blakely were enjoying a drink with Clive Gunnell. Around 9 pm Blakely and Gunnell went to the 'Magdala' public house, South Hill Park, Hampstead, to buy in some fresh supplies of beer. They paid for three flagons of light ale, had a drink at the bar, and went into the street to get into the Vanguard. While Gunnell waited at the passenger side of the car, Blakely — carrying a flagon of ale — looked for his car keys. Ruth approached, appealed to him, and when he ignored her, shot him. Looking for cover, Blakely staggered to the back of the car where Ruth fired another bullet into him. Finally, as he lay face down, she put four more bullets into his body. An off-duty policeman, Alan Thomson, emerged from the 'Magdala' and took the gun from Ruth. At Hampstead Police Station she admitted, 'I am guilty' and said that the gun 'was given to me about three years ago in the club by a man whose name I do not remember' (though she later said that Desmond had given her the gun).

During her time at Holloway Prison, Ruth kept a Bible and a photograph of Blakely by her. Two days after the murder she wrote to Blakely's mother saying, 'The two people I blame for David's death, and my own, are the

Findlaters. No doubt you will not understand this but *perhaps* before I hang you will know what I mean.' After this enigmatic message she added: 'I implore you to try to forgive David for living with me, but we were very much in love with one another. Unfortunately David was not satisfied with one woman in his life. I have forgiven David, I only wish I could have found it in my heart to have forgiven when he was alive . . . I shall die loving your son.'

She seemed to accept the prospect of the death sentence philosophically, telling her solicitor, 'An eye for an eye, a life for a life. I took David's life, and I don't ask you to save mine'. Moreover, she told her mother, 'I won't go to prison for ten years or more and come out old and finished. I'd rather be hanged.' Her trial at the Old Bailey began on 20 June 1955 and ended two days later. Ruth showed no interest in her defence and freely admitted that she intended to kill Blakely. She was found guilty and sentenced to death.

Before she died she asked her mother to put pink and white carnations on Blakely's grave in Penn. On 13 July 1955 she received the Last Sacrament from the Roman Catholic chaplain at Holloway, took a drink of brandy, and went to her death. In 1971 her remains were taken from Holloway Prison and reburied at St Mary's Church, Amersham, not far from Blakely's grave at Penn.

HENRY FAUNTLEROY

1785-1824

HENRY FAUNTLEROY'S father was a respected and distinguished banker in the city of London. When Henry was fifteen he started work in his father's bank — Marsh, Stracey, Fauntleroy and Graham — in Berners Street. From 1807 until his arrest in 1824 he was a partner in the firm.

He lived a double life. On the surface he was the ideal young city gentleman and a pillar of society. His father had died and Henry lived quietly at home with his mother and sisters. His only eccentricity was the affectation of a somewhat Napoleonic appearance and of a gravity rather beyond his years. But he had a hidden life, which involved gambling, racing, mistresses, fast company and the *demi-monde*. He was seen in fashionable circles in Brighton, where he kept spacious accommodation. Rumours began to circulate about his extraordinary spending powers. All this cost a lot of money. But money he seemed to have.

The essence of his swindling was breathtakingly simple. As a banker he was in a position of trust. Considerable sums of money and securities of various kinds — mostly government stock of one kind or another — regularly passed through his hands in the course of business. The basic principle of the banker's trade is the safe-keeping of funds, which are invested on the client's behalf, and the regular payment of interest to the client from the profit made by investing the client's funds. Fauntleroy perceived that a system which enabled him to remove the stock he held for clients — which he could sell to his own advantage — would go undetected as long as the clients or their trustees continued to receive interest.

If he was proficient enough he would even be able to cover his tracks if clients or their trustees wanted the stock returned or transferred, as he would have sufficient time (in the normal course of events) to shift funds from another deposit. This would only require the correct signatures on the appropriate documents. The basic trick was forgery. Henry Fauntleroy was a skilled penman.

He would forge documents which gave him powers of attorney to wealthy clients who had placed large deposits in the bank. His skill lay in moving funds about from one account to another, each time covering his transactions with seemingly legal documents, all duly signed and witnessed. He used government bonds in the main, such as long annuities, consols, exchequer bills, so that in effect his swindling involved the Bank of England. If a client died, then Henry Fauntleroy replaced the missing stock with new forgeries in a new account. As long as clients regularly received an income from their interest the whole system ran as smoothly as clockwork. It was estimated that he took approximately £500,000 in this manner. He spent £10,000 on himself and used the rest to keep the various accounts in the bank properly stocked up.

While his enterprise was at its height he was renowned as one of the most profligate spenders of the day. He had an insatiable desire for expensive works of art and for expensive mistresses. His dinner parties were celebrated, his balls the most lavish. He was frequently seen dazzling the crowds as he whizzed by in splendid carriages. Among his most persistent associates was Mary Bertram, sometimes known as Mary Kent. She was the daughter of a Brighton bathing-woman. Mary was considered among the most fashionable, up-to-date and bang-on females around, and for this reason was called 'Mrs Bang'. Bernard Blackmantle (Charles Molloy Westmacott) in *The English Spy* (1825) wrote of her; 'Everybody knows *Bang*; that is everybody in the fashionable world. She must have been a delightful creature when she first *came out*, and has continued *longer in bloom* that any of the present *houris of the west*.'

Fauntleroy was wild about her and purchased a large house for her in Brighton in 1821. He was very often seen mixing with the most well-to-do members of society circulating at the royal watering-place. But it seemed it was no easy matter constantly to engage Henry Fauntleroy's amorous attentions, as he soon seduced a young schoolgirl, Maria Forbes, and provided a household for her in South Lambeth. He continued to enjoy the gay social whirl, unconscious that discovery was lurking just around the corner.

His exposure was the result of an accident. A certain J D Hulme was trustee of the estate of Francis William Bellis. Hulme was checking the investments of the estate and realised that £10,000 in consols was missing. The sum had been raised by sale of stock authorised under power of attorney. The document, on examination, revealed that the names of Mr Fauntleroy's co-trustees and one of the witnesses had been forged. Henry Fauntleroy was apprehended on 10 September 1824 on a warrant issued at Marlborough Street police office.

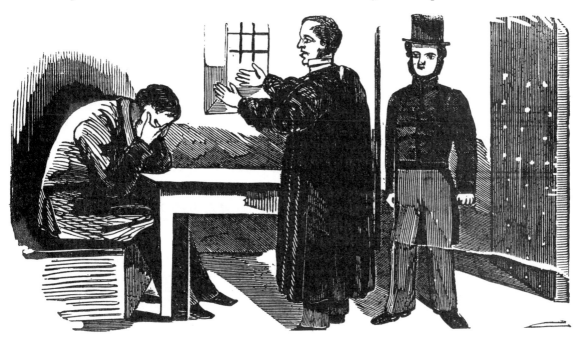

Henry Fauntleroy pleads for mercy.

Panic ensued and there was a run on the bank, which was only checked by a suspension of payments and eventually by a commission of bankruptcy. Newspapers fanned the story far and wide. Accounts of Fauntleroy's wild private life proliferated, including his sexual proclivities and the news of his clandestine marriage to a girl named Young (who had already borne him a child). It is ironic that he was eventually tried for defrauding this young lady's family of £5,000. His trial at the Old Bailey was a sensation.

As early as seven o'clock on the morning of 30 October 1824 there were crowds waiting to get in to the courtroom. Fauntleroy tried to argue in his defence, in the face of the terrible pile of evidence accumulated against him by the prosecution, that he had acted as he did mainly to protect the good name of the bank by propping up its tottering fortunes. There is indeed some evidence of this motivation behind his actions, for — astoundingly enough — among his private papers there was an acknowledgement of his guilt attached to one of the transactions which listed the sums involved and described what he had done. This statement concluded: 'In order to keep up the credit of our house, I have forged powers of attorney for the above sums and parties, and sold out to the amounts here stated, and without the knowledge of my partners. I kept up the payment of the dividends, but made no entries of such payments in our books. The Bank [the Bank of England] began first to refuse to discount our acceptances and to destroy the credit of our house: the Bank shall smart for it.'

In his concluding remarks to the court Fauntleroy said, throwing himself on the mercy of the jury, that he would not consent to be pictured as 'a cold blooded and abandoned profligate, ruining all around me for the selfish gratification of vice and sensuality, and involving even my confiding partners in the general destruction'. At the end of this address, which he read from a prepared statement, he sat down and wept with considerable agitation.

He was found guilty and sentenced to death. In spite of numerous petitions for mercy, he was hanged at Newgate before a crowd of over 100,000 people on 30 November 1824. He was dressed in a black coat, waistcoat and trousers, with silk stockings. He was perfectly composed. The *Newgate Calendar* comments, 'An almost universal sympathy was excited in his favour, in consequence of the melancholy termination of his career; but many . . . have but too powerful reasons to mourn the crimes of which he was guilty, depriving them as they did, in many instances, of every shilling of what otherwise would have been comfortable competencies, sufficient to maintain them in respectability through life.'

MARY FRITH, (MOLL CUTPURSE)

1584-1659

A GREAT DEAL is known about this extraordinary woman, who was a robber, thief and notorious fence, who manifested strong transvestite tendencies. She made a considerable impact on her period, featuring in two plays of the day — Middleton and Dekker's *The Roaring Girl* and Nathan Field's *Amends for the Ladies* — and being the subject of an anonymous biography — *The Life and Death of Mrs Mary Frith commonly called Moll Cutpurse* — which was published in 1612, over forty years before she died.

Moll was born in Aldersgate Street, the daughter of a shoe-maker. She was a tomboy from her very earliest days, and loved wearing boy's attire and joining in violent games and rough and tumble more suited to the young males of the species than to a young girl. She soon drifted into crime, and graduated from picking pockets and other forms of street robbery, to the much more lucrative profession of the fence. She actually opened a shop in Fleet Street. There was a

need and she supplied it. People who had been deprived of their property wanted it back; thieves wanted to get rid of the things which they had stolen. An agency was the obvious answer. She bought up the stolen goods and sold them for a good mark-up. Her most satisfied customers were usually those who had lost the items in the first place, but that is only understandable. Her service was so good that other fences just shut up shop, and those who had been robbed no longer bothered to advertise for their goods, they simply went to Moll's place. If the property had not yet reached her, she took the customer's name and address, and assured them she'd contact them as and when the goods came in! A considerable part of her success was due in a strange way to her honesty — the dishonest thief and the ordinary citizen trusted her equally.

She may be ranked an early pioneer of female emancipation as she attempted not only to muscle in on a male-dominated profession, but refused to wear 'female' clothes or act in the socially accepted 'female' manner — she wore men's clothes, smoked a pipe, drank like a fish and swore profusely. The heroine, Grace Seldom, castigates her in *Amends for Ladies*:

> Hence lewd impudent
> I know not what to term thee, man or woman,
> For nature shaming to acknowledge thee
> For either, hath produced thee to the world
> Without a sex; some say thou art a woman,

Others a man, but I think rather neither
Of man and horse, as the old centaurs were feigned.

The Life and Death of Mrs. Mary Frith calls her 'a notorious baggage that used to go in man's apparel, and challenged the field of diverse gallants . . . a very tom-rig or rumpscuttle she was, and delighted or sported only in boys' play and pastime, not minding or companying with the girls: many a bang and blow this hoyting (*sic*) procured her, but she was not so to be tamed or taken off from her rude inclinations; she could not endure their sedentary life of sewing or stitching; a sampler was as grievous as a winding sheet; her needle, bodkin, and thimble she could not think on quietly, wishing them changed into a sword and dagger for a bout at cudgels.'

In 1612 she was sentenced to undergo public penance at St Paul's Cross, and was observed to be tearful and distressed. There may well have been good reason for this, as by her own confession she drank three quarters of sack before hand and was certainly maudlin. During the English Civil War she pulled off one of her most daring escapades, holding up General Fairfax on Hounslow Heath, shooting him in the arm and killing two of his servants. The Parliamentary officers followed her. Her horse failed her at Turnham Green and she was captured and taken to Newgate.

She was condemned to be hanged, but she bribed her way out for an alleged £2,000. She was clearly a royalist at heart, for when she died she left a provision in her last will and testament that £20 of her fortune should be spent to celebrate the return of the King. She died in 1659 and Charles II was restored the following year.

GENGHIS KHAN

1162-1227

GENGHIS KHAN, the Mongol conqueror and tyrant, was born at Deligun Bulduk on the river Onon. He was the son of a Mongol chieftain, Yesukai, who was absent at battle when his son was born. He was victorious against his Tartar enemies and when, on his return, he was greeted by the news that he had a son, he was delighted to find the babe clutched in his hand a clot of blood like a red stone. He took this to refer to his victorious nature and a celebration of his recent triumph. It was really a symbol of the child's bloodthirsty and warlike propensities, as he was to grow into one of the greatest conquerers the world has ever seen. Genghis was to live to see his warriors victorious from the China Sea to the banks of the Dnieper. The very presence of the Turks in Europe is testimony to his armies' conquests — it was their advance which drove their Osmaanli ancestors from their original home in northern Asia, and led to their invasion of Bithynia under Othman, and to their advance into Europe under Amurath I.

Genghis served a hard apprenticeship. He succeeded his father when he was merely thirteen and for many years struggled to organise his armies against hostile tribesmen. His early success whetted an appetite for conquest which was never to leave him. For six years he subjugated the Naimans, between Lake Balkhash and the Irtish. He conquered Tangut, south of the Gobi Desert. The Turkish Uigurs voluntarily submitted to him and from these people he derived the Mongol civilisation, laws and alphabet. In 1211 he overran the empire of North China and within six years he had annexed the Kara-Chitai empire which stretched from Lake Balkhash to Tibet.

In 1218 he invaded the powerful empire of Kharezm, bounded by the Jaxartes, Indus, Persian Gulf and the Caspian. He took Bokhara, Samarkand and Kharezm (now Khiva, a province of USSR). The sacking of Bokhara must rank among the most bloody engagements of the early Middle Ages. The invading army was initially divided into two armies. One was commanded by Genghis Khan's second son, Jagatai, and marched against the Kankalis, the northern defenders of the Khwarizm empire. The second army was commanded by his eldest son, Juji, and advanced by way of Sighnak against Jand. Shah Mohammed led an army of 400,000 men against Genghis's armies. They were totally routed and left the bodies of 160,000 dead upon the field. Mohammed then fled into Samarkand. Genghis and his sons pursued them, besieging, sacking and pillaging city after city, returning home in 1225. His armies had penetrated northwards from the southern shore of the Caspian, through what is now Georgia into southern Russia and the Crimea, returning by way of the Volga. Another of his generals had completely conquered all northern China, except Honan. Genghis Khan's final conquest was a punitive expedition against the king of Tangut, north-east Tibet. He died on 18 August 1227. His empire stretched from the Black Sea to the Pacific, and was well-organised and administered.

He was remarkable not only for the immense rapidity of his conquests, the vastness of his empire and the tyranny of his rule, but also for the barbarity of his armies. To punish an act of rebellion at Herat, Afghanistan, he dispatched an army to besiege it. For six months it held out against his 80,000 men. Eventually the city surrendered and then for the space of a week rape, pillage and killing went on unabated until 1,600,000 persons had been massacred.

While on his last campaign in western China, five planets appeared in a certain conjunction which he believed foretold that evil was soon to befall him. When he died soon after this, it was considered so important that his death should be kept secret on the return journey, because his very existence was sufficient to command obedience, that as the funeral procession moved northwards the escort put to death everyone that they met. His body was finally laid to rest at the valley of Kilien, and his successor, Ogotai, was proclaimed. Genghis Khan had once announced his ambition: 'There are many kings in the world, I will carry slaughter and cause devastation to my enemy . . . and so my name will live.' It lives almost as a synonym for tyranny.

JOSÉ VALDÉS GUZMÁN

1891-1939

The horses are black.
The horshoes are black.
On their capes gleam
Patches of ink and wax.
They have skulls of lead
Which is why they cannot weep.
With their patent-leather souls
They drift along the road.
Deformed creatures of the night,
When they are near they make
Silences of dark rubber
And terror of fine sand.
They go where they please
And hide in their heads
A nebulous astronomy
Of pistols.

THESE LINES by the Spanish poet Federico García Lorca open his sinister 'Ballad of the Spanish Civil Guard', from *Gypsy Ballads* (1928). They suggest that Lorca's sympathies were with the oppressed and the ballad was, in fact, received by the reactionary Right as an assault on their ideals. As late as July 1936, eight years after the publication of *Gypsy Ballads*, Lorca was summoned to answer a charge that the ballad was politically offensive. On 19 August 1936 the poet was executed in Granada. Although the Civil Guard were not physically responsible, the killing was carried out by those who modernised their methods, who had 'skulls of lead/Which is why they cannot weep'.

José Valdés Guzmán was the son of a General in the Civil Guard. He fought with the Spanish Army in the Moroccan War from 1918-23 and became a War Commissioner when the Republic was established in 1931. An enthusiastic Falangist, he was well placed to represent Franco in Granada. When the Nationalists seized Granada on 20 July 1936, Valdés was appointed Civil Governor. His first official act was to set up a machine-gun at the entrance to the Civil Government building, in order to intimidate the townspeople. He then ordered all the provincial mayors to swear allegiance to the Nationalist rebels and accept the authority of himself as Civil Governor.

As Ian Gibson says, in his authoritative account of *The Assassination of Federico Garciá Lorca* (London, 1979), 'Commandant Valdés was surrounded by a mixed group of Falangists, policemen, Army officers and thugs who devoted themselves to organising the Granada repression'. During interrogations in the Civil Government, prisoners were tortured. 'An instrument known as the "aeroplane" had been set up in one of the rooms,' writes Gibson. 'On this, victims with their arms tied behind their backs were hoisted to the ceiling by their wrists. The screams of men being tortured were often heard by the concierges . . . and on several occasions prisoners threw themselves from top windows in an effort to kill themselves.' Once a prisoner had been interrogated he was handed over to 'The Black Squad', a group of psychopaths who carried out the killings.

Lorca, a native of Granada, had returned to the town on 14 July, six days before Valdés assumed control as Civil Governor. He went first to the Huerta de San Vicente, his father's country house. His homecoming was naturally noted in the local press as he was Granada's most famous son, a lyrical poet with an international reputation. Lorca was not definitely identified as a 'Red' though he had republican sympathies. In fact he was conducting himself with some caution in a difficult political situation. In early June 1936 he had written to a friend asking for an alteration to be made in an interview intended for publication. 'Remove the question and answer,' Lorca asked, 'because it's an aside and it's a question about Fascism and Communism that seems to me indiscreet at this juncture.' However a sergeant in the Civil Guard visited the Huerta and informed the Civil Government that the author of the 'Ballad of the Spanish Civil Guard' was in residence. While the Civil Guard sergeant was at the Huerta some of his men beat up Gabriel, the caretaker, and pushed Lorca around. The poet decided to go into hiding.

Understandably Lorca appealed to his friend, the poet Luis Rosales, for assistance since Luis's brothers were Falangists and their house would presumably be above suspicion. Luis came to the Huerta by car and took Lorca home with him. Ironically, the Rosales house was only 300 yards from the entrance to the Civil Government. By intimidating Lorca's family and threatening to take his father away, the Falangist bully-boys discovered where the poet was hiding. On Sunday, 16 August 1936, Lorca was arrested. At the time he was living on the second floor of the Rosales house and contemplating a new poem, *Adam*, which he projected as his masterpiece. To cite Ian Gibson again, 'There is not the slightest doubt that the poet's arrest, carried out on 16 August 1936, was an official, large-scale operation. Not only was the street surrounded, but armed men were placed on the rooftops to prevent a possible escape by that unlikely route. The Civil Government was determined to arrest Lorca.'

By the time Lorca was in Valdés's power, the Civil Government had executed at least 236 people. Lorca was treated as one more victim and, at dawn on 19 August was shot at the Fuente Grande, on the orders of Valdés. In April 1937 Franco relieved Valdés of the Civil Governorship as the appallingly high incidence of executions was considered to be counter-productive. Valdés died on 5 March 1939, probably from cancer.

KENNETH HALLIWELL

1926-67

IN THE LIGHT of his early lofty ambitions Kenneth Halliwell was a nonentity whose one hope of achieving notoriety was in the manner of his death. He was unsuccessful as an actor, a failure as an author, and unable to cope with the pressure of being 'just another prop in an Orton production', to cite a description from John Lahr's *Prick Up Your Ears* (London, 1978). Joe Orton, Halliwell's lover, was — in sharp contrast — a man who first came to theatrical prominence in 1963 with his play *Entertaining Mr Sloane* and subsequently took the English stage by storm. A critical sensation and commercial smash, Orton was widely accepted as the wittiest dramatist of his time and as the creator of an entirely new mode of black comedy.

Halliwell's father was a chartered accountant who worked in Liverpool and kept his family in a semi-detached home at Bebington. The focus for the family was Mrs Daisy Halliwell, a doting mother and powerful personality. When Halliwell was eleven-years-old, in September 1937, he went to Wirral Grammar School. The same month he was overwhelmed by tragedy. His mother was stung in the mouth by a wasp and choked to death while Halliwell was watching. Though he later cultivated an arrogant exterior, Halliwell was always insecure and cruelly haunted by memories of this traumatic experience.

In 1943 Halliwell left Wirral Grammar School and enrolled at Liverpool Playhouse. He had some local recognition as an actor but little happiness at home where he and his father shared a house but little else. One morning in 1949 Halliwell came down for his breakfast and found his father dead with his head in the oven. 'When he discovered his father in the kitchen,' says Lahr, 'Halliwell stepped over the body, turned off the oven and put on the kettle. After his morning tea and shave, he reported the suicide to the next-door neighbours.'

For Halliwell the most pertinent fact of his father's death was the financial independence it gave him. An inheritance of more than £4,000 enabled him to enrich his theatrical plans with a polish from the Royal Academy of Dramatic Art in London. Failing to get a scholarship to RADA he had to pay his own fees and, though this embarrassed him, he projected an aura of authority to his fellow students most of whom were several years younger than him. Behind him Halliwell had experience in theatres in Liverpool, Perth and Dundee; before him he could look forward to a new life of lording it over Joe Orton, seven years his junior.

Like Halliwell, Orton began his course at RADA in 1951. Unlike Halliwell, however, he was a popular student: amusing and extremely accomplished. The staff at RADA predicted a promising career for Orton while they found Halliwell too tense an actor. Some of the students at RADA disliked Halliwell intensely: his odd appearance, often combining a beret with a black pin-striped suit emphasised his aggressive approach to colleagues, and once he struck a female student. Orton, however, admired Halliwell, moved into his West Hampstead apartment, and soon shared his bed. In 1953 Orton

graduated from RADA with his Diploma while Halliwell was given the
Certificate of Merit, which meant that he had gone through his course without
achieving the required RADA standard.

After leaving RADA Orton got a job as an assistant stage-manager with
Ipswich Rep while Halliwell, changing his name to Kenneth Marlowe, did a
summer season in Wales. At this stage Halliwell was still the dominant partner
in the relationship. He had, after all, enough money to keep himself and Orton
in some comfort. Accordingly, Orton moved back to London to live with
Halliwell and assist his friend by typing for him. Halliwell was working on a
novel and the experience of typing it encouraged Orton to commit his own
ideas to paper. Halliwell encouraged Orton to read the novels of Ronald
Firbank and generally took fraternal care of him. Halliwell and Orton also
collaborated on novels which were sent to publishers, and rejected. Later,
however, Orton incorporated some of the material in his own work. *The*

Ruffian on the Stair, for example, drew on *The Boy Hairdresser*, a novel by Orton and Halliwell.

In 1959 Halliwell bought a second-floor bed-sitting room at 25 Noel Road, Islington, and the two men set up home there. It was a rather bizarre relationship that depended on cheap thrills as much as mutual admiration. The year they moved into the new house, Halliwell and Orton started stealing books from Islington and Hampstead libraries. When they got the books they defaced them, pasted mildly obscene photographs over extant pictures, and removed plates from art books. Orton also wrote offensive blurbs which he inserted in library books. The prank was to prove costly to them. They were arrested in 1962, found guilty of damage amounting to £450, and sentenced to six months in jail, first in Wormwood Scrubs then in open prisons.

Halliwell was mortified by his term in prison and felt that he and his friend had been 'utter fools'. Released in 1962 the two men paid £200 for damages and went on the dole. It was at this time that Halliwell tried to kill himself by cutting his wrists.

Orton's *Entertaining Mr Sloane* was accepted for production in 1963 and this too was a blow to Halliwell. His own writing was undistinguished: an early play, *The Protagonist*, was turned down and novels, including *Priapus in the Shrubbery*, were rejected. He also did collages but these attracted little attention. Halliwell became, in fact, an appendage to Joe Orton, his live-in boyfriend. Although Halliwell boasted that he had supplied the title *Loot* for Orton's play nobody took him seriously and when he came to rehearsals of Orton's productions the stagehands referred to him as 'Mrs Orton'. He became a pitiful figure, a bore who imposed himself on Orton's admirers in a search for sympathy and understanding.

In June 1967 Halliwell went to Morocco with Orton, now a wealthy and famous playwright. Whereas Halliwell wanted Orton largely to himself, Joe wished to enjoy homosexual affairs with any young boy who took his fancy. Already jealous of Orton's dramatic success, Halliwell now became furious about Orton's sexual conquests. There was a quarrel on 27 June 1967 during which Halliwell hit Orton on the head. The two men returned to London and on 1 August Orton went to see his family in Leicester as the local theatre was putting on *Entertaining Mr Sloane*, the first Orton play to be produced in his home town.

Left behind physically, as well as artistically, Halliwell became unbearably depressed. After contacting the Samaritans he went to a doctor for anti-depressant drugs. Orton returned to the flat but seemed so preoccupied with his career must have occurred to Halliwell that there was a danger of Orton leaving him. On 9 August he murdered Orton by striking him on the head with a hammer nine times. He then took his own life by swallowing twenty-two Nembutals washed down with grapefruit juice. Pinned to Orton's diary was a note from Halliwell: 'If you read his diary all will be explained. KH. PS. Especially the latter part'.

The diary revealed the breakdown of their relationship. For instance, on 5 May 1967 Orton recorded that Halliwell had written in large letters on the wall, 'JOE ORTON IS A SPINELESS TWAT'. Orton left behind a body of work, Halliwell left behind six unpublished novels and the body of Orton.

'Halliwell, who had once taken Marlowe as his stage surname, had dispatched Orton with a frenzied brutality typical of that Elizabethan playwright's blood-lust,' wrote John Lahr. 'He had walloped Orton's head so furiously that the vault of his skull had been bashed open and several lacerations on the scalp held the shape of the hammer.'

JOHN HATFIELD

1759-1803

BORN IN MOTTRAM, John Hatfield developed a smooth line in patter by working as a travelling salesman for a linen draper. Subsequently he served, in the American colonies, as a soldier, and added a military swagger to his repertoire of confidence tricks. He loved the company of women but always regarded them as a means to a financial end. His first wife was the illegitimate daughter of Lord Robert Manners-Sutton of the wealthy Rutland family. Hatfield gained not only a wife but her dowry of £1,500.

Once he had his hands on the money, Hatfield left his wife behind and she supposedly died of a broken heart. He lived in style, in the hope of attracting more rich women to him. Eventually, however, his credit ran out and he was imprisoned, in 1782, for a debt of £160. Hatfield's plight persuaded the Duke of Rutland to bail him out with a loan of £200.

When the Duke of Rutland was appointed Lord-Lieutenant of Ireland, Hatfield moved to Dublin where he boasted about his influential connections. Back in England, he was arrested again but once more the Duke of Rutland bailed him out though he insisted that Hatfield leave the country. Hatfield accepted the condition then ignored it by going to Scarborough where he was arrested for defaulting on a hotel bill. He was sent to Scarborough Jail and remanded there until 1800.

That year Michelli Nation, a young woman from Devonshire, took her holiday in Scarborough. Fortunately for Hatfield, her lodgings looked onto the prison and she was greatly distressed by the sight of Hatfield's handsome face behind bars. Greatly taken by him, she paid his debts and the morning after his release, on 13 September 1800, he married Michelli.

The couple went to live at Hele Bridge, near Dulverton, where Michelli's father was steward on an estate. Hatfield had high hopes of establishing himself as a prominent member of the community so he borrowed £3,000 from a Mr Nucella, of London, and bought himself into a business in Tiverton. Before long Nucella was after his money and Hatfield was on the move, again leaving his wife behind.

Hatfield eventually came to the Lake District where he passed himself off as Colonel the Honourable Alexander Augustus Hope, MP for Linlithgowshire and brother of the third Earl of Hopetoun. He was soon on the lookout for suitable female companions. On a visit to Buttermere, in 1802, he went to the Fish Inn to survey the landlord's daughter Mary Robinson. Mary had been a celebrity since being written about as 'Sally of Buttermere' in a travel book of 1792 by Joseph Budworth. The beauty of Buttermere was won over by Hatfield and he also exercised his charm on Mary's father who was pleased to lend money to 'Colonel Hope' — a member of parliament and brother of an earl.

Meanwhile, Hatfield — or 'Hope' — was keeping his options open. In Keswick he spotted a young woman whose guardian was Colonel Nathaniel Moore, a prosperous tourist. 'Hope' proposed marriage to the girl and Colonel Moore was delighted at the prospect of a connection with such a distinguished family as the one Hatfield claimed. Colonel Moore asked 'Hope' to clear the forthcoming marriage with Lord Hopetoun and looked forward to the expected aristocratic approval. On Friday, 2 October 1802, Colonel Moore received a request to cash a cheque for 'Hope' who was in Buttermere before going up to Scotland. Colonel Moore obliged and was stunned to learn the next day that 'Hope' had just married Mary Robinson, the beauty of Buttermere.

The Reverend John Nicholson, who married Hatfield and Mary, wrote to 'Hope' to report the rumours that he was an imposter. Hatfield brazenly returned to the Lake District, partly because he enjoyed a challenge and partly because he hoped to extract more money from Mary's father. At the Queen's Head, Keswick, he was apprehended by George Hardinge, a magistrate who knew the real Colonel Hope. Hatfield was held in the Queen's Head but managed to escape, in a fishing boat, by promising money to the local man who rowed him to safety. In November, with a price of £50 on his head, he was captured in South Wales.

In August 1803, Hatfield was tried in Carlisle for the crimes of impersonation, forgery and fraud. As the first two charges carried the death sentence, Hatfield was hanged at Carlisle — before a large crowd — on 3 September 1803.

Mary, the beauty of Buttermere, gave birth to Hatfield's child but it died. She became a farmer's wife but could not easily ignore her fame as the tale of Mary and Hatfield was told in journals, in ballads and in plays. Joseph Budworth, who had first brought her to public attention, inserted an apologetic note in the 1810 edition of his *A Fortnight's Ramble*: '[The Author] takes this opportunity of deploring that he ever wrote in commendation of any young living creature, as vanity, alas, is the most intoxicating of human plants! and too apt to spread, when unfortunately introduced to public approval.' After Mary died in 1837, Wordsworth remembered the beauty of Buttermere and how Hatfield, 'the spoiler'

> . . . wooed the artless Daughter of the hills,
> And wedded her, in cruel mockery
> Of love and marriage bonds.

FRANCES HOWARD, COUNTESS OF ESSEX

1593-1632

IN 1606 Frances Howard, daughter of the Earl of Suffolk, was married at the Chapel Royal of Whitehall before the Court of James I. Her husband was Robert Devereux, third Earl of Essex, and the spectacular wedding included a performance of Ben Jonson's masque *Hymenaei*. This union was not only a visual delight, it was a diplomatic triumph as it brought together two great families — the Devereux and the Howards — previously divided by the death of the second Earl of Essex, Elizabeth I's favourite.

The new Countess of Essex was beautiful and, at thirteen years of age, seemingly innocent. Because of her youth, the couple were advised not to consummate the marriage after the ceremony. Instead, Frances remained at Court while her husband went abroad for four years to pursue his military career.

Frances was a great attraction at the Court. She was no blushing bride, though, but a precocious young woman conscious of her sexuality. She displayed herself provocatively and was regarded as an object of desire. Arthur Wilson, the Earl of Essex's secretary, described her as being 'of a lustful appetite, prodigal of expense, covetous of applause, ambitious of honour, and light of behaviour'. In her husband's absence she had made a sexual conquest of Prince Henry, the king's son. She then turned her amorous attentions to Robert Carr, Viscount Rochester, the king's favourite.

Once a page at the Scottish Court, Carr had been knighted by James I in 1607. When he took his seat in the English House of Lords in 1611 he was the first Scot to do so. There is no doubt that the king loved him, though it seems that Carr rejected the royal homosexual advances.

Carr was not conspicuously intelligent but shrewd enough to retain Thomas Overbury as his secretary. An imaginative, scholarly man with a minor poetic gift, Overbury assisted Carr in his duties as a Privy Councillor. He also composed the love letters Carr sent to Frances. Nevertheless Overbury had doubts about Frances's integrity and felt that Carr was foolishly compromising himself. One evening he was heard to ask Carr, 'Will you never leave the company of that base woman?'

In 1608 Overbury was knighted and a year later Frances's husband returned to England to claim his conjugal rights. Frances was unwilling to accept any situation that separated her from her beloved Carr and did not wish to accompany Essex to Chartley. When she was persuaded to do so she came up with a plan that would secure the love of Carr and protect her from the sexual overtures of Essex.

Frances turned to Anne Turner, a widow whose Hammersmith house was at the disposal of those with sexual affairs to settle and who was in the business of selling aphrodisiacs. Mrs Turner's associate was Dr Simon Forman, an apothecary by profession and a magician by inclination. His speciality was the concoction of drugs designed to induce impotence. So from Mrs Turner, Frances had the wherewithal to further enchant Carr, while Dr Forman provided her with drugs to debilitate the Earl of Essex.

At home with her husband in Chartley, Frances administered the drugs but they did not seem to put Essex off his marital plans. Frances complained to Mrs Turner, 'I had rather die a thousand times over [than lie with my husband]; for beside the sufferings, I shall lose [Carr's] love if I lie with him . . . As you have taken pains all this while for me, so now do all you can, for never was I so unhappy as now; for I am not able to endure the miseries that are coming on me, but I cannot be happy so long as this man liveth'. The appeal must have been effective for Arthur Wilson claimed that Frances 'got [by her virtuous agents] an artifice, too immodest to be expressed, to hinder penetration. And thus she tormented him, till he was contented to let her steer her own course.'

Essex abandoned hope of winning his lawful wife and went back to London. When Frances returned to London, she was anxious to be back in the arms of Carr and used her own charm and the magical arts of Turner and Forman to ensure this. She also claimed that as her marriage had not been consummated it should be annulled. Obligingly, James I set up a commission to consider the nullity suit. Frances knew, though, there was one obstacle to her eventual triumph in the person of Sir Thomas Overbury, who was not only aware of her relationship with Carr but was in a position to do something about it. When he suspected, rightly, that Carr was planning to marry Frances, after her divorce from Essex, he told him, 'If you do marry that filthy, base woman you will utterly ruin your honour and yourself; you shall never do it by my advice or consent.'

Frances decided that her interests would best be protected by eliminating Overbury. First, she tried to have him murdered but this scheme came to nothing. Cunningly, therefore, Frances involved Carr in his downfall. The king was persuaded to offer Overbury an Embassy abroad (the Low Countries or France or Russia). Thinking he could count on Carr's support, Overbury turned down this offer gracelessly. In fact he told Sir Dudley Digges, who approached him with James I's suggestion, 'I know my precious chief [Carr] better than you do, and my precious chief knoweth the King's pleasure better than any other doth. And therefore I rely upon my precious chief and will not go.' For the king the refusal was 'a matter of high contempt' for which Overbury was sent to the Tower.

This was not enough for Frances, as she had to ensure that Overbury was silenced. Through Mrs Turner, she was put in touch with Dr James Franklin, an apothecary skilled in the making of poisons. In order to get the poison into Overbury's body she needed her own man in the Tower. She recommended that Richard Weston, a friend of Mrs Turner, should be appointed as Overbury's servant in captivity. Sir Gervase Elwes, the Lieutenant of the Tower, accepted Weston in good faith and the plan was put into operation. As Dr Franklin later admitted, 'Sir Thomas never ate white salt, but there was white arsenic put in it. Once he desired pig, and Mrs Turner put into it *lapis costitus*. At another time he had two partridges sent him from the Court, and water and onions being in the sauce, Mrs Turner put in cantharides instead of pepper. For these poisons the Countess sent me rewards . . . She was able to bewitch any man.'

Astonishingly, Overbury survived this slow poisoning so Frances hired another man — William Reeve, assistant to the physician who cared for the prisoners in the Tower. For a fee of £20, Reeve stole a solution of Mercury Sublimate and incorporated it in an enema he administered to Overbury on 7 September. This time there was no mistake and Overbury died on 13 September.

Meanwhile, Frances's nullity case was going through the legal motions. Her case was that 'in hope of lawful issue, and desirous to be made a mother, [she] lived together with the said Robert at bed and board, and lay both naked and alone in the same bed [and] again and again yielded herself to his power, and as much as lay in her offered herself and her body be known ... notwithstanding all this, the said Earl could never carnally know her, nor have the copulation in any sort which the marriage bed allowed.'

As proof of her assertions Frances agreed to an examination of her virginity by twelve ladies. To protect her modesty she was allowed to appear before the ladies in a veil and, as she passed the test, it is obvious she used a virginal substitute. Overbury could have told the commission that Frances was no virgin, but a woman who had enjoyed a sexual relationship with Carr. Still, on 25 September — twelve days after the death of Overbury — the king's commission concluded that Essex and Frances were not man and wife. She was free to marry Carr.

The marriage of Frances and Robert Carr — now elevated to the Earldom of Somerset — was planned for 26 December 1613. In honour of this great event, John Donne composed an eclogue:

> May these love-lamps we here enshrine
> In warmth, light, lasting, equal the divine.

Frances's hair was worn loose at the ceremony, a symbolic declaration of her virginity. The whole scenario was based on deception and the Countess of Somerset may have been haunted by the terror of being exposed as the woman who had Overbury put to death. Her worst fears materialised in the summer of 1615. Reeve, the poisoner, was dying in Brussels and had confessed his sin. On 18 October 1615, Somerset and Frances were arrested for the murder of Overbury.

The trial was delayed until 24 May 1616 to allow Frances to give birth to a daughter. In view of the overwhelming evidence against her, she admitted her guilt and was condemned to death. Quite rightly, Somerset insisted on his innocence but was found guilty of being an accessory and likewise sentenced to death. As a measure of the king's mercy, the couple were spared execution and imprisoned in the Tower until 1622 when they were released.

On regaining a limited amount of freedom, Somerset and Frances went to Greys Court where they endured each other unwillingly. Somerset, after all, had been brought down by a murder he knew nothing about. He detested his wife yet was condemned to live with her. Frances's death, in 1632, must have come as something of a release for him. 'Her death was infamous,' wrote Arthur Wilson, 'for that part of her body which had been the receptacle of most of her sin, grown rotten (though she never had but one child), the ligaments failing, it fell down and was cut away in flakes, with a most nauseous and putrid savour, which to augment, she would roll herself in her own ordure in her bed [and] took delight in it.' Somerset died three years later.

Frances is remembered with mixed feelings. Christopher Simon Sykes, introducing his *Black Sheep* (London, 1982), called her 'almost the wickedest person in the book'. Caroline Bingham, on the other hand, said in *James I of England* (London, 1981), 'The tragedy of Frances Howard is that in all her evil doings she was inspired by her basically blameless desire to be the wife, not the mistress, of Robert Carr.'

WILLIAM HENRY IRELAND

1777-1835

IN THE LAWYER'S chambers where he worked, William Henry Ireland handled Elizabethan parchments and became familiar with the look and feel of sixteenth-century documents. As his father Samuel, an engraver, told William that his greatest desire was to obtain a manuscript in Shakespeare's own hand the young man obliged. William translated his father's dream into apparent reality: using an Elizabethan rent-roll he fabricated a lease signed, supposedly, by Shakespeare. Samuel Ireland was delighted.

William realised he had a flair for faking literary period pieces in Shakespeare's name. He wrote Shakespearean letters and notes, forged a Shakespearean 'profession of faith' and produced a transcript of *King Lear*.

In February 1795 Samuel Ireland put on an exhibition of his son's pseudo-Shakespearean concoctions and invited eminent men to inspect them. Henry James Pye, the Poet Laureate, was convinced of the authenticity of the manuscripts; James Boswell went down on his knees and kissed what he took to be genuine Shakespearean relics.

Eventually William composed a 'new' Shakespearean play, *Vortigern and Rowena*. It was produced, by Richard Brinsley Sheridan, on 2 April 1796 (William refusing to have the première on April Fool's Day). It was a total disaster and taken off after one performance, a spectacle punctuated by the jeers of the audience.

It was assumed by sceptics that Samuel Ireland was responsible for the Shakespearean deception. To clear his father, William admitted his responsibility for the whole affair and published *An Authentic Account of the Shakespearian MSS*. Nevertheless, the critics still considered Samuel, not William, as the guilty party. Samuel died in 1800, William carried on as a minor man of letters.

CLIFFORD IRVING

born 1930

HOWARD HUGHES (1905-76) was once one of the most public men in America. His exploits as an aviator were celebrated, his business acumen was legendary, and he not only produced and directed the movie *The Outlaw* (1943) but designed the brassiere that was Jane Russell's main support in a story involving Billy the Kid, Doc Holliday and Pat Garrett. Fabulously wealthy, Hughes gradually withdrew from public life, refused to give interviews and used his fortune to protect his privacy against the curiosity of the press. He became the world's most reclusive millionaire.

In 1971 Clifford Irving, novelist and author of *Fake!*, persuaded his publisher, McGraw-Hill of New York, that he had been commissioned to ghost the autobiography of Howard Hughes. Such a book would obviously be a publishing sensation and McGraw-Hill were naturally anxious to bring matters to a contractual conclusion though they wanted some proof of authenticity.

Irving had seen, in *Newsweek* magazine, a reproduction of Hughes's handwriting. On this flimsy foundation he concocted a correspondence containing more than twenty pages of forged letters by Hughes. Five of the leading handwriting experts in the USA examined these letters and pronounced them as genuine specimens of Hughes's holograph.

During the course of 1971 Irving was shown a manuscript, on the life of Hughes, by journalist James Phelan. He photocopied all the material and used it as a factual source for what he later admitted was a 'wildly imaginative' text. Still, the publishers were led to believe this was Hughes's story in his own words. Friends and associates of Hughes were completely convinced by the manuscript and argued that only Hughes could have expressed the story in that way.

As a result of this, Irving was given $750,000 for the book, the bulk of which was made out in cheques to H R Hughes.

McGraw-Hill announced the book on 7 December 1971, a revelation that disturbed James Phelan who approached *Time* magazine with his suspicions. *Time* contacted Hughes, who flatly denied he was writing any book. Realising that it would be difficult for anyone to prove otherwise, given the secretive nature of Hughes's lifestyle, Irving suggested that *Time* had not spoken to Hughes but merely to some badly informed assistant. McGraw-Hill were content to support Irving's interpretation of events. Not only had he shown them documentary evidence of his story, but the cheques they made out to H R Hughes were being deposited in a numbered Swiss account.

In January 1972 an indignant Hughes held a press conference and talked to reporters from his hotel in Nassau. He utterly refuted any suggestion that he was collaborating with Irving. Furthermore both McGraw-Hill and the Hughes organisation approached the Credit Suisse bank in Zurich. It transpired that the H R Hughes who held the numbered account was not a man, but a woman. Not Howard Hughes, the millionaire, but Helga

Rosencratz Hughes — Irving's wife Edith by another name.

Irving was exposed and charged for his astonishing confidence trick. He went to prison for seventeen months, his wife Edith for fourteen months. When he was released he owed McGraw-Hill $500,000 and his marriage was ruined. To help clear his debts he wrote, naturally, his own version of the Hughes affair.

JUDAS ISCARIOT

1st century

JUDAS ISCARIOT, meaning 'Man of Kerioth', is the most notorious figure in the New Testament, the archetypal embodiment of treachery. It is likely, however, that the Apostles treated him retrospectively as a convenient symbol rather than an actual individual. Certainly from the Gospels it is possible to assemble only an incomplete picture of his career.

In the biblical narrative Judas is introduced as the villain of the piece. He is 'Judas Iscariot, who also betrayed him' (Matthew 10:4), 'Judas Iscariot, which also betrayed him' (Mark 3:19), 'Judas Iscariot, which also was the traitor' (Luke 6:16). These classifications of Judas enable him to be seen as a complete contrast to Christ in a battle between evil and good.

According to John, Judas was the man who kept the money donated to the disciples. When Mary anoints the feet of Jesus, Judas indignantly demands to know why the ointment was not sold for three hundred pence and given to the poor. 'This he said,' John (12:6) tells us, 'not that he cared for the poor; but because he was a thief, and had the bag'. This monetary motivation is endorsed by Matthew: 'Then one of the twelve, called Judas Iscariot, went unto the chief priests, and said *unto them*, What will ye give me, and I will deliver him unto you? And they covenanted with him for thirty pieces of silver.'

Having made Judas the rotten apple in the barrel of disciples, the Apostles then confer a conscience upon him. Matthew explains that Judas 'repented himself' and attempted to return the thirty pieces of silver because he had 'betrayed the innocent blood' (27:3-4). When the chief priests refuse his offer 'he cast down the pieces of silver in the temple, and departed, and went and hanged himself' (27:5). Peter, however, gives a more lurid account: 'Now this man purchased a field with the reward of iniquity; and falling headlong, he burst asunder in the midst, and all his bowels gushed out' (Acts 1:18). Judas's soul thus sinks, dramatically, into the 'field of blood'.

It is an effective scenario shaped by a sense of justice and has held the imagination of Christians ever since. It is not, however, clear from the Gospels why Judas turned against Jesus. If he was a thief with access to the funds of the disciples he could not have been urgently in need of thirty pieces of silver. Moreover, Christ apparently knew about Judas's plan, for he said, at the Last Supper, 'One of you which eateth with me shall betray me' (Mark 14:18).

The most rational explanation of the whole affair is that Judas was attached to the Zealot party who believed in the violent overthrow of the Roman government. Around 4BC one Judas of Galilee organised a bloody revolt against Herod: 'After this man rose up Judas of Galilee in the days of the taxing, and drew away much people after him: he also perished' (Acts 6:37). Judas was a name traditionally carried by militant Jewish nationalists and the man from Kerioth may have been named in accordance with this. He could have infiltrated Jesus' group and seen Jesus as a man who could be made an example of, thus demonstrating the impossibility of peace through persuasion. Thus his betrayal of Christ would have been part of an attempt to create a climate of violence and he can be assessed as an early exponent of the ruthless political philosophy of means justifying ends. For Judas, Christ was to be sacrificed for a political, not a theological, cause.

GEORGE JEFFREYS, FIRST BARON JEFFREYS, LORD CHANCELLOR OF ENGLAND

1648-89

JUDGE JEFFREYS has the unenviable reputation of being the most unmerciful and barbarous of our chief justices. John Campbell, first Baron Campbell (1779-1861), author of the *Lives of the Lord Chancellors 1845-7* describes how he set out in writing the life of George Jeffreys 'in the hope and belief' that he would find his misdeeds had been exaggerated, and that he could rescue 'his memory from some portion of the obloquy under which it labours'. But he had to admit his hopes were not realised. The best Lord Campbell could do was praise Jeffreys' 'high talents' and singularly agreeable manners, and note that 'his cruelty and political profligacy have not been sufficiently exposed or reprobated'.

He was the son of John Jeffreys, a Welsh country gentleman, born in Acton Park, Denbighshire. He was sent to school at Shrewsbury, St Paul's and Westminster and graduated at Trinity College, Cambridge. He entered the Inner Temple in 1668. He had not been three years at the Bar before he was elected common serjeant of the City of London. He was very early noted for his extraordinary abilities in cross-examination — a skill he perfected by constant exercise. He had risen into practice at the bar of the Old Bailey, where advocates traditionally used a licence unknown in Westminster Hall. For years his main business was the examination and cross-examination of the most hardened criminals and miscreants of a great capital city — robbers, thieves, murderers and prostitutes, the floating debris of the sewer of humanity. This was excellent training for a man who was to become the most consummate bully ever produced by the legal profession. Whatever tenderness for his fellow human beings he might still have had was surely burned out of him here.

He developed a huge-toned voice and command of a relentless rhetorical technique with which to express hatred and contempt. Even in an age remarkable for the intemperance of its language, Jeffreys stood out as a master of vituperation which could not have been rivalled in the armed forces, the fishmarkets or the bear gardens of the day. His rages were notorious and amounted to fits of paroxysm never forgotten by those who witnessed them. His voice could make the rafters ring, and his eyes shone with an unnatural and venomous luminosity.

His ambition was patent. As common serjeant he continued his career at the

Bar and sought to ingratiate himself with the court party so as to gain preferment. He sensibly befriended William Chiffinch, closet-keeper to Charles II, often employed by the sovereign in secret and confidential transactions and thus one very close to His Majesty. He obtained an introduction to Charles and at once attached himself to Louise Renée de Keroualle, Duchess of Portsmouth, the king's beautiful young mistress. By 1672 he was employed in confidential business by the court. In 1677 he was knighted and became solicitor general to James, Duke of York, the king's brother. He was made recorder of London the following year.

It was at this time that Titus Oates began his startling revelations of the Popish Plot. These proceedings threw Jeffreys into the limelight, the glare of which he was never to escape. His zeal in the persecution of those 'exposed' by Oates's testimony earned him the office of chief justice of Chester in 1680. Parliament met in October that year and a hostile resolution caused him to resign his recordership. The king commented, 'Jeffreys is not parliament-proof.'

In 1683 the Rye House Plot occurred. This was a conspiracy to murder Charles II and his brother James, named after the place at Hoddesdon in Hertfordshire where it was intended the killings should be done. The centre of the plot was the most disaffected section of the Whig party, which was adamant for the exclusion of James from the succession. The actual conspiracy probably only concerned a few men but popular feeling was now vehemently directed against many supporters of the exclusion party, the Whigs. This was Jeffreys' moment and he felt he was being pushed on by destiny to punish the would-be assassins. William, Lord Russell, Algernon Sidney and the Earl of Essex were held in custody pending trial — Essex committed suicide. Jeffreys presided at the trial of Algernon Sidney in 1683 and of Sir Thomas Armstrong the next year. Russell, Armstrong and Sidney were all beheaded. In 1685 Jeffreys passed sentence on Titus Oates (see *TITUS OATES*) and in the same year he presided at the trial of Richard Baxter on the charge of libelling the church in his *Paraphrase of New Testament*. Jeffreys was here the tool of James II, who intended to make quite clear his feelings about Protestant Non-Conformists. Jeffreys poured scorn on Baxter, who was a learned cleric, and abused him to the extent that people wept in court. Jeffreys kept up a torrent of ribaldry and invective, calling him a rascal and a factious, snivelling Presbyterian. 'Richard! Richard! Richard! dost thou think we will let thee poison the court?' he bellowed. 'Richard — thou art an old knave. Thou has written books enough to load a cart, and every book as full of sedition as an egg is full of meat. By the Grave of God, I'll look after thee . . . I will crush thee all!'

Even then, Richard Baxter had the courage to complain about the way his trial had been handled. 'Does your Lordship think,' he asked, 'that any jury will convict a man on such a trial as this?' Jeffreys, who had not even allowed Baxter's defence counsel to speak and had overruled character witnesses time after time, answered, 'I warrant you, Mr Baxter, don't trouble yourself about that.' It was rumoured that the sentence Jeffreys wanted was that the old man should be whipped through London at the cart's tail, but he was outvoted by the other judges. Baxter was fined and imprisoned.

Jeffreys' most notorious activities were now at hand — his putting down of the Monmouth rebels. James, Duke of Monmouth was the son of Charles II by Lucy Walters. As James II's tyranny became more and more apparent, many looked to Monmouth as the possible leader of a Protestant insurrection. He was urged on by the Duke of Argyll and landed at Lyme Regis to raise the rebellion, but his forces were routed at Sedgemoor. Jeffreys opened the 'Bloody Assizes' in Winchester. The number of people sentenced to death at these proceedings is uncertain. Many more were transported and sold to slavery in the West Indies and American colonies. King James could not have wished a more zealous scourge for his wrath than Jeffreys. Two of the rebels, John Hickes, a Non-Conformist divine, and Richard Nelthorpe, a lawyer, sought refuge at the house of the Lady Alice Lisle, widow of John Lisle, who had sat in the Long Parliament and had been a Commissioner of the Great Seal during the Commonwealth. In Jeffreys' eyes Lady Alice had harboured renegades against the Crown, and was therefore an accessory. He stormed and fulminated and cursed throughout the proceedings. She was sentenced to be burned alive. After some special pleading her sentence was changed to beheading.

The day after her beheading Jeffreys reached Dorchester. He ordered the court to be hung with scarlet to indicate his bloody purpose. He let it be known that the only hope of mercy was to plead guilty. Many did. Two hundred and ninety-two received the death sentence. He reserved his special anger for Somerset, the seat of the rebellion. Two hundred and thirty-three prisoners were hanged, drawn and quartered. At every point where two roads met, at every market place, bodies were hung in chains or heads stuck up on poles.

As his work continued he seemed to grow more and more pleasantly excited by it, and observers wondered whether he was drunk from morning to night as he seemed in such fine spirits. Accused and witnesses attempted in vain to argue with him. He could better them all. His language became even more foul and his authority was backed up by the full panoply of the state. Lord Stawell, a Tory peer, who tried to defend friends and neighbours from this butchery was rewarded by having a corpse hung in chains at his park gates. Jeffreys transported over eight hundred prisoners, and many were sentenced to savage public whippings. He also made a fortune out of trading pardons and plundering the wealthy Whig families disgraced by the Monmouth rising. For his service to the Crown James II rewarded him with the seal of the Lord Chancellor.

His total identification with James did not serve him well when his sovereign fled the country and William of Orange became king. Jeffreys tried to escape disguised as a common seaman, but he was recognised at a tavern in Wapping and imprisoned in the Tower. He had long suffered from the stone and while imprisoned his condition deteriorated. He died on 18 April 1689. Charles II's verdict on him was simple: 'That man has no learning, no sense, no manners, and more impudence than ten carted streetwalkers.' Lord Macaulay wrote of him that he had the most odious vice 'which is incident to human nature, a delight in misery merely as misery. There was a fiendish exultation in the way in which he pronounced sentence on offenders. Their weeping and imploring seemed to titillate him voluptuously; and he loved to scare them into fits by dilating with luxuriant amplification on all details of what they were to suffer. Thus, when he had an opportunity of ordering an unlucky adventuress to be whipped at the cart's tail: "Hangman . . . I charge you to pay particular attention to this lady! Scourge her soundly, man! Scourge her till the blood runs down! It is Christmas, a cold time for Madam to strip in! See that you warm her shoulders thoroughly!" He was hardly less facetious when he passed judgement on poor Lodowick Muggleton, the drunken tailor who fancied himself a prophet. "Impudent rogue! Thou shalt have an easy, easy, easy punishment!" One part of this easy punishment was the pillory, in which the wretched fanatic was almost killed with brickbats.' To enter his court, Macaulay stated, was to enter the den of a wild beast, which none could tame.

WILLIAM KIDD

1645-1701

OF ALL THE pirates and sea-rovers who contribute so much to our colourful sense of the turn of the seventeenth and eighteenth centuries, not one has ever fascinated the imagination as much as the figure of William Kidd. This may be partly a result of the legend of his fabulous treasure — some £14,000 of it was recovered off the east end of Long Island — and also of the never-ceasing debate as to whether he was actually guilty of piracy or not. Though his later career and notorious trial put in permanent circulation all the elements of romance — buried gold, walking the plank, piracy on the high seas, hand-to-hand fights on board ship and all the rest of it — William Kidd's early life was humdrum enough. He was a Scottish seaman of obscure birth. He earned a name for bravery in war, he married a wealthy woman and seemed likely to settle down in New York.

He received an award of £150 for his services in aiding the colony during the disturbances which occurred in the revolution of 1688. In 1695 he came to London in a sloop of his own in order to trade. At this time King William III was anxious to clear the oceans of piracy. Part of his strategy was to make the Earl of Bellomont, Governor of New England, responsible for putting an end to illegal trading, piracy, smuggling and mayhem on the high seas: 'For several years two very pernicious things had been growing in our American colonies,' a state paper of the time reported, 'an unlawful trade in fraud of the Acts of Navigation and the Plantations, infinitely prejudicial to England; and the cursed practice of Piracy, utterly destructive of all commerce . . . Some Governors having found a way to share in the profits have been obliged not only to connive at but protect the criminals.' It seemed to the newly appointed Governor that William Kidd would be the ideal man to commission to police the seas and bring piracy to heel — after all he was a truly experienced seaman who had served against the French in the West Indies and knew the area very well, and had already served the crown before and been rewarded for his loyalty.

The proposition was put to Kidd and he agreed, provided he was equipped with a good ship, plenty of guns and an able crew, to lead a privateering expedition to cruise against the pirates in the eastern seas. The galley *Adventure* was fitted out for him, and he received the royal commission to arrest all pirates, and — a state of war existing between France and Britain — a commission of reprisals against the French. He sailed from Plymouth in May 1696.

The capital for this venture was put up by some very respectable people, among them the Lord Chancellor, the Duke of Shrewsbury, the Earl of Rumney and Lord Orford. William III himself wished to contribute, but was unable to raise the capital. The crew were not to be paid, but were to receive a quarter of the booty. This, it was hoped, would keep them from mutinying. Kidd's brief was very specific: 'That whereas information has been given to the King that Thomas Too, William Maye, John Ireland, Thomas Wake and others of his Majesty's subjects, had associated themselves with many wicked persons, and committed great piracies in the parts of America and elsewhere, in Violation of the Law of Nations, to the discouragement of Trade, and to the dishonour of his Royal Authority, in case any of his subjects guilty of such detestable enormities should go unpunished, His Majesty did therefore give power to Captain Kidd, commander of the *Adventure* galley, and to the commander of that ship for the time being, to apprehend and seize the persons above named, and that all other pirates whom he should meet with on the coasts of America, or other seas, with their ships and goods; and in case of resistance to fight with, and compel them to yield, and to bring them to a legal trial, in order to suffer the punishment of the law.' He was also ordered to keep strict accounts, a journal of his voyages and details of all ships, ammunition and booty that he should take from the pirates that he was able to apprehend.

In spite of all the legalities and the precautions taken by the authorities (including making many of the officers in Kidd's ship married men domiciled in England, so they would want to return home), as soon as Kidd set sail, instead of hunting down the pirates, he joined in the trade himself. In fact, he became the most successful of all. Stories soon began to reach London of his exploits. The East India Company complained to the government about the increase of piracy and its severe effect on trade. Using the account of Kidd's eventual trial for piracy and murder, some of the details of his voyages can be filled in. His men boarded a French ship on the Atlantic and when they arrived in New York on 4 July 1696 they sold off their takings and recruited more men. The *Adventure* then sailed for Maderas, Bonavista, the Cape of Good Hope, Madagascar — plundering ships all the way along — and then to the Red Sea. Kidd gave chase to a fleet of worthy-looking vessels, but gave up when he found they were British and escaped in good time. Then to Malabar, where he fought with two Portuguese men-of-war. He robbed Moorish ships. He killed one of his own crew by striking him on the head with a bucket during an argument.

He captured and boarded a magnificent ship of four hundred tons, the *Quedah Merchant*, possessed it and fired his own ship, the *Adventure*. He then sailed for the West Indies. He had now amassed a considerable fortune, but the authorities were after him. He had been proclaimed a pirate. His taking another ship and destroying the *Adventure*, which had been fitted out for his expedition, was really the final proof of his having abandoned all intentions of chasing pirates, and having gone over to the enemy himself.

In trading and putting in to various ports for supplies and water, Kidd gradually came to realise what a peril he now stood in. He decided on a bold plan. He would get a smaller vessel — a sloop — transfer his crew and possessions from the *Quedah Merchant* on to this new ship, and sail to New York Sound. He had decided that if he returned with all the treasures he had collected it would look very suspicious, but on the other hand, if he sailed in with enough to placate those who had staked him in the first place, his explanations of his behaviour would be more likely to be believed. He concealed much of his treasure, and took the rest with him.

The ruse did not work. When he landed in Boston he was tricked, and brought back to England to face trial. He was confined for two years and then tried at the Old Bailey in May 1701 for murder and piracy. He was found guilty but said to the judge, 'My lord, it is a very hard sentence. For my part I am the innocentest person of them all, only I have been sworn against by perjured persons.' He was hanged on 23 May 1701. The rest of his treasure is supposed to be still buried somewhere under tropical sands. This famous son of Greenock may well be the original Captain Flint whose treasure is central in the narrative of Stevenson's *Treasure Island*.

MAJOR KRIVTSOV

19th century

DOSTOEVSKY, the great Russian novelist, was arrested in St Petersburg in 1849 as a result of his connections with the Petrashevsky circle of Russian radicals. After some time in the Peter-and-Paul Fortress he and his fellow prisoners were, on 22 December 1849, taken to Semenovsky Square where they underwent a ritual execution: at the last moment, the prisoners were given a reprieve. Three days after the traumatic incident in Semenovsky Square, Dostoevsky was taken to Omsk to begin four years of Siberian exile.

For two of these years he lived in absolute terror of Major Krivtsov, the camp commandant at Omsk prison. Krivtsov was a sadistic creature with a hatred of political prisoners. It was his desire to terrorise the whole camp and he did this in various ways. For example, he would crash into the prisoners' barracks at nights and order a flogging for those who slept on their right sides. He reasoned that Christ slept on his left side so all should follow this sacred example.

When Dostoevsky arrived at Omsk, Krivtsov assured him he would be subjected to corporal punishment at the first opportunity. Dostoevsky, a highly imaginative and hypersensitive man, was terrified that the threat would be carried out. It has, in fact, been assumed that the onset of Dostoevsky's epilepsy in 1850 was a direct result of some humiliation inflicted by Krivtsov.

According to Joseph Frank, in his reliable *Dostoevsky: The Years of Ordeal, 1850-1859* (London, 1983), Dostoevsky was never actually flogged, though he came close to the brutalising he dreaded. One day Krivtsov noticed Dostoevsky resting on a pallet instead of working. It was explained to Krivtsov that Dostoevsky had been given a day's rest because of illness. Krivtsov was adamant, however, that Dostoevsky was to be flogged and insisted that his order should be carried out immediately. Fortunately, Krivtsov's superior, General de Grave, came to the scene of the commotion, reversed Krivtsov's order, and rebuked the camp commandant for his attitude to a sick prisoner.

Eventually Krivtsov was arrested and forced to resign from government service because of his misconduct. Dostoevsky saw Krivtsov, after his disgrace, as a pitiful figure 'wearing a shabby coat'. Yet he was haunted by this man and in *House of the Dead* (1860-2) recalled how Krivtsov's 'spiteful, purple, pimply face made a very depressing impression: it was as though a malicious spider had run out to pounce on some poor fly that had fallen into its web.'

GEORGE HENRY LAMSON

1850-82

ON FRIDAY, 2 December 1881, Percy John, a pupil at Blenheim House School, Wimbledon, received the following letter from his brother-in-law Dr George Henry Lamson:

> My dear Percy, I had intended running down to Wimbledon to see you today, but I have been delayed by various matters until it is now nearly six o'clock, and by the time I should reach Blenheim House you will probably be preparing for bed. I leave for Paris and Florence tomorrow, and wish to see you before going. So I propose to run down to your place as early as I can, for a few minutes even, if I can accomplish no more. Believe me, dear boy, your loving brother, G H Lamson.

Percy must have looked forward to the visit as a welcome intrusion into his life. He was, as the result of curvature of the spine, paralysed from the waist down. His parents had died when he was seven and he depended on what family was left to him. His sister Margaret had married, in 1877, a Civil Service clerk, William Chapman, who acted as Percy's guardian. His sister Kate had married, in 1878, Dr Lamson who had recently been in charge of a military hospital in Bucharest.

Percy was not without financial means. On the death of his brother Hubert

— in 1879, officially from 'enteric fear' but perhaps by poison — he and his sisters had inherited the family property. In 1881, as was revealed at the trial of Dr Lamson, Percy 'was possessed of, in India four per cents, £1,991 5s 11d and £1,078 18s 7d in Consols, producing about £109 per annum'. In the event of Percy's death his fortune would be shared between his sisters Mrs Chapman and Mrs Lamson.

Dr Lamson had used the money his wife had inherited from Hubert John, in November 1879, to buy a practice in Bournemouth. Often irrational, Lamson was unable to keep his patients and his difficulties were increased by his reckless spending. He fell behind with the rent on his house 'Hursley' and when he quit Bournemouth he left many debts behind him. He was in the habit of borrowing money with no hope of repaying it and cashing cheques certain to bounce. Some of the time he seemed unaware of the implications of his actions.

In fact Lamson was a morphia addict. He became addicted in 1877 when he ran the Red Cross Hospital in Bucharest. If he was eccentric before becoming dependent on drugs his condition deteriorated rapidly with the onset of addiction. In his own words: 'Real worries and troubles, however slight, became terrible in their awfulness, and anticipations were even more dreadful and horrible. The imagination seemed to pierce years into the future; colossal successes or failures would either cause a rush of warm feeling and joy, or a despondency impossible to realise.' He experienced a 'complete inability to draw distinctions between truth and falsehood, right and wrong; a loss of knowledge of time and distance; to a very great extent, the power of distinguishing or discriminating; a tendency, quite unconquerable, to put off things; and my memory for names, places and events, almost annulled.'

After leaving Bournemouth to escape his debts, Lamson went to New York. There, as he later admitted, he frequently found it impossible to distinguish between fact and fantasy: 'I would stop at an all-night eating house for slight refreshment, and then return to my room; or else I would read, and always some highly exciting story which became at once reality to me, and then, exhausted, when nearly time for rising, would sink into uneasy sleep, fully believing I was to carry on myself the event of the narrative. When alone (and I always sought solitude for the greater part of the time, the presence of others in a measure interfering with the portentous work the diseased brain was doing), I took neither breakfast nor lunch; but the only meal in the twenty-four hours was a late dinner, with a very little wine or beer.'

In November 1881 Lamson, deeply in debt and under the influence of his addiction, stayed at Nelson's Hotel, Great Portland Street. While he was there he sent the proprietor, James Nelson, a note:

> Dr Lamson (from room No 30) begs that someone may be sent to Mr Buzzard's, Confectioner, etc., Oxford Street, and the following articles procured and brought here for Dr Lamson, viz. one Dundee cake, 3s size, 2 lbs crystallised fruits, assorted. Dr Lamson begs that there may be no delay for these articles, as he wishes to take them with him to Harrow as a birthday gift. As Dr Lamson does not know the price of the articles he has ordered, he begs they may be paid for him, and he will settle when he comes down to breakfast.

Knowing how unreliable Lamson was in monetary matters, Nelson did not carry out these instructions. When Lamson left the hotel on 2 December he did so without settling his account. He did, however, acquire his confectionery.

Another item that Lamson was keen to have in his possession was aconitine, a poison so deadly that one grain will kill within a few hours of absorption. It has the advantage, for a murderer, of being almost impossible to detect. Lamson had once studied under the toxicologist Dr Christison, whose opinion was that aconitine was 'one deadly agent which we cannot satisfactorily trace in the human body after death'. Lamson believed in the beneficial medical uses of aconitine. As Giles St Aubyn writes, in *Infamous Victorians* (London, 1971), 'Although aconitine is a powerful cerebro-spinal poison, doctors in America and Europe advocated its use, in minute doses, for a variety of afflictions ... Some authorities recommended it for paralysis of the limbs and defects of the spine. The medical profession in England, however, remained more convinced of its dangers than its promise. Lamson, who received part of his training in Paris at the time of the German invasion in 1870, so far from sharing his suspicion of aconitine, regarded it as an appropriate remedy for most diseases and injuries.' An American surgeon who worked with Lamson in Bucharest said that 'without regard to the character of the disease or injury to the patient, Lamson seemed possessed of a mania for administering aconitine'.

This doctor, then, with a morphia addiction and 'a mania for administering aconitine', arrived at Blenheim House School on Saturday, 3 December 1881. He wanted to see his brother-in-law and when Percy John was carried into the dining-room remarked, 'Why, how fat you are looking, Percy, old boy'. Percy was eighteen and, looking forward to his Christmas holiday, was in good spirits. William Henry Bedbrook, the Principal of Blenheim House, offered Lamson a glass of sherry. Lamson accepted this but asked for some sugar which, he said, would counteract the effect of alcohol. Castor sugar was brought to him and he stirred it in his glass with a penknife.

Thus refreshed, Lamson opened his Gladstone bag and took out crystallised fruits, a bottle of sweets and a three-shilling Dundee cake full of nuts, currants and raisins. He cut the cake with his penknife and passed it round. Percy enjoyed his slice of cake as, indeed, did Lamson and Mr Bedbrook. Lamson then produced some capsules which he had brought from America. 'By the way, Mr Bedbrook,' he said to the Principal, 'when I was in America I thought of you and your boys; I thought what excellent things these capsules would be for your boys to take nauseous medicine in.' He took two boxes of capsules from his bag and offered one to Mr Bedbrook who swallowed it. Lamson then filled a capsule with the sugar and told Bedbrook, 'If you shake it, it will bring the medicine down to one end.' Turning to his brother-in-law he said, 'Here, Percy, you are a swell pill taker; take this, and show the Headmaster how easily it may be swallowed.' Percy did as he was told.

At 7.20 pm Lamson left the school to go to Paris. Half-an-hour later Percy had to be carried to bed feeling, he said, 'as I felt after my brother-in-law had given me a quinine pill at Shanklin'. After four hours of excruciating agony, Percy was dead. The newspapers took up the story of the strange case of poisoning at Wimbledon and on 7 December Lamson wrote a letter from Paris to William Chapman:

Early this morning I saw the *Evening Standard*. I read therein the dreadful suspicion attached to my name. I need not tell you of the absolute falsity of such a fearful accusation. Bedbrook was present all the time I was in the house, and if there was any noxious substance in the capsule it must have been in his sugar, for that was all there was in it. He saw me take the empty capsule and fill it from his own sugar-basin. However, with the consciousness that I am an innocent and unjustly accused man, I am returning at once to London to face the matter out. If they wish to arrest me, they will have ample opportunity of doing so. I shall attempt no concealment.

On 8 December Lamson was back in London and took a cab to Scotland Yard. He was charged 'with causing the death of Percy Malcolm John at Blenheim House, Wimbledon, on December 3rd'. Lamson's trial, lasting six days, opened at the Old Bailey on Wednesday, 8 March 1882. The case against him was summarised by the Solicitor General: 'You have the death of this lad [Percy John] occurring after an illness of two to three hours' duration, and after suffering of the most severe and terrible character. You have not only the causes to account for the death, but you have the symptoms of death from vegetable poison; you have the presence in the body of the deceased — as I think I shall satisfy you beyond the shadow of a doubt — of that most deadly poison aconitine; you have such a poison purchased by the prisoner shortly before; you have the prisoner's own hand administering the last thing he was ever known to have swallowed; you have the prisoner in desperate straits and need of money; you see him in a position to gain a considerable acquisition of fortune by the death of the deceased.'

Lamson was found guilty of murder and sentenced to death. Because of the difficulty of detecting aconitine in a corpse, it was not clear exactly how the crime had been carried out. However at the post-mortem a raisin skin, impregnated with aconitine, had been found in Percy's stomach. As he cut the Dundee cake in front of witnesses, including the Principal of Percy's school, Lamson had most probably injected the poison in a raisin and thus cut for Percy a piece of cake he had somehow marked as the one deadly portion.

The day before his execution, on 28 April 1882, Lamson admitted his guilt to the chaplain at Wandsworth Prison. 'Sitting in the condemned cell,' he wrote, 'face to face with death, I can truly and solemnly say, that in my right and normal state of mind encompassing and committing such a crime as that for which I must now die, would have been utterly and absolutely impossible, and altogether foreign to my whole nature and instincts.'

It is possible that Lamson also poisoned Percy's brother Hubert despite his denial of that. Though he claimed that he acted as a criminal only because of his morphia addiction, the manner of Percy's murder shows a great deal of cunning and calculation and demonstrates that Lamson knew exactly what he was doing.

TOM KEATING
1918-84

THE BRITISH admiration for a rogue is well demonstrated by the case of Tom Keating who was, at the end of his life, a television personality with a programme of his own. During the course of each programme Keating gave a detailed stylistic analysis of the pictorial mannerisms of a master. He was well equipped to do so since he was one of the most successful art forgers of the century.

By profession an art restorer, Keating realised he had enough artistic ability to duplicate — at least superficially — the style of cerain artists he admired. He was particularly good at forgeries by Samuel Palmer (1805-81), the English visionary painter whose work was in great demand. At least thirteen works sold as original Palmers were in fact by Keating. By his own calculation Keating produced some 2,500 fakes in a career spanning quarter of a century. As his work was credited to such greats as Degas and Renoir he commanded high prices.

When Keating's activities were exposed in 1976, by *The Times*, he was regarded by the public as something of a hero. Keating, it was felt, had put one over the self-styled art experts and the pompous art investors. He was to be applauded for doing so, many thought. With his white beard and articulate enthusiasm Keating conformed to the public image of the painter. He became an increasingly popular figure and liked to use cockney rhyming slang to refer to his fakes as Sexton Blakes.

Keating's trial for conspiracy and criminal deception took place in the Old Bailey, London, in 1977 but was abandoned after five weeks because the artist was judged to be too ill to undergo a legal ordeal. His final years were spent as a celebrity and in December 1983 Christie's auctioned 150 of his pictures, in London for £75,000. Two months later Keating died, in Colchester, of a heart attack.

In September 1984 Christie's held a second auction of Keating's work and his posthumous reputation ensured a staggering success at the saleroom in South Kensington. More than 1,000 people attended (one hundred of them being accommodated in a downstairs gallery to watch the sale on video) and £274,610 was paid for 200 pictures. For example, a 1983 painting of 'Monet and his Family in their Houseboat' was sold for £16,000 and a double portrait of the artist and Jane Kelly (with whom Keating lived in the 1970s) raised £6,000. David Collins, director of Christie's picture department, said, 'I am absolutely amazed at the prices being paid, and at the number of people here. Keating had a tremendous groundswell of public support.' A spokesman of Christie's added, 'He always hoped his paintings would be of public interest. These paintings were not fakes. They wouldn't fool anyone. They are just in the style of the artists, but they are by Tom Keating.' It was generally agreed that Keating had had the last laugh.

JOHN LOGAN

1748-88

MICHAEL BRUCE (1746-67), the 'Gentle Poet of Lochleven', had a short but triumphantly creative life. Born in Kinnesswood, a village in Kinross overlooking Loch Leven, he spent summers tending the sheep on the Lomond Hills and went to Edinburgh University to study for the ministry. Although he was unable to achieve publication in his lifetime his poems were circulated in manuscript among his admirers. One of his most popular poems was 'Ode to the Cuckoo' which begins:

> Hail, beauteous Stranger of the wood!
>   Attendant on the Spring!
> Now heav'n repairs thy rural seat
>   And woods thy welcome sing.

When Bruce died, at the age of twenty-one, his papers passed to his father, Alexander Bruce, a Kinnesswood weaver. In 1767 Alexander Bruce was visited by John Logan, a divinity student, who claimed to have known Michael Bruce at university. Alexander Bruce showed Logan the manuscript 'Poem-book' he had in his possession and was innocent enough to entrust this to the persuasive visitor. Logan then approached other locals in Kinnesswood and extracted from them the Michael Bruce manuscripts in their possession. Before leaving the village, Logan assured the people of Kinnesswood that he would undertake an edition of Michael Bruce's poetry. Since then the Bruce manuscripts have never been seen.

Eventually, in 1770, Logan produced a volume entitled *Poems on Several Occasions, by Michael Bruce*. The edition was eccentric. First, it omitted Bruce's sacred poems; second, it purported to be an anthology by various authors. A preface by Logan stated that 'To make up a miscellany some poems wrote by different authors are inserted, all of them original, and none of them destitute of merit . . . The reader of taste will easily distinguish them from those of Mr Bruce, without their being distinguished by any mark.'

Worse was to follow. In 1781 Logan, minister of South Leith since 1773, published a collection of his own verse and arrogantly included 'Ode to the Cuckoo' as his own work. From this readers were encouraged to conclude that the best poems in the 1770 Bruce volume were also by Logan. When Logan learned, in 1782, that William Anderson, a Stirling bookseller, and John Robertson, an Edinburgh printer, had printed a new edition of Bruce's verse he obtained an interim interdict against them. Undeterred, Anderson and Robertson decided to defend their edition and so the case of Michael Bruce was clarified by litigation. It was Logan's contention that as the 1770 volume was for private circulation, the book had been entered at Stationers' Hall and therefore the copyright was exclusively his. Logan was unable to substantiate his claims and so lost the Court of Session case. It was established that Logan had no copyright control of Bruce's poems, a decision that paved the way for various editions.

Literary evidence also confirms that Logan could not have written 'Ode to the Cuckoo'. His tragedy *Runnamede* was performed in Edinburgh in 1784 and showed no poetic powers of invention. Still, the play had some commercial success which encouraged Logan to indulge his taste for drink and debauchery. His literary and religious reputation in ruins — as a result of the Court of Session case and his obstreperous activities after *Runnamede* — Logan left Edinburgh for London where he died. The Bruce-Logan controversy continued for some years but the whole issue was settled in the Reverend T G Snoddy's *Michael Bruce: Shepherd Poet of the Lomond Hills* (1947).

VICTOR LUSTIG

1890-1946

VICTOR LUSTIG'S criminal career included many profitable ventures, among them selling fake investments which he claimed would print money, and counterfeiting very passable $100 bills. But the one trick he deserves to be remembered for is his brilliant scheme of selling the Eiffel Tower.

He had served a long apprenticeship in petty crime and had picked up some extremely useful professional tips from working with Nicky Arnstein, the American con-man. Lustig was an accomplished actor and spoke several languages. He used many different names and managed to escape serious

trouble. He knew Paris well as he worked there throughout the First World War. He tried to make a living in the USA but returned to Paris in 1925 with the American confidence trickster, Robert Tourbillon, 'Dapper Dan Collins'. Lustig read in the newspaper that there was a serious possibility that the Eiffel Tower might have to be dismantled. Here was a golden opportunity!

He had some headed notepaper printed and wrote to five of the most considerable scrap-metal dealers in Paris, passing himself off as the Deputy Director General of the French Post Office. The dealers were invited to meet the Deputy and his assistant at a leading Paris hotel to discuss the submission of tenders for the purchase of the Eiffel Tower as seven thousand tons of scrap-metal. At the meeting he put on a superb show, replete with flowing spiel full of technical details to support the astounding announcement that there were very good reasons why — sadly — Paris's great landmark would have to be taken down. Lustig scrutinised the dealers very carefully, deploying his innate skills as psychologist and sociologist. He resolved that André Poisson was to be his target.

André Poisson was the perfect victim for a con trick like this; he was well off but rather insecure. Lustig rightly sensed that Poisson would feel the purchase of the Eiffel Tower would help him arrive in Parisian society. He had detected the basic insecurity in Poisson's personal make-up. The various dealers sent in their tenders to the 'Deputy Director General' and Lustig then put the next part of the plan into effect. André Poisson was sent for. Dapper Dan, posing as the Personal Private Secretary to the Deputy Director General of the French Post Office, told him that his tender had been accepted, but that the Deputy expected a little kick-back for the deal. They were both men of the world, and he was sure that Monsieur Poisson would understand that a man in the

Deputy's position etc. etc. Of course Poisson understood perfectly, and handed over a considerable sum as an additional incentive to urge the sale. Lustig also received a huge sum — never disclosed — for the sale of the Eiffel Tower, in return for which the hapless Poisson got a bill of sale on official paper for the Eiffel Tower. Lustig then disappeared. It was said that he went to Vienna.

In 1927 he pulled off the same trick a second time and again escaped. He then went to America where he enjoyed a successful career as con-man and counterfeiter, at one time working with Al Capone. In 1935 he was sentenced to twenty years for putting over a thousand fake $100 bills into circulation. He died in Alcatraz in 1946.

JAMES MACPHERSON

1736-96

THE SON of a Ruthven crofter, Macpherson was ten years of age at the time of Culloden and watched the aftermath of the defeat as the English army burned the homes of the clansmen. When he began to write poetry it had a cutting edge to it, for in 'The Hunter' the Highlander's 'light reflexive blade/Sings through the air, and cleaves the Saxon's head.' Macpherson dreamed of literary victories and in 1759 met John Home, author of the tragedy *Douglas* (1756), taking the waters at Moffat. When Home asked Macpherson about Gaelic poetry he was asked, in turn, if he knew any Gaelic. He answered in the negative and so Macpherson showed him an imitation of a Gaelic poem. Home was impressed and Macpherson was encouraged to seek out the epic Gaelic muse.

In 1761 Macpherson published *Fingal*, presenting it as a translation of Ossian, son of the ancient hero Fingal. The lost paradise associated with Gaeldom now had its heroic voice and Macpherson's translations — *Temora* followed in 1763 — became the literary sensation of Europe where they were admired by such as Napoleon and Goethe.

What Macpherson actually did was to concoct his epic by improvising on the basis of a few authentic fragments of Gaelic poetry. Ironically enough, Macpherson's stylistic source was not Ossianic but Miltonic. In *Paradise Lost* Milton wrote, 'Let each/His adamantine coat gird well, and each/Fit well his helm . . . . for this day will pour down [a] rattling storm of arrows'. Macpherson echoed this in *Fingal*: 'Let each assume his heavy spear, and gird on his father's sword. Let the dark helmet rise on every head; and the mail pour its lightning from every side.' Dr Johnson exposed the element of fakelore and Macpherson was treated as another Scottish pretender in pursuit of Highland glory — a poetic equivalent of Bonnie Prince Charlie. An unrepentant Macpherson ended his life as a wealthy landowner in Badenoch and paid for his body to be buried in Westminster Abbey.

MATTHEW C McKEON

20th Century

STAFF SERGEANT McKEON was a drill instructor at Parris Island, South Carolina. His court martial in 1956 for a whole series of charges, including oppression, culpable negligence and manslaughter, was a notorious case in the history of the US Marines. He was an unhappy and intolerant man at the best of times. This was not the best of times. Platoon 71 was his first drill assignment and unfortunately he took up this posting as he was suffering from a pulled leg muscle which caused him continuous agony. His first view of his men in April 1956 was not a happy sight. They were lying on the grass playing cards, smoking, fooling around and cracking jokes. His first attempt at the shock tactics by means of which he intended to stamp his personality on these young recruits, and assert his ruthless authority, was the immediate instigation of fatigues. Scrubbing and cleaning the barracks did not somehow seem enough.

When darkness came on the evening of 8 April he put a better plan into action. A night march. The men were ordered into kit as they were going into the swamps that night. He asked if any of the men couldn't swim. Several men replied, 'Yes'. The sergeant retorted, 'Well, all recruits who can't swim will drown. And those who can swim will be eaten by the sharks.' In the pitch dark he marched them through the swamps and on into Ribbon Creek, which had a thick muddy bottom unsuitable for marching, as well as a very strong current. Many men got into difficulties and six men drowned, including Tom Hardeman, the best swimmer in the platoon, who tragically gave his life trying to help those in trouble in the murky waters.

Sergeant McKeon was arrested and an investigation was put underway. General Randolph Pate, Commandant of the US Marine Corps, is on record as having said, 'It is our first military and moral obligation to see that Sergeant McKeon is punished to the full extent allowed by the Uniform Code of Military Justice.'

McKeon was court-martialled in the school house on Parris Island in August that year. His charges ranged from possession of alcoholic beverages in barracks and drinking in the presence of recruits, to oppression for leading a platoon into water which he knew to be over their heads, culpable negligence in the deaths of six men, and manslaughter. The chief prosecuting officer was Marine Major Charles Sevier. As he outlined the case against McKeon, a fairly clear picture emerged of an ill-tempered martinet, drunk with power and full of vodka, who had deliberately led his men into danger from an almost motiveless desire to punish them. Sevier demonstrated that night marches were not only not part of Marine training, but that they had been prohibited by a general order posted in the very camp where McKeon was a drill instructor. He also categorised the strong tides which were a feature of Ribbon Creek, and took the court to view the place where the march had ended with such appalling results. He asked them whether a reasonable instructor would have taken a group of untrained young recruits on such a march.

Sevier next put the survivors on the stand to testify. The general opinion was that McKeon was drunk at the time. Some had seen him swigging from a bottle of vodka.

McKeon was lucky in his defence counsel, a man with the unlikely and ironically appropriate name of Emile Zola Berman.

Berman had the knack of using the media and of stage-managing the administration of justice. He gave a press conference and asked all US Marines and ex-Marines to send in their views of the McKeon case. He was democratising justice by using the popular press and broadcasting as means of mass communication, in much the same way as a famous Presidential candidate cleared himself and gained mass support in the midst of serious personal scandal (see *NIXON*). The Marines' letters and telegrams poured in. Their verdict was unanimous. Marines had to be tough. Therefore their training had to be tough. Tough drill instructors such as McKeon had made the Marine corps the elite unit that it was. Berman then went to General Randolph Pate and asked him to appear as a witness for the defence. He also enlisted the aid of another tough witness, Lieutenant General Lewis B Puller, a well known military hero. He aimed to prove McKeon was no sadist, but a man determined to produce a really crack platoon.

Berman's defence was skilfully conducted and he steered the witnesses through a carefully constructed series of questions which indicated that McKeon was a strict but reasonable disciplinarian who trained his men to respect authority and obey orders. McKeon admitted that he sometimes slapped recruits, but explained that it was necessary. He had been slapped himself, by his parents and by nuns at his school: 'It was a slap to show I disapproved of what they were doing. It was proof that we were trying to learn them something and that we are their superiors.' When Berman asked General Pate how he would have dealt with the matter himself, Pate answered that it was probable that McKeon had drunk some vodka and done other things against regulations: 'I think I would take a stripe away from him, for that is a fairly serious thing when dealing with recruits. As to the remaining part of this I suspect I would have transferred him away for stupidity or for lack of judgement. I would probably have written in his record book though, that on no condition was this sergeant to drill recruits again.'

This was a very significant answer, as this distinguished commander was advocating a light punishment, bearing in mind that McKeon was being tried for manslaughter, among other serious charges. General Puller relieved himself of these options: 'The most important thing in training is discipline. It was not oppression of the recruits to order them out . . . the march was good military practice. The main thing that I have learned here as a recruit that I have remembered all my life is that I was taught the definition of *esprit de corps* — love for one's military legion. In my case, the US Marine Corps. It means more than self-preservation, religion or patriotism.' He added that the night march was a terrible accident, but he asserted that the main reason for American troops' poor show during the Korean war was their inexperience of night training: 'Americans are so used to electric lights they're practically night blind.'

Public opinion was now behind McKeon and the court had been won over to a different view of the events. The verdict was that McKeon was guilty of drinking in barracks and simple negligence in the death of six recruits. He was not guilty of manslaughter and oppression. The sentence was however a severe one — to be discharged from the drill service, to forfeit certain pension entitlements, to be confined at hard labour for nine months and to be reduced to the rank of private. This was later reviewed, resulting in the harsh sentence being considerably relieved and the bad conduct discharge removed. McKeon still served his nine months hard labour and was demoted to a private.

WILLIAM MAITLAND OF LETHINGTON

16th Century

WHEREAS John Knox was the undoubted theological leader of the Scottish Reformation — which triumphed in 1560 when the Scottish Parliament approved the Protestant confession of Faith and abolished the Mass — the main political mover was William Maitland of Lethington. He was a man quick to seize any advantageous opportunity, a schemer accurately named 'the Chameleon' by George Buchanan.

Maitland rose to prominence as Secretary of State to Mary of Guise. In 1555, however, he accepted, in a public debate with Knox, that Catholic rituals should be avoided. Opportunistically he associated himself with the Lords of Congregation, as the Protestant nobles called themselves, and was thus well placed when Mary of Guise died in 1560, leaving the Scottish throne vacant for the inexperienced Mary Queen of Scots.

The new Scottish queen inherited Maitland from her mother and trusted him on important missions. Craftily, he used his position to further his own power in the country. After Mary's disastrous marriage to Lord Darnley, in 1565, Maitland and his friends sought to exploit an unstable situation. On 10 February 1567 Darnley was murdered at Kirk o' Field, outside Edinburgh. The likelihood is that the murder was planned and executed by James Hepburn, Earl of Bothwell, with the encouragement of Maitland and other conspirators. When Bothwell appeared at his trial, for the Darnley murder, he was accompanied by Maitland and acquitted. While Mary watched Bothwell's procession from her window, at Holyrood Palace, she was attended by Mary Fleming, one of the Four Maries and now Maitland's wife.

Three months after the murder of Darnley, on 15 May 1567, Mary married Bothwell in a Protestant ceremony at Holyrood. She believed she would be secure in the protection of her third husband but was, as usual, wrong. Though Maitland had ostensibly approved of the marriage he undermined Mary's confidence in Bothwell and then plotted against her. Maitland was prominent among the men who confronted Mary at Carberry Hill, on 15 June, and forced her to surrender to them and abandon Bothwell. The devious Maitland assured the Queen he was not happy with the rebellion and still well-disposed to her. In fact Mary was taken, by jeering soldiers, to the home of Maitland's brother-in-law. As she looked out of the window she saw Maitland and appealed to him for help, calling pitifully 'Lethington, Lethington'. Pulling his hat over his ears, Maitland acted as if he had not heard her. Worse was to follow.

Mary was imprisoned in Lochleven Castle but escaped to England where she was placed under house arrest. In October 1568 an English Commission enquired into the charge that Mary had been responsible for the murder of Darnley. The most telling evidence against her was a collection of papers purportedly written by Mary though she claimed, 'I never writ anything concerning that matter to any creature. There are divers in Scotland, both men and women, that can counterfeit my handwriting.'

It was the Earl of Morton, Mary's Chancellor — and probable plotter, with Maitland, in the Darnley murder — who claimed to have come into possession of the so-called Casket Letters. On 19 June 1567, according to his version, he was dining in Edinburgh with Maitland when he heard that three of Bothwell's servants had been captured. One of these servants had, under a bed in an Edinburgh house, 'a certain silver box, overgilt, containing diverse missive writings, sonnets, contracts and obligations for marriage between the Queen . . . and James sometime Earl of Bothwell'. The casket contained eight personal letters, two marriage-contracts and a love-ballad in twelve stanzas. The Scottish Parliament were impressed and pronounced that 'her privy letters written wholly with her own hand [prove that Mary Queen of Scots] was privy, art and part, of the actual devise and deed of the fore-named murder of the King, her lawful husband'.

When the English Commissioners saw the letters they told Elizabeth I that 'the said letters and ballads, do discover such inordinate love between her and Bothwell, her loathing and abhorrence of her husband [Darnley] that was murdered, in such sort as every good and godly man cannot but detest and abhor the same'. There was no doubt of Mary's guilt, they added, 'if the said letters be written with her own hand'. That, of course, is the question.

Though the original documents conveniently disappeared from history there is little doubt that Mary was 'framed' by Maitland. Four of the eight letters were written by her and none of these was in any way criminal. The other four letters and the love-ballad were written to Bothwell by another woman, probably his Norwegian girlfriend Anna Throndsen and naturally these letters declare a passionate love for Bothwell. By mixing the two sets of letters together, it was made to look as if Mary had been in love with Bothwell while Darnley was still alive.

Maitland probably tampered with the letters to give Mary a clear motive for murdering Darnley. He could easily have had Anna's letters forged in Mary's hand. Not only did he, Mary's Secretary, know her handwriting well, he had also married one of the four Maries, Mary Fleming, who had been taught by the same writing master as the Queen of Scots.

Although the English Commissioners were not convinced of Mary's guilt, she was to serve what amounted to life imprisonment in England before her execution in 1587. For his part, Maitland reconverted to Mary's cause in 1569, was involved in the plot to marry her to Norfolk, and took refuge in Edinburgh Castle which he held on behalf of the Scottish queen. When the Castle was taken in 1573 Maitland avoided execution, it is thought, by committing suicide. On hearing of the death of her former Secretary of State, Mary made little show of grief though the Earl of Shrewsbury noted that 'it nips her very dear'. Maitland had turned his coat so many times he must have driven Mary to despair but at the end she retained some fond memories of 'the Chameleon'.

HANS VAN MEEGEREN

1889-1947

HANS VAN MEEGEREN, the most artful forger of them all, was a man motivated by a pride in his professional skill and a desire to live in the style he felt appropriate to his talent. His early exhibitions attracted attention, on account of his technical prowess and pictorial precision, but Holland's leading authority on art — Dr Abraham Bredius — dismissed his work as unimaginative and derivative. As Van Meegeren later said, in his own defence, 'I had been so belittled by the critics that I could no longer exhibit my own works under my own signature'.

Despite Bredius's critical indifference to his painting, Van Meegeren seemed to prosper. He became a man of property in Holland and acquired his own nightclub. He had expensive habits to indulge, for he drank heavily and became addicted to morphia. His money, he liked to claim, was won in three state lotteries. He was, to all appearances, a man with some personal problems but considerable financial and emotional resources.

In 1945 the Allied Military Government Art Commission were looking for art treasures that had gone missing during the war. Hidden in an old salt mine, near Salzburg, they found a collection of paintings stolen by the Nazis from European collections. One of the paintings was *Christ with the Woman Taken in Adultery* signed by the great Dutch master Vermeer whose pictures were highly prized because of their scarcity. This particular Vermeer had been acquired by Field Marshall Goering. He had, the Commission ascertained, given a Bavarian banker more than 200 paintings, stolen from Holland, for this single example of Vermeer's sublime art.

Further research showed that the painting had once been the property of Hans Van Meegeren so, in May 1945, two Dutch security officers called on the artist to assess his part in the sale of a masterpiece to a leading Nazi. Van Meegeren agreed that he had sold the picture during the war but insisted that he had only done so on condition it would never be resold to the Germans. Van Meegeren explained that he had bought the Vermeer from an Italian family forced, by circumstances, to part with their most valuable possessions.

As the story was highly suspicious, Van Meegeren was arrested on a charge of collaborating with the Nazis by putting a Dutch national treasure at the disposal of the enemy. For days Van Meegeren refused to co-operate with the authorities then, probably suffering from morphia withdrawal, made an astonishing confession. 'I sold no great national treasure,' he said, 'I painted it myself.' Moreover, he boasted that he had painted four more Vermeers — *Christ at Emmaus, Head of Christ, The Last Supper, The Washing of Christ's Feet* — as well as *Interior of Drinkers* by Peter de Hoogh.

This confession had important repercussions. In 1937 *Christ at Emmaus* had been sold in Rotterdam for £180,000. At the time it was praised, by none other than Dr Abraham Bredius, as Vermeer's most important work. If Van Meegeren had really produced *Christ at Emmaus* then Dr Bredius was not only fallible but a bit of a fool.

Goering's Vermeer, *Christ with the Woman Taken in Adultery*, was x-rayed, an examination that confirmed Van Meegeren's claim — the finished product was painted indeed over an extant painting on an old canvas. The Dutch authorities were not yet convinced. They challenged Van Meegeren to make a copy of Goering's Vermeer by way of demonstrating his ability to simulate the seventeenth century idiom. Van Meegeren said he would do better than that. If the authorities would let him return to his studio, and supply him with morphia and gin as well as the art materials he needed, he would paint an entirely new pseudo-Vermeer. Before the eyes of two officials, Van Meegeren took two months to complete his latest Vermeer. *Young Christ Teaching in the Temple* was not as good as the other fake Vermeers but it was good enough to show that Van Meegeren was telling the truth about his forgeries.

On 29 October 1947 Van Meegeren went on trial, in Amsterdam, accused of obtaining money by fraud and of putting false signatures on works of art. He admitted both charges. Though he had made a fortune from his share of the £730,000 his fakes had realised, he said that money was not his main concern. Asked why he had sold the fakes at such high prices Van Meegeren replied, plausibly enough, 'I had no alternative. If I had sold them at a low price it would have been an indication that they were false.' As for the ethics of falsifying signatures Van Meegeren stated that he painted not to deceive others but to delight himself.

The press and public warmed to him as a rogue who had outwitted the art experts. The authorities, too, were sympathetic to his predicament. On 12 November, Van Meegeren was found guilty on both charges and sentenced to one year in prison. If he had lived it is likely that Queen Juliana would have recommended his release after a petition for clemency had been forwarded to her. However, Van Meegeren suffered a heart attack and died, in a clinic, on 29 December 1947.

JACQUES MESRINE

1937-1979

JACQUES MESRINE, gunned down by a squad of French policemen specially trained for the task in Paris in November 1979, seemed to be in real life the kind of character portrayed on screen so well by Alain Delon. A closer inspection of his career reveals a far less attractive figure. For years France's Public Enemy Number One, Jacques Mesrine possessed in abundance the qualities of daring, enterprise and intrigue so valuable in military exploits in time of war but such a menace to society in times of peace. A cold-blooded killer who boasted of his approximately forty murders, a master of disguise and an undoubtedly brilliant escapologist, he squandered his many gifts in criminal and destructive activities.

He was born in Paris in 1937 and showed early in his behaviour at school his hatred of authority and authority figures. He drifted from job to job, then leaped at the chance to serve in the army and volunteered for service in Algeria. Here he underwent an intensive apprenticeship in barbarity and the lessons were not lost on him. The Arab population was sympathetic towards the Front de Liberation Nationale. Terrorism was rife, and Mesrine, like most Frenchmen who served there, soon developed a hatred for Algerians. The army acted as if they were answerable to none but themselves, and Mesrine's hardihood and immense strength made him an outstanding soldier. For a personality like his, the Algerian war was an adventure holiday. For the first time in his life he was a success. It was a feeling he liked.

When he was demobilised he was proud to show his father his medals, but the pace of civilian life soon bored him. He worked as a salesman for a lace-manufacturer, and soon began to crave excitement. He knew he had the personal qualities to lift himself out of the rut. Crime offered him two things he needed in endless supplies — money and thrills.

Safe-breaking, robbery with violence and work for the anti-Gaullist OAS replaced 'working for a living' in the usual sense. He teamed up with a prostitute, Jeanne Schneider, as his activities got bigger and braver and indeed more and more violent. The couple fled to Canada in 1968. A kidnap attempt went wrong and they were arrested. He made one of his famous escapes with another criminal, Jean-Paul Mercier, and killed two forest rangers who recognised the two escaped prisoners. This brutal crime earned them immense publicity in Canada and they had a price on their heads. Carey Scholfield, Mesrine's biographer (*Mesrine – The Life and Death of a Supercrook*, 1980) reports that he was upset at seeing a photograph of one of the ranger's sons weeping beside his father's coffin, 'but . . . he had wondered whether the boy realised his father was authorised to kill in the name of the law'. His attitude was that it was unfortunate for all of them that they had encountered each other.

He picked up a new female partner, an ex-call girl, and set off for New York. They then found their way to Venezuela where more robberies were committed. Then in 1972 he returned to France. Signs of megalomania had already shown themselves in his behaviour. He seemed to believe he lived a charmed life. Even when he knew he was the most wanted man in the country, he would pull up by a police car and ask the officer at the wheel the way to such-and-such a street. Another trick which revealed his arrogance was robbing the same bank twice, just to show he wasn't afraid. Danger made him drunk. He worked with a group of about a dozen fellow criminals but it would not be correct to term this a 'gang'. They worked in small groups and each job was meticulously planned. While not actually 'working' the group acted as watchmen and security men to ensure that Mesrine was not under surveillance from the police. In the world of crime Mesrine was treated as a head of state.

He was captured in 1973 and charged in Compiègne of numerous crimes including robbery, murder and the attempted murder of a policeman. He made a spectacular escape. For weeks he had been feigning dysentery, a performance he kept up with considerable conviction, making frequent demands to be taken to lavatories. At the Palais de Justice he requested to be taken to relieve himself. Outside an accomplice waited in a car. Behind the cistern a 9mm Luger was hidden. He concealed the gun on his person and went into court. When the charges were read out he produced the Luger and threatened to shoot the judge. Then using the judge as a human shield, he made good his escape. He remained in hiding while his companions organised false tip-offs for the police. He was free for 108 days and then captured again. He was placed in the security block of Paris's La Sainte prison. Here he wrote and was able to smuggle out for publication his autobiography, *The Killing Instinct*.

Another escape plan succeeded in springing him and further robberies followed. He relieved the casino at Deauville of thirteen thousand francs and lifted four hundred and fifty thousand francs from a bank. The authorities now began to train a special squad of policemen for the final reckoning.

Mesrine was growing more and more unstable and reckless. A journalist was beaten up when interviewing him and this gave police several vital clues to his whereabouts. In November 1979 his apartment in Paris was surrounded and he died trying to escape a hail of bullets. This time no chances were taken. Mesrine's charmed life was over.

When his apartment in the Rue Beilliard was searched it was found stocked for a siege. There was an arsenal, a machine gun, a rifle, numerous hand guns, canisters of gas and plenty of ammunition; also eight bars of gold and two hundred thousand francs. In some ways he chose this manner of ending his career — a dramatic death at the hands of a unit of the police whose very existence testified to his unique importance. 'They will never take me alive' had become his motto. He had even stage-managed his end, which was replete with a tape recorded message to his girlfriend. Police found a cassette in the flat, where, with romantic music in the background, Mesrine's voice declaimed: 'My love, it is certain that if you are listening to this, that I am dead . . . I prefer to die from the bullets of the police than waste away in some cellar . . . They are going to make a hero of me. It is not me who fabricates this hero. There are no heroes in crime. But I am richer than any of them. I have the soul and the courage that they lack.'

MESSALINA

AD 25-48

AFTER THE assassination of Caligula, the Roman Emperor, in AD 41, the Roman soldiers decided that his uncle Tiberius, Claudius Drusus Caesar, should succeed him. It is probable that Claudius was spastic: he stammered when he spoke, slavered when agitated, and walked with some difficulty. Physically he was more imaginative than many Romans. He was an enthusiastic author but had little luck with women. One fiancée opted out of a marriage, another died on the projected wedding day. He then divorced two wives before marrying Messalina in AD 40. He was forty-eight, she was fifteen.

Claudius became emperor the year after his marriage to Messalina who bore him two children, a daughter Octavia and a son Britannicus. There was no doubt who was in control of the domestic empire: Messalina easily dominated Claudius and felt it was her right to seek sexual satisfaction wherever she pleased. She was a nymphomaniac who used her power and position to get her way with anyone she fancied. Mnester, a celebrated ballet dancer, was one man she wanted. To get him into her bed she asked Claudius to issue an order insisting that Mnester was to obey Messalina. This he did and apparently discharged his sexual duties as well. When he was subsequently seduced by the beautiful Poppaea Sabina, Messalina became insanely jealous. She concocted a plot that would get rid of her rival and also, as a bonus, allow her to acquire the most coveted gardens in Rome — the Gardens of Lucullus, owned by ex-consul Asiasticus.

Messalina instructed two of her toadies to persuade Claudius that Asiasticus was a threat to his imperial rule since he had declared himself proud to be numbered among the men who had killed Caligula. Actually, Asiasticus had merely expressed approval of the assassination but Claudius was not to know that. As it was the emperor's policy to eliminate those interested in assassinating emperors, he had Asiasticus arrested and put on trial — in Messalina's presence and in, appropriately enough, a bedroom.

During the interrogation of Asiasticus, Messalina excused herself as if overcome by sadness at the spectacle. She used this opportunity to convey threatening messages to Poppaea who was thus persuaded to take her own life rather than face the consequences of Messalina's fury. Asiasticus also killed himself after being condemned to death.

Messalina was sexually insatiable. When she was not summoning lovers to her side she worked, purely for pleasure, in a Roman brothel where she put on a flaxen wig to disguise herself as a blonde lady of pleasure. She was always on the lookout for new thrills and moved quickly when she chose Julius Gaius Silius, consul designate, as her next target. At Messalina's behest Julius divorced his wife Junia. A delighted Messalina then moved in with Julius who was not slow to see the political possibilities of his great affair. He suggested to Messalina that she should make a break with Claudius by marrying himself. He reasoned that when Claudius died he, Julius, would adopt Britannicus and take over as emperor. And, of course, the question of Claudius's premature death could always be discussed.

Messalina agreed to the marriage which duly took place in AD 48. She also amused herself by arranging the murder of Claudius's son-in-law and, for good measure, the boy's parents. By way of celebration she held a Bacchanalian orgy in the Gardens of Lucullus. Claudius was away in Ostia while all this was going on and when he heard the news of his wife's bigamy, and her indifference to his authority, he returned to Rome in a rage.

While Narcissus, an ex-slave, denounced Messalina, the lady's lovers were brought before Claudius. Silius was put to death as were others less guilty. When Mnester, the dancer, was accused of enjoying Messalina he reminded Claudius of his command to obey Messalina and showed the marks on his back made by the whip Messalina used on him while urging him onto sexual heroics. The explanation was in vain and Mnester died.

Claudius was, nevertheless, inclined to spare Messalina but Narcissus took the imperial law into his own hands. He ordered one of the soldiers to kill Messalina, insisting that this was the emperor's wish. Messalina was given a dagger in order to inflict an honourable end on herself but she was in a state of such terror that the officer had to do the deed for her. News of Messalina's death was then brought to Claudius at his meal. His response was to continue eating and order more wine.

CHARLES MOHUN,
5th BARON MOHUN
OF OKEHAMPTON

1675-1712

CHARLES MOHUN was one of the most notorious duellists and rakehells of his day. He was the son of the 4th Baron Mohun, who died in 1677 from wounds he received in a duel. Young Charles lacked a regular guardian and enjoyed a thoroughly misspent youth. While still in his mid-teens he had earned a reputation for drunkenness, debauchery and fornication. He fought his first recorded duel in 1692, when he was seventeen, but in 1693 the slaying of the actor William Mountfort in a street brawl earned Mohun a reputation that has lasted down the centuries. However, even the part he played in this affair was to be eclipsed in a subsequent fight to the death.

One of Mohun's fellow roisterers, Captain Richard Hill, fancied himself deeply in love with Anne Bracegirdle, the celebrated actress, made famous in roles in plays by Congreve and Wycherly. It was rumoured that William Mountfort, although a happily married man, was enjoying Mrs Bracegirdle's favours. Richard Hill's jealousy was inflamed to fever pitch, and he and Mohun hatched a plot to abduct Mrs Bracegirdle from the house of her mother, or as she left the theatre after a performance, bundle her into a carriage and take her to a house in the country which Hill had prepared to receive her. Here he intended to take by force what the lady would not willingly part with. On the evening of the proposed abduction the two plotters drank deeply in several taverns, working themselves into the right mood. They then staggered off to Drury Lane Theatre. Here the playbills outside the doors told them that Anne Bracegirdle was not in fact to appear that night. They entered the theatre and learned that the object of Hill's desires was at dinner with friends nearby.

By now they had gathered with them a few companions who were all willing to take part in this reckless escapade, and the party moved off to wait outside the house in Drury Lane where Anne and her mother were at supper. Mohun waited in a coach with the coach-door ready and open, while Hill and the rest lurked in the shadows. Eventually the dinner party broke up, and Anne Bracegirdle, her mother, and their host, a Mr Page, came out on to the street. The trio walked towards the coach, not realising what had been planned for them. Hill leaped upon Mrs Bracegirdle and tried to force her inside the coach, but her mother had instantly gathered something was amiss and grabbed her daughter round the waist. Page tried to interfere, but was easily floored. The shouting and struggling aroused the watch, who now arrived on the scene.

Lord Mohun came down from the coach and attempted to calm the situation, explaining that his companion, Captain Hill, had had rather too much to drink, and offering to take the party home. They wisely declined, and accompanied by Mr Page, Anne and her mother began to walk the short distance to their house in Howard Street. Mohun and Hill followed, as it was still Mohun's intention to gain access to Anne's house if possible. The door was shut in his face. For a time they kept up a riotous din in the street, shouting and waving their swords. Candles were lit in darkened houses and faces appeared at the windows. Anne and her mother, safely indoors, talked things over and Anne realised that it was Hill's jealousy which was the cause of the evening's events. She decided the best thing was to warn Mountfort and to this end a servant was secretly dispatched with a message to the actor not to go home, or at least to get protection. Sadly the message failed to get through.

Inexplicably, Mountfort had decided not to take his usual route home to Norfolk Street from the theatre. His wife received the warning message for a husband she was never to see alive again. Mountfort turned down Howard Street, which crosses Norfolk Street, and was thereby accosted by Hill and Mohun. The Baron went up to him and demanded to know what he was doing in the street at this time of night. Mountfort answered that he came down the street quite by chance. Mohun then said: 'I trust you have heard about the lady?' The actor answered: 'I hope that my wife has given you no offence?' Mohun then retorted: 'Damme! It's Mrs Bracegirdle I mean!' Just as Mountfort was murmuring that Mrs Bracegirdle was no concern of his, Hill struck him on the side of the face and as he reeled from this unexpected blow, ran him through with his sword before Mountfort had even had a chance to draw his own. Hill then ran off in the confusion as several citizens of Howard Street, aroused by the brawl, as well as the local watch, gathered on the pavement. Mohun stood there alone, shaken and pale. He was taken away by the authorities and made two curious statements, which were dutifully recorded at the time. When he heard that Hill had fled and left him to fend for himself he exclaimed: 'I don't care a farthing if I hang for him!' To which he added: 'I'm sorry to learn that he has no money. I'd have given him some had there been time.'

Charles Mohun claimed the right to be tried by his peers. His trial at Westminster Hall opened on 31 January 1693. His charge read that he did 'with malice and aforethought, aid, abet, comfort, assist and maintain Richard Hill to kill and murder one William Mountfort'. The penalty would be death.

A peer charged with a capital offence was not entitled to legal counsel. Mohun conducted his own defence and by all accounts he carried it off very well. His main tactic was to discredit witnesses, successfully implying that the prosecution's main testimony was given by drunks or women of low repute — these were the witnesses who it was claimed had heard Mohun and Hill plotting in the taverns the night of the crime. In his summing up he said: 'My Lords, I hope it will be no disadvantage to me in my summing up that I have made it clear, by various questions to the witnesses, that there was no quarrel or malice between Mountfort and myself. I hope, too, that I have made it abundantly clear that the reason why I stayed so long in the street with Captain Hill was because he was my friend and I wished to persuade him to approach Mrs Bracegirdle in all humility and beg her pardon for an offence against good taste. My conscience is clear of all other motive, and I commit myself to the honourable House.' Sixty-nine peers voted for his aquittal, and fourteen voted him guilty. He was discharged.

But the scandal tainted his name. Given time he might have lived it down, but he could not change his character or his ways. In 1699 he again appeared before the House of Lords on a murder charge. Once again it was a drunken quarrel. He and a group of associates had spent the night on the town, much of it at a tavern named the Greyhound in the Strand. There was a violent disagreement over a woman, and a party of six of them had themselves taken by sedan chair to St Martins-in-the-Fields and there fought it out. The result of this night's excitement was the death of a certain Captain Coote. Lord Mohun and the Earl of Warwick, who had both been engaged in the fight, were arrested.

This was a serious blemish on Mohun's name as he had in other respects rendered his country good service. He had volunteered for the Brest expedition in 1694, had been made captain of horse and gone on to distinguish himself in Flanders. But he could not leave fighting to his career in the army, he had to bring his aggression and energy into civilian life. Once again his peers voted him not guilty. This time their Lordships took it upon themselves solemnly to recommend him to mend his ways.

For some years it truly seemed that he had taken their advice to heart. His companion, Edward Rich, the Earl of Warwick, had been found guilty of the manslaughter of Captain Coote, and this seemed to shake Mohun into some serious mood of reform. He became a staunch supporter of the Whigs and often spoke on the Whig cause in the House of Lords; he attended Charles Gerard, second Earl of Macclesfield, as envoy extraordinary to Hanover in 1701. But his end was bloody and typical. For some time he had been in dispute with James Douglas, fourth Duke of Hamilton, a supporter of James II and of the high Tory political preacher Henry Sacheverell, over a longstanding debt claimed by Mohun. Mohun had given him the lie to his face and was thereby challenged to a duel of honour. They fought a long and ferocious duel in Hyde Park in November 1712. Mohun drew the first blood. Hamilton was clearly very badly wounded and Mohun called upon him to yield his sword, but Hamilton declined. They fought on and Hamilton seemed to gain his second wind. Taking Mohun off his guard, he ran him through the stomach, killing him instantly. James Duke of Hamilton died the same day. The duel was alleged at the time to have been a Whig plot.

On Mohun's death the barony, which had been created to honour his great grandfather, John Mohun (1592-1640) became extinct. Mohun appears in Thackeray's novel *Henry Esmond* (1852) which contains a vivid account of the Mohun-Douglas duel. Thackeray wrote that Lord Mohun had 'an air of fixed fatality' and it does seem to some extent true that he set out on a self-destructive career.

RICHARD NIXON

born 1913

AFTER NARROWLY losing the Presidential election of 1960 to John F Kennedy, Richard Nixon failed to secure the governorship of California in 1962 and was cast into the political wilderness by his critics. 'You won't have Nixon to kick around anymore,' Nixon told reporters at what was supposed to be his farewell press conference. Nixon, the man you wouldn't buy a used car from (as the Kennedy camp insisted), was widely regarded as a spent political force.

Then Nixon made an astonishing comeback. Partly due to the intervention of a third candidate, George Wallace, Nixon managed to defeat Hubert Humphrey and become President of the USA in 1968. He and his Vice-President, Spiro Agnew, fought the campaign as Republican law 'n' order candidates. Nixon projected himself as the embodiment of American decency. He denounced 'campus bums' and others who broke the law. He spoke up for the 'silent majority'.

In 1972 Nixon was returned for a second term after a massive victory against George McGovern. But two years later he was forced to resign over what has been called a 'second-rate buglary' — the break-in, in June 1972, at the Democratic National Committee Headquarters in the Watergate complex in Washington.

Thanks mainly due to *Washington Post* reporters Bob Woodward and Carl Bernstein, the Watergate story was fully explored. The five Watergate burglars had intended to install wiretapping equipment yet the public could not, at first, comprehend the reason behind the operation. Nixon, in 1972, was virtually certain of re-election, so why bother with the break-in?

Nixon himself denied any knowledge of it. When he was compelled to surrender tapes of White House conversations he (it seems certain) erased sensitive sections and would have erased all the conversations had he the time to do so. Nixon kept trying to evade responsibility for the break-in and eventually dismissed his two key advisers, John Ehrlichman and Bob Haldeman on the grounds that they had arranged the cover-up. Even after his resignation Nixon took the line that he knew nothing about the Watergate burglary, did not participate in the cover-up, and was only guilty of excessive loyalty to Haldeman and Ehrlichman by keeping them on the White House staff when they should have been dismissed. Nixon portrayed himself as a martyr.

A more plausible explanation is that Nixon actually instigated the whole Watergate scenario. A notoriously vindictive man, Nixon had long wanted some ammunition he could use against Larry O'Brien, chairman of the Democratic National Committee. In his book *The Ends of Power* (London, 1978) Haldeman describes the grudge Nixon had against O'Brien and how Nixon suspected O'Brien of being on the payroll of Howard Hughes, the enigmatic millionaire. Nixon apparently wanted to nail O'Brien and so ordered his phone to be tapped. Haldeman says unequivocally, 'Richard Nixon, himself, caused those burglars to break into O'Brien's office.' As for the cover-up, Haldeman says, 'The President was involved in the cover-up from Day One.'

Nixon, the champion of law and order, treated the law with contempt when he was President. He also tried to wriggle out of his reponsibilities by putting the blame on his colleagues. Haldeman regrets the fall from grace of Nixon, a man he admired, a complex man terribly insecure 'about his truly humble background. He never let us forget that his mother had to scrub bedpans, for example.'

Nixon's nastiness was nothing new. He first came to prominence as a member of the House Committee on Un-American Activities, an *ad hoc* organisation dedicated to hounding anyone who seemed the least bit Leftish. Nixon had Gerhard Eisler cited for contempt of Congress for refusing to testify before the Committee. He also had Alger Hiss sent to jail in 1950. Hiss, president of the Carnegie Endowment for International Peace, was accused of passing secret State Department papers to Whittaker Chambers, a senior editor with *Time* magazine and a man with a Communist past. Chambers told the Committee he kept the secret papers in a pumpkin. When the pumpkin papers were examined in 1975 they were shown to contain no sign of secrets.

Yet Hiss went to prison while Nixon eventually went to the White House. Lilian Hellman, whose *Scoundrel Time* (1976) tells of her struggle with the Committee, describes Nixon as a man who 'invented when necessary, maligned even when it wasn't necessary'.

TITUS OATES

1649-1705

PERIODS OF national insecurity and paranoia often bring forth those who denounce the enemy within, and achieve fame and sometimes fortune thereby. Recent American history shows this in the case of Senator Joseph McCarthy. The end of the seventeenth century in England gave us Titus Oates, one of the greatest perjurers in history. His early life promised very little, but it did show his unreliability, dishonesty and duplicity. Had the times been other than they were, he might never have become notorious, but there was a fear of Roman Catholics and of an international Catholic conspiracy, possibly led by Louis XIV of France, to overthrow Protestant government in Britain and restore the old faith. King Charles II, it was believed, was a sound Protestant, but his wife was a Catholic. Suppose there *was* something in the conspiracy theory and the rumours that circulated?

Titus Oates was expelled from Merchant Taylors' School during his first year there in 1665. But he went on to Gonville and Caius College, Cambridge, and later to St John's College. He did not take his degree but appears as the vicar of

114

Bobbing in 1673. Shortly after this he was imprisoned at Dover for making serious accusations against a schoolmaster in Hastings. Before being brought to trial he escaped and was for a time a chaplain in the navy. He was soon expelled and then served as chaplain to the Protestants in the household of the Duke of Norfolk. It was here that he first came into contact with Papists. A vital element in his story is his contact with Israel Tonge (1621-1680) whom he met in 1676, and whose willing dupe he became in the Popish Plot.

Israel Tonge initially simply employed Oates to produce diatribes against Roman Catholics, but Oates was to develop into a master Catholic baiter without parallel. Oates himself became a Catholic in 1677 in order to get further information about the organisation of the faith in Britain. He entered the Jesuit College at Valladolid but was expelled within six months. He then went to St Omer and by 1678 he and Tonge believed they were ready for their major effort against the Papists. The basis of the so-called Popish Plot was simple: Charles II was to be murdered and the country was to be run by Jesuits. The conspiracy, they were to claim, was organised by a group who frequented the White Horse Tavern in Fleet Street. The plot was vivid in its details: all the shipping in the Thames was to be fired and the gutters would run with good Protestant blood.

Titus Oates made these sensational revelations before the magistrate, Sir Edmundbury Godfrey. Soon afterwards, Godfrey's body was found on Hampstead Heath, having been run through by his own sword. This would seem to confirm the plot as detailed by Oates. It was believed that the Jesuits had begun to take their revenge.

Three men were executed for Godfrey's murder. The evidence was not very strong, but they were the first of what was to become a procession of sacrificial victims to the machination of Titus Oates, who now accused a man named Edward Coleman of bribing assassins to murder Charles II. Coleman was tried and executed at Tyburn. Oates named Charles II's Queen, Catherine of Braganza, in the conspiracy but was not believed. However, others whom he named soon met their ends at the hands of the executioner. The execution of William Howard, first Viscount Stafford, who was accused by Oates of being the paymaster of the Catholic army, and of complicity in the plot to murder Charles II, caused a revulsion of public feeling. Up until then Oates had been doing rather well. While his accusations were bearing fruit, and suspected traitors were being hauled away to trial and many of them to their deaths, Oates was living luxuriously in Whitehall, next to the Court, on a pension of £1,200 a year. But cracks were beginning to appear in Titus Oates's fabrications.

There was something to hold the story of the plot together, or so it seemed. James, Duke of York, the King's brother, *was* a Roman Catholic, and so was Charles II's wife. It was possible that Coleman had corresponded with Jesuits abroad . . . but was there really a plot to murder Charles II, put leading Protestants to the sword, and hand the nation over to foreign Catholic powers? Sir William Scroggs, the Lord Chief Justice of England seemed willing enough to go along with Oates's denunciations. His view was: 'It is better to be warm on the bench (condemning Catholics) than in Smithfield' (burnt as a martyred Protestant after a Catholic restoration).

Then five Jesuits stood before the dock in London accused of conspiracy. Their defence was that Oates could not have known about their activities at the stated times, as he himself was not in London. He was actually at the Jesuit retreat at St Omer, and they could prove it. The Jesuits themselves had been at St Omer in France and had seen Oates there at the time. In fact, they had taken their meals with him . . . Nevertheless these unfortunate men were executed. But doubts had begun. The next turn of events against Oates was his arrest for libelling James, Duke of York. He was fined £100,000, but had no money and so was imprisoned for life.

When Charles II died, James came to the throne. It was time to deal with Titus Oates. On 8 May 1685 he appeared before the King's Bench, charged with 'perjury, in that he had, on the seventeenth day of December 1678, sworn there was a treasonable consult of Jesuits held at the White Horse Tavern in the Strand, in the County of Middlesex, the twenty fourth day of April in the said year 1678, at which the Jesuits Whitebread, Fenwick, and Ireland, the said Titus Oates, and forty or fifty more Jesuits were present; and that they separated themselves into several companies, or clubs, and came to a resolution to murder the King; and that he, the said Titus Oates, carried the said resolution from chamber to chamber to be signed by the said Jesuits; whereas, in truth and fact, he, the said Titus Oates, was not present at any such consult on the 24th of April, 1678, nor carried any such resolution from chamber to chamber to be signed: and so he, the said Titus Oates, on the said 17th of December, 1678, did commit wilful and corrupt perjury.' Many witnesses were brought against him to discredit his testimony and prove that he could not have been privy to the intrigues he claimed to denounce in others. He was exposed as a liar and a fraud. His sentence was a severe one:

> That the defendant should pay one thousand marks upon each indictment; that he should be stripped of all his canonical habits; that he should stand in the pillory before Westminster Hall Gate on the Monday following for an hour with a paper over his head declaring his crime, but that first he should walk it round all the Courts in the hall.
>
> On the second indictment he should stand in the pillory, the Tuesday following, at the Royal Exchange; that the next Wednesday he should be whipped from Newgate to Tyburn, at the hands of the common hangman; that the ninth of August every year of his life, he should stand in the pillory before Westminster Hall Gate; the tenth of August at Charing Cross; and the eleventh over against the Temple; and the second of September, at the Royal Exchange; on the twenty-fourth of April every year at Tyburn.

These sentences came at the end of several very long and complex trials. His first day at the pillory nearly killed him. He was pelted with dead rats, dogs, cats, as well as stones and rotten vegetables. His friends tried to encircle him the next day so as to save him. The whipping at the hands of the hangman was horrendous; he was nearly flayed alive. The sentence was duly carried out over the months, but what saved him was the deposition of James II. In 1689, after being imprisoned for over three years, he was released. He was granted a pension of £300 a year after friends had interceded for him with William III.

116

He published an attack on King James II, called *Eikon Basilike*, in 1696. Two years later he entered the baptist church and on occasion preached at Wapping. A financial scandal caused his dismissal in 1701 and he died on 12 July 1705.

Part of Oates's success was the result of articulating what all men *knew*, namely that the Jesuits would like to restore the old faith in England, and of claiming that he was cognisant of various genuine plots to put this *into effect*. Thus when he exposed Coleman, he was doing little more initially than exclaiming what many had whispered — and it was upon such foundations that his larger fabrications were so convincingly constructed. John Evelyn wrote in his journal:

> I do look on Oates as a vain, insolent man, puffed up, with the favour of the Commons, for having discovered something really true; as more especially detecting the dangerous intrigue of Coleman, proved out of his own letters; and of a general design, which the Jesuitical party of the papists ever had, and still have, to ruin the Church of England; but that he was trusted with those great secrets he pretended, or had any solid ground for what he accused divers noble men of, I have many reasons to induce my contrary belief.

One interesting theory which might account for Titus Oates's obvious familiarity with Roman Catholic circles which would normally have been barred to a rather disreputable clergyman of the Church of England, is the fact that he was beyond doubt a practising homosexual. His denunciations and betrayals then seem even more blackguardly. During the trial of Stafford Evelyn it was recorded that the testimony of a man such as Oates should not be taken against the life of a dog. Drawing on contemporary sources the historian Macaulay wrote this description of Oates:

> . . . his short neck, his legs uneven, the vulgar said, as those of a badger, his forehead low as that of a baboon, his purple cheeks, and his monstrous length of chin, had been familiar to all who frequented the courts of law. He had then been the idol of the nation. Wherever he had appeared men had uncovered their heads to him. The lives and estates of the magnates of the realm had been at his mercy. Times had now changed; and many who had formerly regarded him as the deliverer of his country, shuddered at the sight of those hideous features on which villainy seemed to be written by the hand of God.

Similarly unfavourable portraits of Oates are to be found in Dryden's *Absalom and Achitophel* (1681) and in Roger North's *Examen*, which was published in 1740, though written by an eye-witness to these terrible events. The persecutions of Catholics which resulted from Oates's denunciations were the talk of Europe, and there was something almost of universal joy when it was known that justice had overtaken him. It was said that since his forehead was too low to blush, it was only right that his back should be made to do so.

ARTHUR ORTON
1834-1898

THE TICHBORNE CASE is a prime example of the art of false representation made possible — and indeed successful — because there are those who desperately wish to believe what is represented to them.

Lady Tichborne, wife of Sir James Francis Doughty Tichborne, wanted with all her heart to believe that her eldest son, Roger Charles Tichborne, who was reported drowned at sea in 1854, was really still alive, despite the fact that his will was proven in 1855. Lady Tichborne put advertisements in newspapers in Australia in her attempts to trace her long lost son. Arthur Orton saw one of the these advertisements, and when he returned to England, Lady Tichborne professed to recognise him as Roger Charles Tichborne. Orton brought an ejectment action in 1871 against Sir Henry Tichborne, twelfth baronet, and posthumous heir of Sir Alfred Tichborne, Sir James's younger son, who had succeeded as the eleventh baronet in 1862 and died in 1866. The trial, which reads like something out of *Bleak House*, lasted 102 days.

Fully to relish the audacity of Orton and his supporters some historical detail is needed. Roger Charles Tichborne, whom Orton later claimed to be, was born in 1829. Until he was fourteen he lived in France (this was later to be significant evidence) and then he was sent to Stonyhurst. In 1849 he received a commission in the 6th Dragoon Guards. He had fallen in love with his cousin, Miss Doughty, but when his love was not returned, he took the rather drastic if romantic step of resigning from the army and retiring to South America. His voyage took him first to Valparaiso and next to Rio de Janeiro. After leaving this port his ship was reported to have sunk at sea.

Arthur Orton was, in fact, five years younger than Roger Charles Tichborne. He was born in Wapping, the son of a butcher. He had a sparse education. He could read and write English passably well and had enough skill in figures to work in his father's business. As a young man he suffered from St Vitus's dance and went on a sea trip for the good of his health. In 1848 he sailed for Valparaiso from Antwerp. At Melpipilla he was befriended by a family called Castro and for some reason he assumed the name Castro. He also picked up a bit of Spanish. In 1851 he was back in Wapping again. But he was restless at home and once again set out in his travels, this time to Tasmania. At Hobart, Gippsland and Wagga-Wagga he plied various trades like butchery, horse-dealing and petty crime, including bushranging and horse-theft. He married a servant girl.

In 1865 a man named Cubitt opened a missing persons office in Sydney. He advertised in *The Times* and came to the attention of Lady Tichborne. Cubitt advertised for the missing Roger Charles Tichborne and Orton, alias Castro, saw the advertisement in a Sydney newspaper. Thus began his career as the Tichborne claimant. He acted the role for friends and greatly amused them by the airs he adopted. He took to signing his name 'Sir Roger Tichborne' in his diary, and then began consistently to claim that he *was* Tichborne. A man named Gibbes heard of the person who called himself Roger Tichborne and reported the matter to Cubitt's agency. There was a reward, of course. In due course Lady Tichborne and the claimant were in correspondence.

Orton's letters were full of nonsense and inaccuracies but the fact is that Lady Tichborne wanted to believe he was the long lost Roger Charles, and therefore she tended to overlook the evidence of her own eyes. His attempts to explain his long absence and silence were feeble, but she accepted them. He made many errors about his supposed family and his career — but she affected not to notice them. One trump card Orton had was a negro named Boyle who lived in New South Wales, who had been a servant of the Tichborne family. He claimed to recognise in Orton the missing son and heir. He was also able to supply Orton with many details of the Tichborne house and estate. When he learned that the Tichbornes were Roman Catholics he married his wife a second time in a Roman Catholic ceremony. Even here he made mistakes, signing his name 'Titchborne' in the register! He returned to England and finally mother and 'son' were reunited. When they met for the first time, Arthur was ill in bed and had his face turned to the wall throughout the interview. In the course of their conversation he made numerous mistakes, including saying he suffered from St Vitus's dance (Roger suffered from rheumatism), that he was educated at Winchester (Roger went to Stonyhurst),

Roger Charles Tichborne.

119

Lady Tichborne.

that he'd been a trooper in the cavalry (Roger had been an officer) and others. But Lady Tichborne asserted: 'He confuses everything as if in a dream, but it will not prevent me from recognising him, though his statements differ from mine.'

Orton then devoted his energies to impersonating Roger Charles Tichborne. He brushed up on knowledge of the family's history, and the biography of the young man he was supposed to be. He even contrived after much practice to make his signature and handwriting look like that of Roger Tichborne. After four years of training, he was ready. The subsequent trial showed how well he had done his homework. He had eighty-five witnesses who averred he was Roger Tichborne — and they included six magistrates, Lady Tichborne, the family's solicitor, four vicars, seven family tenants, sixteen family servants, one baronet, one general, three colonels and one major. Against him were a mere seventeen witnesses, but he lost the first trial as a result of his own poor showing in cross examination when Sir John Coleridge made vast inroads into his insufficient knowledge of his own, alleged, early life, schooling and army career. He had no knowledge of his own mother's maiden name. He knew hardly anything about the family estates. He thought Julius Caesar wrote in Greek. He had no knowledge of Virgil. When shown a text of Virgil he said he believed it to be Greek. Mathematics was a closed book to him. He knew nothing of Stonyhurst school or its customs and mythology. He was totally ignorant of military matters. Roger Tichborne spoke French like a native. Orton was completely ignorant of this tongue. He said he had 'forgotten' it. He was unaware that Roger had vowed to build a votive chapel at Tichborne should Miss Doughty ever agree to marry him. Tattoo marks which Roger was known to possess on his body — a cross, an anchor and a heart — had gone without trace from Orton's arms. The jury, having heard all the evidence and witnessed the cross examination of Orton and the witnesses, returned their verdict — to nonsuit the claimant. Arthur Orton was consequently prosecuted for perjury.

The second trial was equally sensational. The evidence of one of Orton's witnesses, Jean Luie, who claimed to be a Danish seaman who had rescued

'Roger' from the shipwreck, was eventually and sensationally discredited. The judge's summing up lasted for eighteen days, and he justified his vast and complex review of the evidence by saying: 'It is not the business of the judge so to adjust the scales of the balance that they shall hang evenly; but it is his duty to see that the facts as they arise are placed in the one scale or the other according as they belong to the one or the other . . . if the facts make one scale kick the beam it is the fault of the facts, not of the judge . . . It is the business of judicial action to protect virtue, but it is the duty also of the judge to see that the guilty do not escape.' Orton was sentenced to fourteen years penal servitude.

In 1895 he published in *The People* a signed confession of the whole affair, which although he was later to refute it, did explain everything about this extraordinary case. He died in abject poverty in a lodging house in Marylebone on 1 April 1898. By all account he was an exemplary convict, subject to fits of depression and frequent bouts of weeping. The Tichborne claimant remains one of the most fascinating examples of criminal impersonation in British legal history.

LORD WILLIAM PAGET

1803-73

YOUNGER SON of one of the heroes of the Battle of Waterloo, Lord William Paget seemed destined for a safe career in the British navy and a life of some luxury thanks to the generosity of his father, the Marquis of Anglesey. His family credentials were impeccable and he became Member of Parliament for Caernarvon in 1826. Thanks also to his father's eminence William rapidly rose to a position of some authority; the Marquis of Anglesey was created Lord Lieutenant of Ireland and William went to Dublin as Commander of the *Royal Charlotte*, the Vice-Regal yacht. The job was worth £1,000 a year to him and he meant to enjoy it in the style to which he felt he should be accustomed.

In 1827 William married Fanny Rottenburgh despite his father's advice to the contrary. Rightly suspicious of his son's prodigal appetite for ostentatious comforts, Anglesey advised William to marry a woman of financial substance. Fanny had no fortune and was thus unable to contribute to the running of William's life. Nevertheless, William kept a carriage and spent a fortune on clothes, wine and fine possessions. But by March 1829 William was no longer in command of the *Royal Charlotte* and now desperately in needs of funds as he was being pressed to pay his considerable debts. Counting on his father's pride in his own reputation, William told the family solicitor that unless his creditors were satisfied he would have no alternative but to resign his parliamentary seat and declare himself a debtor. The ignominy of this would, of course, embarrass Anglesey who decided to help his son out of a difficult situation. When the family solicitor asked for details of the debts, William wrote 'Dear

Sir, my debts amount to £20,000, yours truly, William Paget'.

Returning to England William did not, as his father urged, accept the loan of a house. He decided, instead, to rent one. Anglesey wrote:

> Is it to be believed that this disgraced and wretched young man, with all his difficulties staring him in the face, and knowing that his tricks and falsehoods must come to light . . . should have impudently taken a house near London, and have expended £1,300 on the furniture!!! Here I stop. It would be endless to attempt to enumerate his extravagances — his folly — his falsehoods — alas what a word to write of one's own son!

William himself had no regrets. When a lawyer, George Thompson, asked him to settle an outstanding debt he replied:

> Sir, on looking over some papers this day, I find one from you, dated 4 May last upon the subject of Mr Curwen's bill. I do not recollect to have seen it before, and certainly a more laughably impertinent production I never received. Who you are, for you sign your name George Thompson (there are a great many George Thompsons in the world) dating your letter (if it deserves the name) Dublin, I am at a loss to guess; neither should I be at the trouble of finding out, excepting for the purpose of informing you, that the next opportunity you give *me*, I shall give *you* the benefit of the postage of your letter back again. P.S. Mr Curwen's bill (by the way) is an impudent extortion, whether I undertook to pay it or not.

Since he had to clear his son's debts, Lord Anglesey made certain conditions. William's £10,000 inheritance was to be put into trust and his possessions were to be sold. In return for this William was to live abroad on an allowance of £500 per annum. William, who had been put in command of a ship bound for the West Indies, insisted that he should retain a London house for his family. He also hinted that he would publicly disgrace himself unless his father cleared all his debts. On 1 January 1830 Anglesey commented, 'As for the threat of . . . his relinquishing his ship and his seat in Parliament and giving his person to his creditors . . . He is his own master, and may do as he pleases.' As Anglesey added that he might cut off William's inheritance the prodigal complied with his conditions and sailed to the West Indies on the *North Star*.

The voyage was an eventful one for William. On his instructions one William Heritage, a boy on the ship, was given twelve lashes for forgetting to put his hammock away. Unfortunately, the boy subsequently forgot to lock the fresh water tank and was sentenced to a further flogging. Unable to endure this, the boy threw himself over the side and drowned. On the ship's return to Portsmouth William was tried by Court Martial and honourably acquitted. Immediately after the trial, though, he was arrested for debts amounting to £772. Anglesey, who was delighted that his son had been cleared by a Court Martial, overlooked this further evidence of irresponsibility and paid off the creditors.

For several years William lived, characteristically above his means, in Belgium and France. He came back to England in 1835 and took up a commission in a mercenary outfit formed to fight in the war in Spain. Back in England in 1836 he was, predictably, arrested as a debtor and imprisoned in

Southwark. Yet again his father came, reluctantly, to the rescue but insisted that 'immediately upon being released from Prison [William] must go abroad and reside there upon his present yearly income of £680'. It was also made clear to William that 'if the aforegoing stipulations, or any one of them, be broken on the part of Lord William, Lord Anglesey will not pay another shilling of debt, but will withhold the said allowance of £500'.

After yet another run in with creditors, William moved to Pau, in France, but returned to England in 1839, having separated from his wife. Anglesey was furious, especially as he had been against the marriage from the beginning:

> At the moment when I had hoped that he was losing his evil ways, and that there was a faint prospect of reform, he comes and as it were intentionally destroys in one breath all further hope ... He has been so long incorrigible that I believe him capable of coming to England (from which he had bound himself in honour to absent himself until he had my sanction to return) to court incarceration for the mere purpose of distressing his family still further.

Anglesey ordered William back to Pau but he was unable to return for, as his wife informed him, creditors were waiting for him.

William doubled back to England to the despair of Anglesey who decided to call for a family gathering to resolve William's financial distress and his marriage. At Uxbridge House, on 16 February 1840, Anglesey summed up the situation. In the last ten years, he pointed out, the sum of £26,916 had been paid to William because of his debts. Anglesey angrily continued: 'What right had he to expect this? Or that his extravagance should be fed at the expense of his brothers and sisters, and towards whom it were injustice to allow it. Promises had been made by Lord William, and on the last occasion, when taken out of the Bench, they were most solemnly made, but, as usual, broken. Again he has incurred debts at Pau, to the extent of upwards of £500 and has left his residence there, and come to England against his father's wishes.'

Having condemned his son in these terms, Anglesey now made a proposal. 'This is what I will do,' he explained, 'and for the last time, I here declare it most solemnly. Lord William asked some short time ago for an additional £20 per annum, on the score of house rent being high at Pau. I will increase that to £100 per annum, in addition to the present allowance of £500 — and I will pay the debts at Pau to the extent stated — nay I will go further and call them £600. This will put Lord William once more free at Pau, with an income of £780 per annum (including his half-pay of £180) having only himself, his wife and two children to maintain.' In the circumstances it was an extremely generous offer which William accepted with alacrity. The debts at Pau were cleared and William promised his father he would never again involve him in the payment of his debts.

Needless to say, William continued to run up debts and this time his father responded by stopping his allowance. William managed to get back to England but had to live in humble lodgings. Now that his appeals to his father were being ignored, he made another attempt to enrich himself. Hearing that his wife was having an affair with Lord Cardigan he hired a private detective, Winter, to obtain evidence he could use to his financial benefit. Winter duly brought back information that enabled William to take legal action against Cardigan. At the trial of February 1844, though, Cardigan was cleared. Sir William Follet, Cardigan's defence lawyer, stated accurately enough that William's motive had been 'to extract money from a wealthy nobleman'.

William's debts continued to pile up, including one that would have led to his dismissal from the navy had not Anglesey spared him this humiliation by bailing him out. By 1846 he was operating a new scheme, pretending he could sell government jobs to those with enough money to pay for the privilege. He made £900 this way but that was not enough to keep him out of trouble and he had to flee to Cadiz to escape the attentions of yet more creditors. His father then intervened to offer him the navy's retired allowance which kept him going. Inevitably there was more debt and further appeals to Anglesey who died in 1854. After this William was left, virtually, to his own devices and presumably lived out the rest of his life in an environment of debt and deceit and in permanent exile from England.

Though an egregious rogue, William must have had a personality attractive enough to attract sympathy. He still does, for Christopher Simon Sykes, in his book *Black Sheep* (London, 1982) writes, 'The truth is that William was the victim of a system which actively discriminated against younger children, and often encouraged idleness and dissipation amongst their elder brothers; the system of primogeniture.'

WILLIAM PALMER

1824-56

WILLIAM PALMER is one of the most notorious poisoners in British criminal history. He was a qualified physician who practised medicine at Rugeley in Staffordshire after serving as house-surgeon at St Bartholomew's Hospital in London in 1846. He poisoned his wife in 1854, his brother Walter in 1855 and his friend John Parsons Cook, also in 1855. All these crimes were committed for financial gain. He was only tried and convicted for one murder — that of Cook — but his trial created enormous public interest. Charles Greville, the political diarist, recorded on 28 May (Derby Day) 1856, that the fascination with the case was almost unprecedented, and that the women in particular were taken up with it, 'though there was nothing peculiar in it or of a nature to excite them particularly. The trial lasted a fortnight, all the details of it were read with the greatest avidity, half the town went one day or other to hear it, and the anxiety that the man should be convicted was passionate . . . This trial has proved more attractive and interesting than anything in the political world . . .'

The face William Palmer turned to the general world was a jolly one. He was a large-faced happy-seeming person with red cheeks and a sporting disposition. But beneath this happy exterior was a tortured soul. He qualified as a doctor and then began his professional career in his home town, Rugeley, in 1846. He married well — or so he thought. He married the daughter of one Colonel Brooks, who had done rather well in the service of the East India Company and had retired and settled at Stafford. Palmer's wife was his natural daughter, and when he died his fortune was successfully claimed by his legitimate heirs. Mrs Palmer did not do well in the division of the spoils. This was unfortunate, for Dr William Palmer had developed rather expensive habits which included owning race-horses and betting on a large scale. His practice was not bringing in a fortune but he saw no reason why he should be forced to change his lifestyle. All he needed was a frequent injection of capital and he set about ensuring such a supply.

His mother-in-law visited him in 1849 and died at his house, rather suddenly. A fellow member of the fraternity of the turf, one Bladon, stayed with the jovial physician in Rugeley in 1850 for a few days. He had just collected a large sum of money in winnings, and he also carried with him his betting book which detailed rather large amounts which Palmer had lost to him. Bladon died suddenly at Rugeley, and a mere £15 was found in his possession. His death certificate was signed by a friendly old colleague of Dr Palmer's. Mrs Bladon was not really satisfied that her late lamented husband had died from natural causes but was restrained by considerations for the feelings of Mrs Palmer. This lady, for her part, was herself somewhat put out by the curious way in which their guests seemed to die on their premises. Witnesses recalled later that Mrs Palmer had been heard to exclaim to her husband: 'Where will it end? Last year my mother! Now Mr Bladon! What will the world say?' It was to end in a manner which she could not have foreseen — some fifteen poisonings in all, with herself one of the victims, and the good-natured Dr Palmer at the end of the hangman's rope.

Despite Dr Palmer's vigorous efforts as dispenser of death-giving substances to unsuspecting victims, his finances did not seem to improve. In fact, they got steadily worse in the face of all his efforts. By 1853 his difficulties were dire indeed. He was forced to borrow from bill-discounters, among them the celebrated Padwick. A year later he borrowed £12,000 on bills with his mother's signature, which he forged himself. He borrowed further sums on the forged signature of John Parsons Cook, who was to become one of his victims. These barely stemmed the tide of Palmer's mounting problems, and were a severe and desperate remedy, as they were discounted at the rate of 60%. As they became due his problems renewed themselves. Desperate problems require desperate solutions. He planned a scheme which would resolve these matters once and for all, but at a considerable personal cost — the life of his wife. He insured her life for a series of handsome sums — £3,000 with Norwich Union; £5,000 with the Sun Insurance Company; £5,000 with the Equitable Company. He attempted to get her insured with other companies but these proposals came to nothing. His wife died a few months after the ink was dried on the contracts and Dr William Palmer was £13,000 better off.

But his problems refused to go away. His brother was the next victim to be sacrificed. He was insured by the good doctor for similar amounts. He died rather suddenly, and William Palmer dutifully completed the paper work and waited for his £13,000. But he was to be disappointed. The insurance companies would not pay up. If he had waited patiently the cheque might have turned up, he might have been able to keep his pressing creditors at bay, and he might have got away with murder. But he panicked. His need for money was immediate. He decided to try the insurance trick yet again. He resolved that his next victim would be his stable boy, Bates.

Palmer threw a dinner party, attended by several of his race-going associates, including John Parsons Cook and Samuel Cheshire, the Rugeley postmaster (he was a very useful friend of Palmer's and had often kept back mail from pressing creditors). At this party Bates was plied with drink and then persuaded to put his signature to an insurance proposal on his life for £25,000. Palmer told him, in fact, that it was for £4,000 and that he'd be able to borrow £500 on its security.

This was too much for the insurance companies and they made enquiries. The result was that they were far from satisfied. Bates had been described as 'a gentleman of independent means', he was in fact a groom with a wage of twenty-four shillings a week. They were not happy either with the claim made on the life of William Palmer's brother Walter and they refused to pay out a penny or to take his further business.

William Palmer was now pushed to the extreme. One of his mistresses, Jane Burgess of Stafford, had kept his letters to her. In one of them he advised her to have an illegal operation to abort their unwanted child. She now wrote to Palmer threatening to blackmail him. To compound this pressure, he also lost heavily at the Shrewsbury race meeting which he attended with Cook. He knew that Cook had £1,000 in winning tickets on his person, for his horse, *Polestar*, had won the cup. What better than a slap-up meal and plenty of booze to celebrate? After dinner and drinks at the Raven Hotel, Cook said that his drink tasted rather bitter, and asked for a different glass. William Palmer egged him on to finish one drink before having another, and Cook tossed off the tumbler and sat down. His throat was burning, he said. The celebration ended and all retired to bed. That night Cook was taken ill. He handed over his money to a colleague, Fisher. Cook recovered by morning, and the group went off for the day's racing. Even so, Cook did not feel his old self, and the considerate Palmer advised him to come with him to Rugeley, where he could stay at the Talbot Arms, just over the road from his surgery, where he would be able to keep an eye on him.

Cook's condition deteriorated and he suffered considerable and distressing pain, in spite of the good Dr Palmer's constant attentions at his bedside, busily administering medicines and cordials. He even called in another physician, probably to allay suspicions. This was old Dr Bamford, who had obliged in the matter of certificating Bladen's death. Palmer explained that his friend Cook was suffering from the effects of too much alcohol, that this was the price he had to pay for all the junketings which accompanied success on the turf. That night Palmer gave Cook some pills to take and the poor man's sufferings increased. Another physician was called in, a Dr Jones. New medicine was prescribed and administered by Palmer. That night Cook died in the most dreadful agony.

Palmer's haste in getting his hands on Cook's money was the last move which brought the whole fabric of his malefactions tumbling down. He dashed to Tattersall's to claim Cook's winnings.

At the same time as his creditors were issuing writs against him for debts forged in his mother's name and now being called in, the authorities became suspicious at the strange and sudden death of John Parsons Cook. Palmer was arrested. At his house in Rugeley the police found full details of all Palmer's terrible financial difficulties, which provided the motive for his crimes, and a treatise on poisons, with notes in Palmer's own handwriting, which gave clear indication as to his methods. As well as the findings of the autopsy on Cook's body, the bodies of Mrs Palmer and of Walter Palmer were exhumed. Clear traces of antimony were found.

It was believed that the local feelings against Palmer would be so considerable that he would not get a fair trial in Stafford, so he was tried at the Old Bailey, on 14 May 1856, before Lord Chief Justice John, first Baron Campbell, author of *Lives of the Lord Chancellors* and *Lives of the Chief Justices*. The prosecution was led by the Attorney-General Sir Alexander Cockburn (see *ARTHUR ORTON*) and the defence was conducted by William Shee, Sergeant-at-Law.

The case against Palmer was wholly damning although it is true to say that the evidence was entirely circumstantial. It was established that he had several times bought poisons and that he had the opportunity to administer poisons to Cook and to change tablets and medicines which had been prescribed by other physicians for potions which he had made up himself. He had sent soup in for Cook to drink which he had made himself, and was most particular to find out whether the unfortunate man had drunk it or not. Nevertheless Palmer's composure throughout the trial was very well maintained. The Old Bailey was packed out with members of society — lords, ladies, princes and other notables — and was the sole topic of conversation. When he was pronounced guilty he blanched for a moment, and wrote on a piece of paper which he handed to his defence: 'The riding did it.' There was a lobby to get him reprieved but he was hanged in public at Stafford Jail on 27 May 1856. Many legends have grown up around the Palmer case. One is that he killed his own children by dipping his fingers into poison, then smearing sugar on top and letting them lick it off while they sat on his knee. It is certainly true that his children by Mrs Palmer died in infancy. Another grisly story is that his activities had made the town of Rugeley so notorious that the citizens petitioned Lord Palmerston, the Prime Minister, to change it. 'Certainly,' he replied. 'Name it after me . . .'

Palmer about to be hanged.

BONNIE PARKER

1911-34

BONNIE PARKER always took liberties with the facts. In her ballad *The Story of Suicide Sal* she said:

> I was born on a ranch in Wyoming,
> Not treated like Helen of Troy,
> Was taught that rods were rulers,
> And ranked with greasy cowboys.

In fact she was born in Rowena, Texas, and drifted to Dallas where she worked as a waitress. She married Roy Thornton and had his name tatooed on her right thigh. For murdering another man, Roy Thornton was given a ninety-nine-year sentence in Eastham prison, a terrifying institution known as the 'Burning Hell' because of the way the prisoners were abused by officials.

Bonnie stood five foot high and had fair hair. 'Bored crapless', as she said, in Dallas she relieved her tedium by seeking out the company of young men. One who entered her life, in 1930, was Clyde Barrow, a small-time crook whose brother was serving a five-year sentence at Eastham prison farm. Bonnie and Clyde were doing some heavy petting when Clyde was arrested and charged with a burglary committed in Waco, Texas. He got two years in Waco prison.

Bonnie sensed that her life was bound up with Clyde Barrow and helped him escape from prison by taping a pistol to her thigh and smuggling it to him. Clyde got out but only as far as Middleton, Ohio, where he was arrested and sent to Eastham, the 'Burning Hell'. He was brutalised, and probably sodomised, in Eastham. When an inmate informed on him, for gambling, Clyde took his revenge by smashing in the man's skull with a lead pipe. Bonnie, in her ballad, saw Clyde as a typical victim of a warped society:

> But the law fooled around,
> Kept tracking him down,
> And locking him up in a cell,
> Till he said to me,
> 'I will never be free,
> So I will meet a few of them in hell.'

In 1932 Clyde was released from Eastham after his mother had made a plea for mercy to the Governor of Texas. Bonnie and Clyde got together and began their careers as robbers with a penchant for violence.

Clyde led the way. In Hillsboro, Texas, he shot the owner of a jewellery store and in Atoka, Oklahoma, he shot two policemen. Bonnie followed suit. In Oklahoma City she drove up to a policeman on traffic duty. As she asked him for directions, she took a shotgun from between her legs and fired both barrels at his head, blowing it off his body. She shrieked with delight and drove off with an impressed Clyde who sat in the passenger seat.

In Arthur Penn's film *Bonnie and Clyde* (1967), Faye Dunnaway portrayed Bonnie as a sensitive and sensuous woman of some intelligence who was able

to bring erotic love into the sad life of Clyde Barrow, played by Warren Beatty. Yet Jay Robert Nash, in *Bloodletters and Badmen* (1973) tells a more likely tale. Clyde's 'real bent', writes Nash, 'was homosexuality . . . It was Ray Hamilton [a member of the gang for some time] who slept with Bonnie . . . and Clyde. Later WD Jones, the gas-station attendant who joined the Barrow gang for kicks, would serve as lover to both.'

In September 1932 Bonnie and Clyde and Ray Hamilton robbed the National Guard Armory at Fort Worth. The machine-guns they stole became part of their legend. Using the guns Bonnie and Clyde took $1,400 from the Abilene State Bank and a few days later Clyde shot a butcher who resisted an attempt to rob him. In November 1932 Bonnie drove the get-away car after Clyde had robbed the Oronogo, Missouri Bank of $200. This sustained them while they drove to New Mexico to see Bonnie's relatives. On the way they took WD Jones on board.

The Barrow gang grew when Clyde's brother Buck joined them, with his wife Blanche, after a pardon. They continued to steal and to shoot their way out of trouble. By now the American newspapers were full of their exploits. In lurid press stories Bonnie was called 'Suicide Sal', Clyde was known as the 'Texas Rattlesnake'. Delighted by the sensational publicity, Bonnie sent *The*

Story of Suicide Sal to the newspapers. After explaining how she 'knew Clyde/When he was honest and upright and clean' Bonnie contemplated their inevitable end:

> They don't think they are too tough or desperate,
> They know the law always wins,
> They have been shot at before
> But they do not ignore
> That death is the wages of sin.
>
> From heartbreaks some people have suffered,
> From weariness some people have died,
> But take it all in all,
> Our troubles are small,
> Till we get like Bonnie and Clyde.
>
> Some day they will go down together,
> And they will bury them side by side.
> To a few it means grief,
> To the law it's relief,
> But it's death to Bonnie and Clyde.

After escaping from the police in Joplin, Missouri, the Barrow gang were surrounded in a deserted fairground in Dexter, Iowa, on 24 July 1933. In the shoot-out Buck was killed, Blanche was captured, Bonnie and Clyde and W D Jones were wounded but managed to get away. On 23 May 1934, Bonnie and Clyde were ambushed at a roadblock near Gibland, Louisiana. Taken by surprise (Clyde was wearing his socks, Bonnie was eating a sandwich) their bodies were riddled with 187 bullets. Texas Ranger Frank Hamer, who headed the posse, said, 'There wasn't much to it. They just drove into the wrong place. Both of them died with their guns in their hands, but they didn't have a chance to use them.'

Clyde was buried in West Dallas Cemetery, Bonnie first in Fish Trap Cemetery then in Crown Hill Memorial Park. On her tombstone are the words:

> As the flowers are all made sweeter
> By the sunshine and the dew,
> So this old world is made brighter
> By the lives of folks like you.

CHARLES PRICE

1727-83

THERE ARE times when wickedness and cunning combine in illegal acts with an effect which is almost comic. In the case of Charles Price, thief, forger and counterfeiter, master of disguise, con-man and fraud, admiration and laughter almost combine in the contemplation of such black villainy. A conservative estimate puts the sum total of his robbing society at £100,000.

Price was born into the drapery trade and it is interesting to note that costume played such an important part in his career, and at such an early age. When still a young boy he stole some gold braid from his father's shop and, when he went to sell it to a 'fence', took the trouble to wear his brother's clothes. When the theft was revealed and a description circulated, it was Charles's brother who took the beating. From this first successful crime on, Charles Price never looked back. He followed one trade after another, and gradually accumulated a fine collection of costumes, wigs, eye patches and various properties which were later to serve him in such good professional stead. He was a servant to a hatter and hosier, clerk to a merchant, clerk to a diamond dealer in Amsterdam, and manager of a brewery in Yeovil.

Portrait of CHARLES PRICE in his usual dress.

His Parson's disguise.

Some of Price's disguises.

When he devoted his energies finally to his criminal career he combined forgery with impersonation. He created false bank notes and false characters to circulate them. Thus he distanced himself safely from his own deeds. His multifarious business, trade and professional experience was thus put to invaluable use. He was a complete professional: he made his own paper and drew and etched the plates he used for printing. The secrets of his craft were thus kept more or less to himself.

One example from quite early on in his career well illustrates his audacity and cunning. He fastened his attentions on a certain wealthy London merchant. He then addressed a forged letter to this unfortunate man, purporting to come from a correspondent in Amsterdam. The fellow businessman in Amsterdam wrote to explain that he had recently been deprived of £1,000 by a villain named Trevors. He wrote to ask if the London merchant, so well known for his probity, would help him recover his loss, as he knew Trevors was due in London that very week. He would be approached by a friend of his soon to be in London. Sure enough, the merchant was accosted by a commercial gentleman in the business quarter of London who was personally acquainted with our friend in Amsterdam. Yes, the London merchant agreed to help in any way he could. Well, it seemed that Trevors was due the next day, and he was furnished with a very good description of Trevors' appearance and costume. A good plan would be to invite Trevors to dinner, then reveal all that was known about his crime and threaten to expose him upon the Exchange if he did not repay the sum of £1,000 on the spot. This advice was given, of course, by Price in disguise. The next day Price appeared in another disguise — as 'Trevors'. The London merchant fell for it. 'Trevors' was invited to his house for dinner and then threatened. He affected fear and promised to repay. He offered £500 down now as earnest of his good intention. This was accepted. The only trouble was that he only had on him a draft for £1,000 and that would leave him without any funds at all in London. The merchant obligingly gave him £500 change, with Trevors promising to contact him soon and leaving a London address. The next day when he went to cash his £1,000 the draft was discovered to be a brilliant forgery and 'Trevors' had vanished into thin air.

As he developed his professional skills his acts became more and more daring. In the guise of an old man he alighted from his coach outside the shop of a prosperous grocer named Roberts, in London's Oxford Street. He made several genuine purchases and left quite an impression. He returned several more times, and each time spent lavishly and acted with great politeness and sophistication. Then one day when he called the shopkeeper was away on business and the premises were in the hands of his assistant.

Price was taken ill and the assistant did all that he could to help him, including giving him some medicine. The old man recovered. The next time he called he gave the man a gift out of gratitude — a ten pound note. He changed £50 in the shop. The next time Roberts was away the old man reappeared, full of praise for the wonderful cure acheived on the premises, and requesting change for five £50 notes. The willing assistant went round to the bank and returned with the money in smaller denominations. The old man thanked him profusely for his trouble and climbed back into his coach. He was never seen again, which was awkward, as the notes were forgeries.

Another fraud of Price's was the phoney business enterprise. The most famous was one in which he deceived no less a personage than Samuel Foote, the actor and dramatist. It is strange to think that a professional thespian of Foote's stature would be taken in by such an impersonator as Price but this must be accounted a tribute to Charles Price's utter professionalism. Under the name of P C Cardigan Head of Charing Cross the confidence trickster put an advertisement in the press for a business partner. The business, it was claimed, would yield 50% with little risk at all. The proposed business was a brewery needing capital investment of between £500 and £1,000. When Foote made contact he met a loquacious master brewer who explained the whole scheme to him. This was Price, of course, putting his experience in the brewing business in Yeovil to good use. Samuel Foote was impressed by Price's obvious first-hand experience of the trade, and willingly advanced Mr Cardigan Head £500 in investment capital, all being safely signed, sealed and delivered and clearly above board. Then Head vanished.

He thrived in smuggling from the continent where his ability to play to many parts and to lie convincingly paid off handsomely. Disguising himself as an elderly man and making himself seem very tall with high heels, and very thin with tight clothes, he named himself Brant and bought a large quantity of lottery tickets. By the time the forged notes were discovered, he'd sold the lottery tickets to other punters and moved on to other things.

He was finally apprehended for forgery and hanged himself in Tothill Fields Prison. Among his possessions were the most astonishing items of equipment — suits for men of all ages and sizes, forging equipment, false noses, wigs and eye patches.

EDWARD WILLIAM PRITCHARD

1825-65

WHEN DR E W PRITCHARD was executed in Glasgow on 28 July 1865, some 100,000 citizens gathered to watch the spectacle. Pritchard was not only notorious, he was known to have no regrets for his homicidal activities. He was a notorious egotist and was portrayed as such in James Bridie's play *Dr Angelus.*

Pritchard, the son of a captain, was born in Southsea, Hampshire, and went to Portsmouth where he was apprenticed to a surgeon. He went to sea in 1846, as a navy surgeon, and visited various places which would later feature in the fantastic tales he concocted as a public lecturer. In 1850 he was in Portsmouth again and met Mary Jane Taylor, daughter of an Edinburgh silk-merchant. Pritchard impressed Mary and her respectable parents and within a few months of meeting Mary, he married her.

Thanks to Mary's parents, Pritchard obtained a practice in Hunmanby, Yorkshire. He flourished, as a result of his imposing appearance and fund of fascinating anecdotes, and expanded his medical practice to Filey, a resort that became the subject of one of his books. Pritchard saw himself as a celebrity and was in the habit of passing round signed photographs of himself. In addition to his social pursuits and medical duties, he also mastered the art of seduction and was well known locally as a sexual adventurer. To complete the picture of the busy man, Pritchard became a prominent Freemason.

After selling his Yorkshire practice, Pritchard spent some time in the Middle East, another source for his stories. In 1860 he settled — with his wife and five children — in Berkely Street, Glasgow. Pritchard failed to make much impression on the medical establishment of Glasgow: he was not accepted into the Faculty of Physicians and Surgeons and his application for the Chair of Surgery at the Andersonian College was rejected. On the other hand he gained some recognition as a formidable character who claimed influential friends like Garibaldi (though the two men never met) and had important contacts in the Freemasons.

While he was making his way in Glasgow society, Pritchard was also anxious to have access to young girls. Like other men in his position he employed servants and it is in character that he would try to take advantage of the pretty ones. In 1863 Elizabeth McGirn, a girl employed by Pritchard, was burned to death in his house. The circumstances were strange enough to cause comment in the *Glasgow Herald* of 6 May 1863:

> It is said that the poor girl, who has met such an untimely death, was in the habit of reading in bed; and the supposition is that, after she had fallen asleep, the gas-jet, which was close to the head of the bed, had ignited the bed-hangings, and that the deceased had been suffocated by smoke. This is the more apparent from the position in which the body lay, because if the deceased had not been suffocated while asleep, she would have made some attempt to escape, and been found in a different position. The neighbour servant of the deceased happened to be out of town with her mistress, and possibly, in her absence, the girl McGirn had read longer than usual, and fallen asleep without extinguishing the gas.

Reading between the lines of that report, with the benefit of hindsight, there is significance in the fact that Pritchard's wife was away when the accident occurred. In view of Pritchard's propensity for murder it is safe to assume that Elizabeth was already dead, or drugged, when the fire broke out in her room. Shortly after the fire Pritchard moved to 22 Royal Crescent and looked for a replacement for Elizabeth. His new servant was Mary McLeod, an attractive girl of fifteen. Before long she was Pritchard's lover.

The year 1864 saw Pritchard in yet another house; his new home, at 131 Sauchiehall Street, was secured for him by his mother-in-law Mrs Taylor. Pritchard was well placed as a medical practitioner but his private life was causing him problems. He was overspending recklessly and when Mary McLeod became pregnant he had to perform an abortion and ensure her silence by promising her that she would be the new Mrs Pritchard when the present one, Mary Jane, died.

Sure enough, Mary Jane was not in the best of health. She had stomach pains which, of course, Pritchard claimed he could cure. In November 1864 he bought quantities of tartarised antimony and tincture of aconite. With these poisons on the premises, Mary Jane's condition deteriorated rapidly. However she went to Edinburgh to stay with her parents for Christmas and immediately there was an improvement in her health. Pritchard continued to accumulate poison for her return.

Back at Sauchiehall Street, Mary Jane's health broke down again. Her mother, alarmed at the bad news, came through to Glasgow to look after her. To settle her own nerves, Mrs Taylor used Battley's Sedative Solution, a

concoction of opium. In recent years she had become increasingly dependent on the opium which she drank in large doses. Soon after arriving at the Pritchard home, Mrs Taylor succumbed to the mysterious illness that seemed to be claiming her daughter. Another doctor, James Paterson, was called in to examine Mrs Taylor and Mary Jane. He was startled by the condition of Mary Jane and her mother. Both women seemed to be dying by degrees; Mary Jane was wasting away while Mrs Taylor showed the signs of drug addiction. Pritchard had an answer to this; he revealed that Mrs Taylor was an opium addict and Dr Paterson left, though he suspected there was foul play.

On 24 February Mrs Taylor died and Pritchard signed the death certificate which gave the cause of death as 'Paralysis, duration twelve hours; secondary cause, apoplexy, duration one hour'. In her will, Mrs Taylor left the bulk of her estate of £2,500 to Mary Jane. Less than a month after the death of Mrs Taylor, Mary Jane was dead. Again, Pritchard completed the death certificate. Mary Jane had died, he recorded, from gastric fever. On 18 March, the day of Mary Jane's death, an anonymous letter was sent to the Procurator-Fiscal in Glasgow. It pointed out that Mary Jane and her mother had died in suspicious circumstances. The author of the letter was, almost certainly, Dr James Paterson.

The bodies of both women were examined and when antimony was found Dr Pritchard was arrested. His trial, in July 1865, lasted five days and Pritchard was duly sentenced to death. He confessed his crimes in the following terms: 'I, Edward William Pritchard, in the full possession of all my senses, and understanding the awful position in which I am placed, do make a free and full confession that the sentence pronounced upon me is just; that I am guilty of the death of my mother-in-law, Mrs Taylor, and of my wife, Mary Jane Pritchard; and that I can assign no motive for the conduct which actuated

me, beyond a species of "terrible madness" and the use of "ardent spirits".'
Pritchard, an Episcopalian, made much of his religious principles in the days
that remained to him. In a broadside ballad, Alexander Allan gave some of the
details concerning the case of Dr Pritchard:

> But when a wretch, in secret hate and guile,
> A foul, cold-blooded human crocodile!
> Plots calmly on for months, from day to day,
> To take his fellow-creature's life away —
> (And that the wife that in his bosom lay);
> Counts out the grains of poison it requires
> To do the deed his hellish heart desires;
> Sees that the deadly drug works grief and pain,
> And yet administers the same again;
> Deals out the poisoned cheese, egg-flip and wine,
> And, smiling, says, 'My darling it is fine!!
> And, when at last he has deprived his wife
> Of precious health and all the joys of life,
> And thinks that now the fitting time has come,
> He sends her to her everlasting home;
> And then declares, his murd'rous deed to hide,
> It was of gastric fever that she died!
> Compared with this, [impulsive] crime is light! —
> This is a mighty mountain — that a mite.

Jack House, in *Square Mile of Murder* (Glasgow, 1961), cites a curious
footnote to the Pritchard story. Years after Pritchard's execution, the South
Prison was replaced with a High Court. Plumbers laying new pipes had to
uncover stones in the murderers' graveyard at the prison: 'Under a stone
marked "P" they found the skeleton of Dr Pritchard. But, by some chemical
freak, the patent leather boots which he wore to the scaffold were still in a
perfectly preserved state. Somebody took these boots and sold them to an
unsuspecting member of the public.'

GEORGE PSALMANAZAR

1679-1763

WHILE STRUGGLING to make a name in the world of letters, and to earn
his daily bread, Samuel Johnson crossed paths with one of the great imposters
of the early eighteenth century. Johnson's biographer John Wain described
George Psalmanazar as 'one of the most successful and shameless imposters
even in that century of splendid bare-faced rogues'. *(Samuel Johnson*, 1974.)
When Johnson met him in London in the early 1740s he was an old man and

Johnson revered him. He listened patiently to everything he said, asserting that he would 'rather have thought of contradicting a bishop'. Taking into account Samuel Johnson's very well documented tendency not to hear other people out, and to be ready to contradict so many people — several of them acknowledged experts in quite specialised areas of study — then this is a truly remarkable piece of testimony, and a credit to the skills of fraud and imposture exercised by the man who called himself George Psalmanazar (his real name has never, in fact, been ascertained).

George was probably born in Languedoc, and was educated by the Jesuits. He had a remarkable gift for languages, which he was later to turn to considerable professional advantage. By the age of sixteen he had resolved to earn his living as a wandering vagabond and mendicant in France, Germany and the Netherlands, in a Europe devastated by recent wars and suffering the effects of having to absorb hundreds of soldiers, sailors, galley-slaves and mariners recently demobilised by the Peace of Reswick (1697). Many of these took to plundering all and sundry and to the life of the road. Often these malefactors were caught and hanged and their rotting bodies were a frequent sight as Psalmanazar passed by. In this social context his act was a good one — he travelled as a wandering pilgrim, with flowing gown and staff.

His education at the hands of priests and monks had given him a vast storage of biblical knowledge and theology, as well as Latin, Greek and Hebrew, and he was able most professionally to deck out his patter with holy writ and convincing religiosity and mumbo-jumbo. His cloak and wandering staff had an authenticity — they were at least genuine and respectable items, as he had stolen them from a church. He posed as a foreigner, a sensible stroke as it would explain his inability to converse in German or Flemish or Low German or whatever the local vernacular. Latin was still to some extent an international language, and he got by. Initially he was an Irishman, but then hit on the idea of being Japanese. Now very few people knew anything about Japan and hardly anyone in Europe had seen a Japanese, so he could incorporate anything he liked into his act. This served him well for a time and he travelled with very good documents, which, of course, he had forged himself.

As a Japanese wanderer he joined the army of the Elector at Cologne. Later in his life he wrote detailed memoirs which gave a colourful account of his days as a pilgrim. Of this period he wrote:

> The liberty that is commonly granted to soldiers to swear, game, drink, whore, etc., is very great among the Germans, and much more among the French . . . Those we had in this regiment were, if possible, still worse, being mostly deserters from the French service, and to the last degree profligate .
> . . This was the unhappy herd I had now got among, and whose company and example completed my ruin . . . I was indeed neither inclined to drinking nor gaming, and was not hardened enough in impudence to follow them in their lewdness; but was bad enough, nevertheless, to indulge myself, in order to appear as vile and abandoned as they, in a shameful habit of uttering such new and fashionable oaths, and monstrous curses, as I had lately rather heard with horror, than learned . . .

This was not all that he learned to do. While in the Elector's army he further developed his Japanese role, and extended it to include all manner of theological and ritualistic embellishments, which impressed his fellow Lutherans and Papists alike. He later wrote in his memoirs that he got so carried away with all this flummery that it was almost as if a fit had laid hold of him:

> This vain fit grew up to such a height, that I made me a little book with figures of the sun, moon and stars, and such other imagery as my frenzy suggested to me, and filled the rest with a kind of gibberish prose and verse, written in my invented character, and which I muttered or chanted as often as the humour took me.

These performances proved so convincing that George was brought to the attention of the regimental chaplain, a Reverend Innes, who attempted to convert him to christianity. Innes gave George some money, which was well received, and they had several conversations about the nature of the true faith. Innes had resolved to take George back to England with him, as a fine example of a heathen who had seen the light — provided, of course, that he was able to effect George's conversion. To this end Innes wrote to his bishop, the Bishop of London. Quite early in this relationship, however, Innes discovered that George was a fake by getting him to translate the same passage of Cicero from Latin into Japanese. George had not taken the precaution of being consistent, and Innes compared the two versions and realised his 'Japanese' would-be convert was an imposter. However, George's religious education continued apace and Innes did not reveal the nature of his young pupil's fraud.

The young convert was baptised 'George Lauder' (named for Brigadier Lauder, the governor of Sluys). Innes had a favourable reply from the Bishop of London, who urged him to return to England and bring his young charge with him. It had been recommended that Psalmanazar should go to the University of Oxford where he could teach budding missionaries his native language to aid them in their mission to spread the gospel in the Far East. At a hint from Innes George had now shifted his nationality to that of the island of Formosa which, it was to be hoped, would be even less well known to the English speaking world than Japan. Psalmanazar exerted himself to perfect the role he was to play and lived wholly on a diet of raw fish, herbs and roots, liberally plastered with pepper and other spices. This proved an impressive element of the total imposture and surprisingly seemed to do George little physical harm.

The arrival of Innes and his ward caused a sensation in London and they were soon surrounded by curious churchmen who were all hoodwinked by Psalmanazar's eloquent patter and apparently vast knowledge of the East. Even when he was taxed on the curious matter of his fair hair and complexion there was a ready answer. It seemed that in Formosa there were two types of people. Those who worked in the sun became dark. Those who toiled indoors or underground remained fair. The news of the Formosan visitor spread like wildfire. He spoke to his guests in Latin with a strange accent, but Innes was able to translate all he said. In his memoirs Psalmanazar comments on the impression he made:

> Thus I remember a remarkable article from London, printed in the Dutch and French papers, that the young Japaner had been presented to the Archbishop of Canterbury, who admired him chiefly for his readiness in speaking a great variety of languages. Whereas I cannot call to mind that I spoke any but Latin, which his grace having either forgot, or being unused to my foreign pronunciation, was forced to have interpreted to him by Dr Innes in English.

Psalmanazar's conversion was going to further Innes's reputation, and he was determined to get as much capital out of him as possible. To this end he persuaded George to write and publish some accounts of his land and countrymen. The indefatigable Psalmanazar then set to and compiled a translation of the church catechism into 'Formosan', a history of Formosa, which included details of religious rituals and customs, and an account of the Formosan language and grammar. It was gibberish, of course, but at the same time it was convincing gibberish. The 'Formosan' alphabet began: 'Am, Mem, Nen, Taph . . .' The theology was a cunning construct of scraps of all kinds. There had been an ancient prophet, named Psalmanazar, after whom George had been named. Their faith required a fairly lavish amount of personal sacrifice. He had commanded the construction of a temple on the altar of which should be sacrificed a hundred oxen, a hundred rams, a hundred goats and the burning of twenty thousand young human hearts under the age of nine. This was the price of one divine appearance. Women were regarded as inferior in the faith of the Formosans, so impure 'that she can never attain to Happiness, until she be Transformed into the Body of a man or some Male Beast'. Young women suffer a strange illness in their late teens, the text claimed, which the Formosans called 'Chataesko' or green-sickness. The only known cure was marriage. As a sop to the Protestant cause the Jesuits were given a very poor press in Psalmanazar's volume. The work was between sixty and seventy thousand words long and dedicated to the Bishop of London. It took him a mere two months to compose.

The first edition sold out in no time and George Psalmanazar was then taken in some considerable triumph to Oxford where he earned a reputation as a good teacher and a tireless scholar. This latter aspect was fostered by his leaving his candles alight all night and sleeping in a chair. The news spread that a light was to be seen in his room all night long and that his bed was never disturbed. Such diligence was unusual in Oxford, at this date at any rate.

But the author of the *Historical and Geographical Description of Formosa* (1704) was compelled at a rather later stage to enter show business and general charlatanism after his mentor the Reverend Doctor Innes — having made *his* reputation — was promoted chaplain general of the English forces and sent to Portugal. Psalmanazar could not keep up the act so well on his own and the nine days' wonder was soon discredited. *The Spectator* of 16 March 1711 gives some indication of his decline from the miracle scholar of Oxford:

> On the first of April will be performed at the play-house in the Haymarket an opera called *The Cruelty of Atreus*. NB — The scene wherein Thyestes eats his own children is to be performed by the famous Mr Psalmanazar, lately arrived from Formosa: the whole supper set to kettle-drums.

He next turned his hand to selling Formosan enamel, a white paint whose secret he claimed to have brought with him from his native land. This too failed. He then worked as a tutor, hack writer, regimental clerk and fan-painter. He reserved plenty of energies for various debaucheries, claiming that women fell for his exotic character rather more readily than for red-coats. He settled in Ironmonger's Row and his knowledge of such genuine languages as Latin and Hebrew earned him a living of sorts. He was brought to repentance by reading William Law's *Serious Call to a Devout and Holy Life*, which was published in 1729.

When Johnson met him he was a saintly old man with white hair. Johnson was impressed by his sincere protestations of religious faith and vast curious learning. The great lexicographer claimed in later life that Psalmanazar was the best man he ever knew. He died on 3 May 1763 and his autobiographical volume, published a year after his death, did not reveal his real name or the where he was born. His French accent, experts claimed, was Gascon. The name he gave himself was a version of the Old Testament King Shalmaneser. It makes one doubt the scholarship of the eighteenth century Lords Spiritual. Henry Compton (1632-1713), the bishop to whom Psalmanazar was introduced, did not recognise a 'foreign' language faked up from Latin when he heard it, nor did he recognise a name lifted from the scriptures.

MARQUESS OF QUEENSBERRY

1844-1900

JOHN SHOLTO DOUGLAS, 8th Marquess of Queensberry, was the man who drew up, in 1867, the rules that govern amateur boxing and, in 1895, won the unfair fight that ended the dramatic career of Oscar Wilde.

Queensberry was an outrageously eccentric Victorian, given to both physical and verbal violence. A dogmatic atheist and accomplished pugilist, he abused his wife and bullied his children and was forever issuing threats to those who displeased him. When he discovered that his third son, Lord Alfred Douglas, was keeping the company of Oscar Wilde — the epitome of histrionic wit — he was outraged. After approaching Wilde, Queensberry was briefly captivated by the conversational charm of the man but soon changed his mind and went all out for vicious victory against the great aesthete.

On 1 April 1894 Queensberry wrote to his son: 'Your intimacy with this man Wilde must either cease or I will disown you and stop all money supplies . . . With my own eyes I saw you both in the most loathsome and disgusting relationship, as expressed by your manner and expression . . . Also I now hear on good authority, but this may be false, that [Wilde's] wife is petitioning to divorce him for sodomy and other crimes . . . If I thought the actual thing was true, and it became public property, I should be quite justified in shooting him at sight.' Douglas responded in a provocative telegram: 'WHAT A FUNNY LITTLE MAN YOU ARE'.

After this Queensberry relentlessly pursued Wilde and Douglas, constantly threatening them both with a thrashing. Wilde was understandably embarrassed and considered taking legal action against the Marquess on the basis of the remarks in his offensive letter to Douglas. Instead Wilde merely asked for an apology which was not forthcoming from the 'scarlet Marquess'.

In June 1894 Queensberry, accompanied by a prizefighter, called on Wilde at his home in Chelsea. After implying that Wilde was having a homosexual affair with Douglas, he told him, 'If I catch you and my son together in any public restaurant, I will thrash you'. Wilde retorted, 'I do not know what the Queensberry rules are but the Oscar Wilde rule is to shoot at sight'. He then had Queensberry, 'the most infamous brute in London', shown out of his house.

Unfortunately for Wilde, Queensberry was not easily silenced. He was determined to end the homosexual relationship between his son and the celebrated writer and Douglas seemed to enjoy taunting his father. In a letter to Queensberry, Douglas said, 'if you try to assault me I shall defend myself with a loaded revolver which I always carry, and if I shoot you, or [Wilde] shoots you, we would be completely justified, as we should be acting in self-defence against a violent and dangerous rough, and I think if you were dead not many people would miss you'.

On 14 February 1895 Wilde's *The Importance of Being Earnest* opened at the St James's Theatre and, though refused entrance, Queensberry left a bouquet of vegetables as a calculated insult to the author. On 18 February, Queensberry arrived at the Albemarle Club and left his visiting card for Wilde, who was a member. The card carried the message 'For Oscar Wilde posing as a somdomite (*sic*)'. When Wilde saw this he wrote to Robbie Ross, on 28 February: 'Since I saw you something has happened. Bosie's father has left a card at my club with hideous words on it. I don't see anything now but a criminal prosecution. My whole life seems ruined by this man. The tower of ivory is assailed by the foul thing. On the sand is my life spilt.' Wilde then saw a solicitor and a warrant was issued for the arrest of Queensberry.

For Wilde, the decision to sue Queensberry for criminal libel was a disaster. Wilde was brutally interrogated in court, at the Old Bailey, by Edward Carson who forced him to admit his fondness for young men. Queensberry was found Not Guilty on 5 April and sent a message to Wilde: 'If the country allows you to leave, all the better for the country! But if you take my son with you, I will follow you wherever you go and shoot you!' Queensberry also instructed his solicitor to contact the Director of Public Prosecutions who ordered the arrest of Wilde. The *National Observer* gloated: 'There is not a man or woman in the English-speaking world possessed of the treasure of a wholesome mind who is not under a deep debt of gratitude to the Marquess of Queensberry for destroying the High Priest of the Decadents. The obscene imposter . . . has been exposed, and that thoroughly at last. There must be another trial at the Old Bailey.'

Wilde was tried twice at the Old Bailey and endlessly by the popular press who delighted in his downfall. He was convicted for homosexuality and sentenced to two years' imprisonment which he served in Pentonville Prison and Reading Gaol. His conditions were miserable and his sufferings are movingly recalled in *The Ballad of Reading Gaol* (1898):

> Dear Christ! the very prison walls
>> Suddenly seemed to reel,
> And the sky above my head became
>> Like a casque of scorching steel;
> And, though I was a soul in pain,
>> My pain I could not feel.

After his release Wilde left England and worked on his ballad and did little else.

Queensberry and Wilde both died in 1900; the Marquess in January, the dramatist on 30 November in Paris. Queensberry is remembered for his pugilistic rules and the ruin he brought on Wilde. After a period of reaction, Wilde was restored to a posthumous prominence as one of the great comic writers in the English language.

ALEXANDER BAILLIE RICHMOND

(died c.1834)

IN THE EARLY nineteenth century the weavers' unions were a powerful force for radical reform in Scotland. Inevitably Alexander Baillie Richmond, a young weaver from Glasgow, decided to join the National Committee of the Scottish union societies and 'entered into the measures of the period with avidity and enthusiasm'. In 1812 the National Committee of the Scottish union societies considered a mass demonstration and the issue was explored by two sides, representing workers and employers. Richmond, a member of the workers' committee, thus came into contact with Kirkman Finlay, Tory MP for Glasgow. When the meeting was over Finlay invited Richmond home to suggest ways in which the explosive situation in Scotland could be defused.

On 20 November 1812 a meeting of magistrates noted the wage demands of the weavers and pronounced them just. The National Committee informed the union societies to withdraw their labour unless the agreed wage scales were implemented. A strike followed and the employers decided to use force against the weavers. As Richmond noted, 'all disposable troops in Scotland were ordered to the western counties and cantoned in the various towns and villages; and it was rumoured that the operatives were to be put down by force'.

As a representative of the National Committee, Richmond went to see Kirkman Finlay and was assured that no military measures would be taken against the strikers. Two days later Richmond was arrested. When Glasgow University students demonstrated in favour of the strike, the windows of

Kirkman Finlay's house were broken. As a result the dragoons cleared the students and turned on the strikers, some of whom were shot dead.

Richmond was released in time to see the strike crushed in February 1813. He was once more summoned to meet Kirkman Finlay and warned that he would be treated as the main malcontent in the imminent trials of the strikers. If Richmond ceased to support the National Committee, he was told, then he would receive Finlay's protection. Rather than risk trial and imprisonment Richmond went into hiding and was declared an outlaw in his absence. He fled to Dublin but, homesick for Scotland, returned to Glasgow and sought out Finlay to see if he could assist him. Having done a great deal with the authorities, Richmond surrendered himself, served a nominal sentence of a month's imprisonment, borrowed £300 from the men who defended him, and set himself up as a manufacturer. He pursued his friendship with Finlay who was convinced there was a conspiracy to overthrow the government.

Having established himself as a manufacturer Richmond decided to expand his activities by becoming, with Finlay's assistance, a government spy. He infiltrated the radical movement and, because of his posture of revolutionary zeal, persuaded Andrew MacKinlay, a weaver, to take an oath expressing allegiance to the radical cause 'either by moral or physical strength, or force, as the case may require'.

This was a breakthrough for Richmond who realised that spying was more suited to his nature than anything else; he found it easier to manufacture false reports than to manufacture goods. On 19 January 1817 he went to Finlay's home to agree on an appropriate salary for his new career as a full-time spy. He continued to infiltrate radical organisations and extract incriminating information which he duly passed to Finlay. In a debate in the House of Commons on 24 February 1817 Finlay communicated the contents of Richmond's oath. The House responded by passing the Habeas Corpus Suspension Act and arresting the leaders of the alleged conspiracy. This led to several sedition trials and, on 23 June 1817, the trial for high treason of MacKinlay. The authorities were unable to get a conviction against MacKinlay but it became generally known that Richmond was in the business of arranging evidence against radicals. Public outrage was expressed in slogans such as 'Beware of Richmond the Spy'.

After the Scottish Insurrection of April 1820 had been brutally suppressed, it was recognised that Richmond had done his despicable work well. A historian, Peter MacKenzie, eventually decided to speak out against the government policy of planting agents amongst the radicals. In 1832 he published *An Exposure of the Spy System Pursued in Glasgow During the Years 1816-20*. An indignant Richmond sued for libel and conducted his own case at a trial in London in December 1834. He lost the case and as P Berresford Ellis and Seumas Mac a 'Ghobhainn point out in *The Scottish Insurrection of 1820* (London, 1970), 'The Government now took note of the revelations and a pardon was granted to all the 1820 Radicals who had been transported'. The same authors also note, 'Richmond claimed that from December, 1816, to February, 1817, he had made a deficit of £27 in his spying activities. At the subsequent libel trial in 1834, it was stated that Richmond received £2,000. On October 17, 1817, Richmond wrote to Finlay saying that Lord Sidmouth had agreed to pay him a substantial annuity. Despite Richmond and his like, freely employed by the Government to infiltrate the various organisation for political reform through the state, the Radical movement began to grow strong, but nowhere did it obtain the strength and organisation that it did in Scotland.'

JACK RUBY

1911-67

JACK RUBY, the man who murdered Lee Harvey Oswald — President Kennedy's alleged assassin — claimed that his act was motivated by patriotic indignation. Describing the events of 24 November 1963 Ruby said, in evidence to the Warren Commission, 'No underworld person made any effort to contact me. It all happened that Sunday morning... the last thing I read was that Mrs Kennedy may have to come back to Dallas for a trial for Lee Harvey Oswald and I don't know what bug got hold of me... Suddenly the feeling, the emotional feeling came within me that someone owed this debt to our beloved president to save her the ordeal of coming back. I had the gun in my right hip pocket, and impulsively, if that is the correct word here, I saw [Oswald] and that is all I can say . . . I think I used the words, "You killed my president, you rat". The next thing I was down on the floor.' Impulsive was not the correct word since Ruby went to the Dallas police station armed, and with the intention of wiping out Oswald. He admitted he intended to shoot Oswald three times though he was overpowered after the first, fatal, shot.

Ruby was not the spotlessly pure patriot he said he was. He was a petty crook connected to the leading figures in the American underworld. He knew, for example, the Mafia leader Santos Trafficante who said, in 1962, 'Mark my word, this man Kennedy is in trouble, and he will get what is coming to him . . . He is going to be hit.' It seems likely that Ruby was chosen to be the Mafia's hitman against Oswald who was thus brutally silenced before he could testify in public about the facts of the assassination.

Ruby was born Jacob Rubenstein in Chicago where he asserted himself, at an early age, as one of the toughest kids on the block. Because of his highly excitable nature and quick temper he was nicknamed 'Sparky'. Keen to get into the world of organised crime, 'Sparky' began his career as an oddjob man for Al Capone. In Capone's world criminal law was enforced by terror and those who posed a threat to the mob were brutally eliminated. 'Sparky' saw how Capone's operation worked and was impressed. In 1937 'Sparky' became an official in the Iron and Junk Handlers Union, a group under the influence of the mob. When a union boss was shot in 1939 Ruby was questioned — and released. However the murder allowed the union to come under the control of Paul Dorfman, subsequently described by Attorney General Robert Kennedy as 'a major operator in the Chicago underworld'.

It seems likely that Ruby was sent to Dallas to soften up the city for Mafia activities. In 1946 Dallas police charged Mafia man Paul Jones after he had attempted to establish, by bribery, a criminal syndicate in the city. As the police knew only too well, the man named by Jones as the local Mafia contact was Jack Ruby. In the aftermath of this affair, Ruby set up the Silver Spur, his first nightclub in Dallas. Mafia types were always welcome at Ruby's clubs — as were Dallas policemen. Ruby cultivated the friendship of many police officers in Dallas, offering them presents ranging from free booze to free broads.

Ruby ran his club with brutal relish. Those who got out of line were beaten up, often personally by Ruby who enjoyed violence. Yet although Ruby was arrested for assault he was never penalised. He was a popular figure with the Dallas police right up to the time of the Oswald murder.

While Ruby was extending Mafia power in Dallas, he was also involved in anti-Castro activities. In 1959 Santos Trafficante was detained by Castro, during the campaign to combat organised crime in Cuba, and it is probable that Ruby visited the Mafia boss when he was over in Cuba. According to Anthony Summers, in *Conspiracy* (London, 1980), Ruby was involved in gunrunning to Cuba. The Mafia was anxious to overthrow Castro and re-establish their empire of vice in Havana.

In June 1963 there was a Mafia convention in Dallas, ostensibly to control prostitution and gambling but it is possible that the Kennedy brothers were discussed. The mob was horrified at Robert Kennedy's campaign against crime. Particularly angry was Jimmy Hoffa, leader of the Teamsters Union, then manipulated by the mob. Hoffa was determined to get revenge against Robert Kennedy who had repeatedly investigated corruption in the Teamsters Union. He talked of shooting and bombing the Attorney General and was heard to utter threats against President Kennedy. One of Hoffa's associates was Barney Baker, a man described by Robert Kennedy as 'Hoffa's ambassador of violence'. Two weeks before the assassination of President Kennedy, Jack Ruby was contacted by Baker.

At the beginning of 1963 Ruby was financially embarrassed, to say the least. He was due $21,000 to the Inland Revenue for unpaid taxes; he was also in arrears for the rent for his club premises. Yet (as Anthony Summers shows) three hours after the assassination of President Kennedy he arrived at his bank with $7,000 in large bills: 'Ruby deposited none of the money, and almost half of it had vanished by the time he was arrested two days later.'

On the night of the assassination Ruby was at the Dallas police station with his gun, though he did not then use it as he couldn't get across to Oswald. On Sunday, 24 November, he did come face to face with Oswald and gunned him down. He had no problem gaining access to the police station and no qualms over the murder.

When Ruby was questioned by the Warren Commission he insisted that he should be taken to Washington so he could speak freely but Earl Warren,

Chief Justice of the United States, thought this was not necessary. Evidently, Ruby felt his life was in danger in Dallas: 'Gentlemen,' he told the Warren Commission, 'unless you get me to Washington you can't get a fair shake out of me . . . Unless you get me to Washington, and I am not a crackpot, I have all my senses . . . Gentlemen, my life is in danger here.' The Warren Commission concluded that President Kennedy was assassinated by a man acting on his own and that Ruby was likewise a lone nut. Ruby had, however, strong criminal credentials and probably took orders from the Mafia when he shut up Oswald. Ruby died in prison, of cancer, but before he died he told a reporter of a conspiracy, adding 'If you knew the truth you would be amazed!'

EMIL SAVUNDRA

1923-76

BORN IN CEYLON, where his father was respected as a judge and popular as a law lecturer, Emil Savundra — or Michael Marion Emil Anacletus Savundranayagam to cite the name his father gave him — was raised as a Roman Catholic and expected to conform to the legal traditions of the family. Savundra took his religion seriously but saw himself as much a man of action as a man of God. During World War Two he served in the Royal Engineers then went to Colombo College to study law. After two years he abandoned his law studies to take a job as a broker with an English trading company based in Ceylon.

Socially ambitious as well as hungry for money and power, Savundra pursued Pushpam Aloysius, daughter of a wealthy Ceylonese aristocrat. Pushpam's father rejected Savundra as an unacceptable son-in-law, but the suitor persisted in a spectacular fashion. He sent vanloads of flowers to Pushpam and stunted in the sky with his Tiger Moth to attract her attention. Eventually Pushpam's father capitulated and put on an ostentatiously grand wedding. Savundra not only had a beautiful wife in Pushpam, he had a woman who could provide him with the capital he needed. He raised £15,000 from the shares Pushpam gave him as a wedding present.

Using just £7 of his capital, Savundra launched his first company, Trans-World Enterprises Ltd, in 1949, and soon set up a second company, Eastern Traders Ltd. On the board of directors of Eastern Traders were reliable names like Pushpam's Uncle Chittampalam Gardiner and R P Senanayake, son of the Prime Minister of Ceylon. With this respectable front, Savundra now negotiated a deal to supply the Chinese Communists with oil at a cost to them of $1 million. Because of the political battle building up in Korea, the West refused to supply the Chinese so Savundra had a clear field for his own brand of intrigue. He invented a bogus company to supply the oil and circulated forged documents to pretend that the oil was on the way to the Chinese. It was a complete fraud, but there was little the Chinese could do to regain their money as the deal was illegal anyway. Savundra had succeeded in duping a government and was considerably richer as a result.

His next big swindle was planned in Paris where he set up another bogus firm, Modern Industries Ltd, in 1953. Once again his deception was on a grand scale involving governments and once again he manufactured documentary proof of his integrity. Savundra arranged to supply the Government of Portuguese Goa with a shipment of rice in return for $865,000. He made elaborate plans, dropped respectable names and produced, as usual, forged documents to suggest the deal was a legitimate one operating from Antwerp. Though the money was paid, there was no rice and no ship to take it to Goa. Interpol investigated the ensuing scandal and the Belgian Government, on learning that Savundra had gone to London, applied for his extradition so he could stand trial in Brussels. This time it was more difficult to extricate himself from his problems.

In London, Savundra acted with his customary style. He had a convenient heart attack — all his life he was to get good mileage out of his coronary condition — and went to the illustrious London Clinic, in Devonshire Place, to recuperate in luxury. There he, literally, held court and was approached by the counsel for the Belgian Government. After various legal ploys Savundra was extradited to stand trial, in Brussels, in January 1956. Found guilty, he was fined 40,000 Belgian francs and sentenced to five years in prison. However he did not serve his sentence; somehow he convinced the authorities that he was a dying man who should be allowed to spend his last few days in freedom with his family. Once released, he headed back to England and had his obituary published in the Belgian press, an act that he rightly realised would put the Portuguese and Goan Governments off his trail.

There is no doubt that Savundra had a flair for fraud; no sooner had one venture failed than he was able to initiate another scheme. When Ghana gained its independence in 1958 it was obviously a lucrative source of money for those who knew how to tap the country's commercial potential. Savundra felt he was the man to do this and arranged an introduction to President Nkrumah. What Savundra wanted was control of the country's mineral rights for the next fifty years and he persuaded Nkrumah and his colleagues that he was not only able to help them but that he did so in a selfless dedication to the anti-colonialist cause. Savundra revealed that he had had dealings with the Chinese Communists and that he had been imprisoned by the Belgians who were hated by African nationalists because of their behaviour in the Congo.

Backed by John Dalgleish's Camp Brid organisation, Savundra set up three companies in Ghana, each with a capital of £100 million. As it took only £7 to register a company in Ghana it cost Savundra next to nothing to make his grandiose claims. Though Savundra's arrival in Accra, in October 1959, impressed the Ghanaians, Geoffrey Bing, Ghana's Attorney General, was suspicious and investigated Savundra's three companies. They were, as usual, elaborate fronts for making money fraudulently. Savundra was deported from Ghana and returned to Ceylon. Yet again he had avoided imprisonment.

Savundra was not content to stay in Ceylon as he had plans to establish himself as one of the most eminent Englishmen of his time — he did, after all, refer to himself as 'the original black Englishman'. He worked gradually

towards his goal. In 1960 he became a naturalised British citizen and simply
assumed two doctorates. Backed by the financial resources of Uncle
Chittampalam, 'Doctor' Savundra formed several companies bearing the
name of his daughter — Jacqueline Holdings, Jacqueline Finance, Jacqueline
Nominees, Jacqueline Securities, Jacqueline Enterprises. Each company was
capitalised to the tune of only £100 but they enabled Savundra to orchestrate
his grand theme of fraud on a massive scale. 'When you English see a loop-hole
in the law,' Savundra said, 'you drive a Mini Minor through it; I, Savundra,
drive a Rolls-Royce.'

In 1963, when Savundra created his Fire, Auto and Marine organisation, it
was possible to register a motor insurance company by convincing the Board
of Trade one had a capital of £50,000. This was not, for Savundra, an
insurmountable problem. He got his friend Count Maxim de Cassan Floyrac
to guarantee £48,000 while Jacqueline Securities — Savundra under another
name — put up £1,000. The remaining £1,000 was provided by Stuart de

Quincey Walker, a smuggler who became Chief Executive of FAM. To give the company respectability, Savundra persuaded Cecil H Tross Youle, OBE, to become Chairman, though he had no idea of the fraudulent nature of the business he was endorsing.

FAM was registered on 14 February 1963 and began to acquire customers by offering cut-price policies and paying a high commission to agents. FAM's motto was 'Benefit through Care' and Savundra covered himself by refusing to accept liability on any car that had been damaged through careless driving.

Savundra flourished while FAM expanded. As Jon Connell and Douglas Sutherland write, in *Fraud: the Amazing Career of Doctor Savundra* (London, 1978), 'The formula of paying higher commissions to brokers than anyone else and charging motorists less than anyone else was proving irresistible. By the end of the first year the flow of money into Orchard House (FAM's first headquarters) had reached a staggering £20,000 a week. While rival insurance companies and Lloyd's underwriters watched with frustration, FAM became the fastest-growing car insurance firm in the country.'

FAM had to be seen to be successful so Savundra moved, in 1964, to an eight-storey office block near Hendon — inevitably, the new headquarters was called Jacqueline House. He had his business computerised and it attracted international attention as a progressive company using the scientific resources of the modern world. To complete the picture of confidence Savundra moved to a new home. White Walls, a mansion with two acres of ground in Bishop's Avenue, Hampstead, was an appropriately ostentatious environment for the man who seemed to have everything, including a Rolls-Royce, two Aston Martins and a Jaguar.

Even as he was proclaiming the merits of FAM, Savundra set up, in 1963, the Merchants and Finance Trust in Leichtenstein to redistribute FAM's income and make it inaccessible to any British creditors. Though Savundra himself could have money transferred to a Swiss bank account, FAM was insolvent by 1965. At first Savundra was able to disguise this fact by his customary repertoire of fraudulent tricks. In 1965 he produced a Government Bond worth, apparently, more than £500,000. The following year he displayed a portfolio of shares worth, apparently, in excess of £800,000. Both the bond and the portfolio were worthless forgeries. Savundra alone knew how hopeless FAM's finances were and had plans to desert the sinking ship. He sold his shareholding to Stuart Walker and, on 22 June 1966, resigned from the board of Fire, Auto and Marine Insurance Company. He then went to Switzerland and took a room in the Hirslanden clinic outside Zurich. Once again his heart was troubling him. Thus he was at a safe distance when, on 2 July, the liquidation of FAM was announced. On 9 July Savundra returned to the safety of Ceylon where he complained of his physical distress and made threats to inquisitive reporters who dared suggest he was a swindler.

Back in Britain, there were 400,000 motorists with FAM policies. 43,000 of those had outstanding claims. With a deficit of some £3 million FAM had not, of course, any way of helping the unfortunates who had trusted in Savundra. Astonishingly enough, Savundra decided to come back to Britain to face the charges against him and the general atmosphere of hostility. He believed, no doubt, that his charm and cheek would prevail. 'I am like General

MacArthur,' he announced. 'He said: "I shall return" when the Japs drove him out of the Pacific. And I, the great Savundra, am returning in likewise fashion.' Incongruously, on 16 January 1967, he went from White Walls, his mansion, to claim his rights at the Labour Exchange. On 23 January 1967 he saw the Official Receiver and was presented, the next day, with a writ for £386,534.

It is a measure of Savundra's arrogance that he felt he could defend himself in the most public way possible. Far from expressing sorrow, Savundra saw himself as a heroic figure. He agreed to appear on television with David Frost, then rated the most penetrating interviewer in Britain. The confrontation took place on Friday, 3 February 1967, and Savundra antagonised an already hostile audience of FAM policy-holders by declaring, 'I am not going to cross swords with the peasants. I came here to cross swords with England's greatest swordsman.' The ensuing verbal battle brought out the best in Frost and the worst in Savundra who said, when a widow told how her cheque for a £7,000 claim had bounced, 'All these and other heartrending stories which I have heard make me realise only too well that my selling out was the wisest thing I ever did.' The audience retorted: 'For you. What about us?' When the interview ended Savundra left the studio with the angry accusation, 'Audience fixed! Audience fixed!'

Savundra was arrested on 10 February. The charges against him were that he had used a forged certificate; that he had made a false entry in a balance sheet to suggest that FAM had British Government Securities of £540,000; that he had conspired to defraud people taking out insurance policies with FAM.

The trial opened at the Old Bailey on 10 January 1968 and Savundra was accused of stealing, with the connivance of his friend Walker, £600,000 from motorists' premiums. Savundra nevertheless looked calm and confident when he appeared in the witness box on 8 February. By 19 February, his final day in the box, he was emotionally exhausted by the ordeal but would not admit any guilt. 'I submit,' he said, 'that I did everything in my power to replace the goose quill with the fountain pen, but was bludgeoned out of existence by the giants. I suppose I should have known better than to engage in war against the enormous forces ranged against me.' He was found guilty on four charges: misappropriating premiums; falsifying his 1966 balance sheet; making a false entry in the 1965 balance sheet; and issuing forged share certificates. For these crimes Savundra was sentenced to ten years' imprisonment.

He served more than six years of his sentence and was released on 4 October 1974. Two years later he died, of a heart attack. While he was in Wormwood Scrubs prison the prisoners had a song about him;

> Oh, Doctor Savundra,
> I know who you are;
> And I know where I'd like you,
> Under my car.

Those must have been the sentiments of the thousands swindled by Savundra in his bizarre career. His wife Pushpam had a different point of view: 'I'm nothing but proud of him. Like all brilliant, progressive men in history he has been persecuted.'

JOHN SCANLAN

1796-1820

LIEUTENANT JOHN SCANLAN was the dashing squire of the castle in the Irish village of Ballycahane, on the river Shannon. He was no longer in the British army, but retained his rank and his former batman, Stephen Sullivan, who lived in the castle and acted as his valet. The two earned an unsavoury reputation for drinking and debauchery. In 1819 Scanlan's roving eye was attracted by the figure of the young Ellen Hanley, at fifteen one of the prettiest girls in the village. She was an orphan who had been brought up by her uncle, a Mr Connery, variously described as a rope-maker and a shoe-maker.

Scanlan's initial advances proved unsuccessful and it was not until he promised the girl marriage that she consented to her seduction. Scanlan was a gambling man, and his wicked treatment of the unfortunate Ellen is compounded by the fact that he also persuaded her to steal her uncle's savings as a dowry. In June 1819 she left her uncle's house, with his life's savings of £120, and the couple were married by a defrocked priest. Ellen believed the marriage was a valid one. Scanlan thought the marriage was an illegal one which he would be able to discount as soon as he wished — as soon as he tired of Elly and had gone through her money. The couple spent their honeymoon on the island of Glin, on the river Shannon. Elly was last seen alive at a remote farmhouse, situated on the island of Carrig, further along the river estuary. Her body was washed ashore seven weeks afterwards.

Elly had soon bored Scanlan and had begun to put on airs. It seemed to the bold Lieutenant that she might be tempted to spend the marriage funds on fancy clothes, and the two men decided callously to get rid of her. It later emerged that they had made several attempts. Stephen Sullivan rowed her out into the middle of the Shannon intending to drown her, but her merry prattle and innocent laughter totally unnerved him and he brought her home again. The two villains talked it over and a further plan was hatched. Sullivan filled himself with whisky to give him the nerve to go through with the deed. He rowed her out again, beat her head in and after weighing her body down with stones he lowered it into the water.

On 6 September, seven weeks after the muder, the naked body of Elly Hanley surfaced again. Although immersed for so many weeks and somewhat decomposed, it was still recognisable, and a search for Scanlan and Sullivan was instigated. The matter was one of considerable political delicacy, as the Irish people identified very much with Elly Hanley, while the figure of Lieutenant Scanlan seemed to stand for the ruling Anglo-Irish class Also it was feared that Scanlan might get off with the murder as a result of his high connections within the establishment. A thorough search was carried out and the erring Scanlan was discovered, hiding in a pile of straw within the walls of Ballycahane castle.

He was tried at Limerick, and although defended by the great and eloquent Daniel O'Connell, he was sentenced to death and hanged.

Stephen Sullivan, meanwhile, had been doing rather well. He had married an heiress after his flight from the scene of the crime, but by a strange twist of fate he had been arrested on suspicion of passing forged currency and imprisoned at Tralee jail. Although he had changed his name, he was recognised as Scanlan's valet, and witnesses came forward to attest that he had been seen in the company of Scanlan and the unfortunate Elly Hanley in June and July 1819. He was tried for the girl's murder and throughout these proceedings he insisted on his innocence. It was not until he stood on the scaffold that he finally admitted his guilt, and confessed that he had been persuaded by John Scanlan to take Elly out in the boat on the Shannon and beat her to death. He was hanged on 27 July 1820.

ISABELLA, COUNTESS OF SEAFORTH

(17th century)

SCOTLAND IN THE seventeenth century, was a land saturated with superstition and there was widespread faith in the precognitive gifts of various prophets. The most celebrated prophet was Kenneth Mackenzie — Coin neach Odhar of Mackenzie — who was born in Uig on the Isle of Lewis. Tradition has it that Kenneth acquired, from the fairies, a white divination stone that enabled him to foretell the future. Whatever the reason for it, his talent was remarkable enough to attract attention from the high and mighty. He was summoned to Brahan Castle, near Dingwall on the Cromarty Firth, as a vassal of the Earls of Seaforth.

Initially, Kenneth worked as a farm labourer and occasionally practised his prophetic art. However, the third Earl of Seaforth elevated Kenneth to the status of Brahan Seer and he was encouraged to peer into the future. Thus Kenneth grimly told people how and when they would die. In fact his predictions were consistently gloomy. Passing Drumossie Moor, the site of the Battle of Culloden in 1746, he said, 'Oh! Drumossie, thy bleak moor shall, ere many generations have passed away, be stained with the best blood of the Highlands.' Culloden was a catastrophe for the clans. Kenneth also predicted the coming of the Highland Railway: 'The day will come when long strings of carriages without horses shall run between Dingwall and Inverness.' More chillingly, as it has not yet come to pass, he said that life in the Highlands 'shall be exterminated and drowned by horrid black rains'.

The third Earl of Seaforth eventually married Isabella Mackenzie, daughter of Sir John Mackenzie of Tarbat. She was an arrogant, overbearing woman animated by a jealous concern for her husband. After the restoration of Charles II, Seaforth was sent to Paris on official business. In his absence the Countess became increasingly agitated and accordingly summoned the Brahan Seer to her presence. Surrounded by her entourage, she asked Kenneth if her husband was well and he answered, smilingly, in the affirmative. When she pressed for more details, Kenneth asked her to be content. But she persisted.

He then told her, 'As you will know that which will make you unhappy, I must tell you the truth. My lord seems to have little thought of you, or of his children, or of his Highland home. I saw him in a gay-gilded room, grandly decked out in velvets, with silks and cloth of gold, and on his knees before a fair lady, his arm round her waist, and her hand pressed to his lips.'

Isabella was appalled at this revelation which, she realised, humiliated her before her own household. She ranted at Kenneth, accused him of evil intent, and concluded: 'You have spoken evil of dignities, you have defamed a mighty chief in the midst of his vassals, you have abused my hospitality and outraged my feelings, you have sullied the good name of my lord in the halls of his ancestors, and you shall suffer the most signal vengeance I can inflict — you shall suffer the death.' On the orders of the Countess, then, Kenneth was executed as a witch by being placed in a barrel of burning tar. A stone at Chanonry Point, Fortrose, commemorates the place of execution.

Before he died, however, Kenneth asked the local ministers to record his final prophecy. 'I see into the future,' he began, 'and I read the doom of the race of my oppressor. The long-descended line of Seaforth will, ere many generations have passed, end in extinction and sorrow.' Mackenzie then specified the fate of the Seaforths. 'I see a chief, the last of his house, both deaf and dumb. He will be the father of four fair sons, all of whom he will follow to the tomb . . . After lamenting over the last and most promising of his sons, he himself shall sink into the grave, and the remnant of his possessions shall be inherited by a white-hooded lassie from the East, and she is to kill her sister.'

This all came to pass. Baron Seaforth of Kintail was twelve-years-old when, in 1766, he became deaf as the result of scarlet fever. His four sons predeceased him; William Frederick died as an infant, George died at the age of six, Francis was killed at sea, the second William Frederick died at the age of twenty-four in 1814. The following year Baron Seaforth died. His daughter Mary married a man called Hood — Sir Samuel Hood — who died shortly after Baron Seaforth. When Mary returned home from the East she was Lady Hood and she wore a widow's white-hood. While driving her younger sister, Caroline, through the woods near Brahan Castle the carriage overturned. Lady Hood escaped with minor injuries; Caroline died.

Thus the Seaforth family ended in 'extinction and sorrow'. Sir Walter Scott sympathised with Lady Hood in a lament for the *Last of the Seaforths:*

> And thou, gentle Dame, who must bear, to thy grief,
> For thy clan and thy country the cares of a Chief,
> Whom brief rolling moons in six changes have left,
> Of thy husband and father and brethren bereft;
> To thine ear of affection, how sad is the hail
> That salutes thee — the heir of the line of Kintail!

Sceptics will always have their doubts but in Scotland the fate of the Seaforths is a direct result of the cruelty of Isabella, Countess of Seaforth.

MADELEINE SMITH

1835-1928

THE TWO PRINCIPALS in perhaps the most notorious murder trial in Victorian Scotland show not only the truth of the old maxim that opposites attract; they suggest, too, that our received notions of Victorian life are wildly inaccurate. According to the popular stereotype of the Victorian Scotswoman, Madeleine Smith should have been a prim, easily shockable female, terrified of sex. According to the stereotype of the romantic Frenchman, Emile L'Angelier should have been an irresistibly erotic force. In fact Madeleine was a dominant woman anxious to indulge her sexual appetite whereas Emile was a neurotic creature uncertain of his own virility.

The eldest child of affluent architect James Smith, Madeleine was born in Glasgow and educated, for a while, in Newcastle when the family lived there. In Glasgow, though, she acquired a Scottish accent and an assertive attitude that her father deplored. Hoping to turn his daughter into a Victorian lady, James Smith sent Madeleine to a finishing school in London — Miss Gorton's School for Young Ladies, Clapham. There her Glasgow-Scots accent was eliminated and she was given a social polish. When she returned to Glasgow in 1851, she was an accomplished young woman of eighteen. She was also intelligent enough to appreciate her sexual impact on men. Using high heels to boost her height of five-feet-four-inches, she was a stunningly good-looking woman. With lustrous dark hair, large breasts and an aura of sensuality, she was one of the most desirable women in Glasgow. Her father's wealth was, of course, an additional attraction.

Pierre Emile L'Angelier was no social match for Madeleine. He was born in 1823 in St Helier, Jersey, where his French father was a market-gardener. Expected to carry on the family business, Emile had hopes of going further than his father though he possessed little more than a little-boy-lost charm that both men and women responded to. Sir Francis Mackenzie, a Scottish landowner, encountered Emile in St Helier and took him back to Edinburgh to work in a firm of nurserymen. Emile arrived in Scotland in 1842 and kept his job after the death of Sir Francis the following year. In 1848 Emile was in Paris as a member of the National Guard and witnessed the fall of Louis-Philippe. He returned to Scotland in 1852, eventually obtaining a job as a packing-clerk in Glasgow with a salary of £26 per year. Already he suffered from depression, a condition he treated with doses of laudanum. He also turned his charm on the ladies of Glasgow. Through friendships formed at St Jude's Episcopal Church, Jane Street, he got new lodgings with the Clark family in the Great Western Road where his landlady, Mrs Clark, doted on him. He likewise made a great impression on Miss Mary Arthur Perry, a spinster living at West Renfrew Street. With Mrs Clark to look after him and Miss Perry to mother him Emile was relatively comfortable and content when, early in 1855, he first caught sight of Madeleine Smith.

Emile immediately went into action, sending Madeleine a single rose on St Valentine's Day and arranging an introduction to her. Predictably, her father was opposed to any deep friendship between his expensively educated daughter and a humble clerk and told Madeleine that Emile would not be welcome at the Smith home. In March Madeleine wrote to Emile from Rowaleyn, her father's country house in Row village, hoping that he would become 'a friend of Papa's'. During the year they became secretly engaged and Madeleine began using the pet name Mimi. On 3 December 1855 she began her letter by addressing Emile as 'My own darling husband' and ended with 'Much much love kisses tender long embraces kisses love. I am thy own thy ever fond thy own dear loving wife thy Mimi L' Angelier.' Emile was entitled to think that his Mimi genuinely wanted to marry him, even if it meant opposing her father.

Emile's attitude to women was confused; he believed that working girls were fair game for seduction but that ladies like Madeleine should be virgins until the day, or first night, of their marriage. Madeleine appeared to agree with this and wrote assuring him, 'I shall not yield to you — you shall marry me pure and innocent as the day on which I was born. You will never deprive me of my honour — I shall be firm on this point dearest — I know you shall love me better for it.'

On 29 March 1856 Madeleine came of age, and could, theoretically, marry Emile despite her father's opinion of him as 'poor and but a clerk'. She gave Emile the impression that she was willing to intensify their relationship even at the risk of parental condemnation. Madeleine was determined to consummate the affair and encouraged Emile to meet her secretly at Rowaleyn where they would be able to come together in a penetrating premarital embrace.

Madeleine met Emile in the woods at Rowaleyn on Tuesday night, 6 May 1856, and had intercourse with him. The letter she wrote in the wee small hours of the morning after give her own account of the experience: 'Beloved, if we did wrong last night it was in the excitement of our love. Yes, beloved, I did truly love you with my soul. I was happy, it was a pleasure to be with you. Oh if we could have remained, never more to have parted. But we must hope the time shall come!' She explained that she was thinking about confiding in her mother but held out little hope of support from that source.

What fascinated Madeleine was the sexual act she had just committed. 'I did not bleed in the least last night,' she told Emile, 'but I had a good deal of pain during the night. Tell me, pet, were you angry at me for allowing you to do what you did — was it very bad of me? We should, I suppose, have waited till we were married. I shall always remember last night. Will we not often talk of our evening meetings after we are married . . . Beloved, have you a doubt but that we shall be married some day . . . God bless you and make you well. And may you yet be very, very happy with your Mimi as your little wife. Kindest love, fond embrace, and kisses from thy own true and ever devoted Mimi, Thy faithful WIFE.'

Emile, on the other hand, was full of remorse. In a draft reply to Madeleine he poured out his sadness: 'I shall never be happy again. If ever I meet you again, love, it must be as at first. I will never again repeat what I did until we are regularly married . . . I am in such a state of mind I do not care if I were dead. We did wrong. God forgive us for it. Mimi, we have loved blindly. It is your parents' fault if shame is the result; they are to blame for it all . . . I do not understand, my pet, your not bleeding, for every woman having her virginity must bleed. You must have done so some other time. Try to remember if you never hurt yourself in washing, etc. I am sorry you felt pain. I hope, pet, you are better. I trust, dearest, you will not be ——. Be sure and tell me immediately you are ill next time, and if at your regular period. I was not angry at your allowing me, Mimi, but I am sad it happened. You had no resolution.' Emile obviously felt like the innocent party erotically overwhelmed by a being more sensuous than his. It was a reversal of the roles he had been taught to play in society.

In July 1856 Emile moved into 11 Franklin Place, Glasgow, where his landlady Mrs Jenkins took the usual maternal shine to him. Madeleine's father was also contemplating a change of address and had taken a house at 7 Blythswood Square. As he thought it too big for his family he intended to let the top storey to William Harper Minnoch. Though he was the same age as

Emile, Minnoch had little else in common with the Frenchman. He was a successful businessman with an income of £4,000 per year and was friendly with Madeleine's father, who saw him as the perfect son-in-law. Before the move to Blythswood Square, in November, Madeleine was on friendly terms with Minnoch though she continued to make assignations with Emile. As the year came to an end Madeleine was becoming weary of Emile's lack of sexual drive. She complained to him, 'I know your love for me is great when I am good but you are cool when I am bad.' Emile, of course, was mainly interested in marriage whereas Madeleine's priority was sex.

On 28 January 1857 Minnoch proposed to Madeleine. She accepted him but asked the family to postpone a public announcement of the engagement. By the middle of the following month Madeleine was writing to Emile explaining that their relationship was at an end and that she intended to marry another man: 'I did once love you truly, fondly, but for some time back I have lost much of that love. There is no other reason for my conduct, and I think it but fair to let you know this, I might have gone on and become your wife, but I could not have loved you as I ought. My conduct you will condemn, but I did at one time love you with heart and soul. It has cost me much to tell you this — sleepless nights, but it is necessary you should know . . . I know you will never injure the character of one you so fondly loved. No, Emile, I know you have honour and are a Gentleman. What has passed you will not mention. I know when I ask you that you will comply. Adieu.'

That letter was in complete contrast to the passionate, sexually provocative messages Madeleine had previously showered on Emile. He had kept these letters and now threatened to send them to Madeleine's father, an action that would expose Madeleine as a sexual athlete and probably destroy her chances of marriage to Minnoch. Madeleine pleaded with Emile to do nothing that would make her a 'public shame' and asked him to visit her at Blythswood Square, giving him directions: 'I cannot get to the back stair. I never could see the way to it. I will take you within in the door. The area gate will be open. I shall see you from my window, 12 o'C. I will wait till 1 o'C.'

Emile visited Madeleine on 19 February and noted, in his diary, 'Saw Mimi a few moments. Was very ill during the night.' Emile was a hypochondriac who liked to dose himself with laudanum, and other substances such as arsenic, but his illness was serious enough to alarm Mrs Jenkins, his landlady. He had severe stomach pains and was violently sick. Next day — Friday, 20 February — he was well enough to visit Madeleine again.

On Saturday, 21 February, Madeleine went to Murdoch Brothers, a druggist in Sauchiehall Street, and bought sixpenny worth of common white arsenic, which she needed, so she said, to deal with rats. It was sold to her in a mixture of soot as the law required the addition of colouring to the poison which might easily be mistaken for a harmless white powder. Next day, in the absence of her family, she entertained Emile in the drawing room at Blythswood Square. After this meeting he was ill enough to need attention from a doctor.

At the beginning of March, Madeleine told Emile she intended to go on a family holiday to Bridge of Allan and advised him to go to the Isle of Wight for the sake of his health. Emile replied, on 5 March, 'The doctor says I must go to

B[ridge] of A[llan]. I cannot trail 500 miles to the I of W and 500 back. What is your object in wishing me so very much to go south?' On 6 March, the day she received this rebellious letter, Madeleine went back to Sauchiehall Street where she bought another sixpenny worth of arsenic, from Currie's, to kill rats. She was given one ounce of arsenic mixed with indigo. In the afternoon she went, with her family, to Bridge of Allan.

Meanwhile, Madeleine's plans to marry Minnoch were advancing. It was agreed that news of the engagement could be published in the press on 26 March. Madeleine knew word of this could send Emile into a rage during which he might send her erotic letters to her father, or even her fiancé. She had to deal with him somehow before the news of her engagement was made public.

While Madeleine was away, Emile turned to the other two women in his life. His landlady Mrs Jenkins listened to his physical complaints and Miss Perry heard of his psychological worries. Emile confided to Miss Perry that his love life was in a mess. He was being cruelly treated by his beloved and could only see her surreptitiously. Moreover, he told Miss Perry that when he visited Madeleine she made a point of giving him excessive amounts of coffee, cocoa or drinking chocolate and that he always felt ill afterwards. He said he could never leave her: 'It is a perfect fascination — my attachment to that girl. If she were to poison me I would forgive her.' Miss Perry rebuked him for this morbid sentiment and asked, 'What motive could she have for giving you anything to hurt you?' Emile observed that 'she might not be sorry to be rid of me'.

On Wednesday 18 March, Madeleine was back in Glasgow and once more went to Sauchiehall Street to buy another sixpenny worth of arsenic from Currie's. In the evening she wrote to Emile, inviting him to visit her the next night, a Thursday. Madeleine's letter did not reach Emile on Thursday morning, however, and only arrived after he had left for Bridge of Allan. He received it on the Friday by which time Madeleine was worried at his failure to come when summoned. She wrote to him on Saturday, 21 March: 'Why my beloved did you not come to me? Oh beloved are you ill? Come to me sweet one. I waited and waited for you but you came not. I shall wait again to-morrow night same hour and arrangement. Do come sweet love my own dear love of a sweetheart. Come beloved and clasp me to your heart. Come and we shall be happy. A kiss fond love. Adieu with tender embraces ever believe me to be you own ever dear fond MINI.' (Sometimes she alternated the name 'Mini' with 'Mimi'.)

Emile received this on Sunday morning at Bridge of Allan, headed back immediately to Glasgow but got off the train at Coatbridge and walked the remaining ten miles, reaching his lodgings in the evening. He asked Mrs Jenkins for a front-door key and told her to call him early in the morning so he could get the first train back to Bridge of Allan. At 9pm he left the house. When he returned at 2.30 am, Monday 23 March, he was in a ghastly condition, shivering and vomiting. A doctor was called in and Miss Perry was brought to his sickbed. At 11.15 am Emile died.

When the contents of his stomach were examined 82 grains of common white arsenic were found, enough to kill some forty men. Madeleine had, of course, purchased arsenic but dismissed this as an irrelevance in her statement of 31 March: 'I remember giving him some cocoa from my window one night some time ago, but I cannot specify the time particularly. He took the cup in his hand and barely tasted the contents, and I gave him no bread to eat with it. I was taking some cocoa myself at the time, and had prepared it myself . . . As I had attributed his sickness to want of food, I proposed, as stated in the note, to give him a loaf of bread, but I said that merely in joke, and, in point of fact, I never gave him any bread. I have bought arsenic on various occasions . . . as a cosmetic, and applied it to my face, neck, and arms, diluted with water . . . I had been advised to the use of arsenic in the way I have mentioned by a young lady, the daughter of an actress, and I had also seen the use of it recommended in the newspapers . . . I did not wish any of my father's family to be aware that I was using the arsenic, and therefore never mentioned it to any of them, and I don't suppose they or any of the servants ever noticed any of it in the basin . . . I never administered, or caused to be administered, to M. L'Angelier arsenic or anything injurious. And this I declare to be the truth.'

Madeleine's trial, in Edinburgh from 30 June to 9 July, ended on a verdict of Not Proven, a conclusion that admitted an element of doubt to the case. So it has remained. Theories abound. In his *Madeleine Smith* (London, 1975), Henry Blyth referred to the rumours that 'Madeleine and Emile performed acts of oral sex. This led to the supposition that she might have poisoned Emile by using an arsenic paste or ointment on her vulva. This seems possible and indeed probable . . . Above all it would explain how Emile failed to detect the flavour of arsenic in the cocoa; for in this theory it is not suggested that *all* the poison was sexually administered, but that it was so administered first — with the co-operation of Emile, an addicted arsenic-eater — and then, without his knowledge, in large doses in the cocoa.'

However she achieved it, it seems likely that when Emile kept his appointment with her she managed to get a lethal dose of arsenic into him. She may have silenced him but must have realised his death would lead to the discovery of her own erotic letters. In the event, she accepted this and brazened out the trial.

After her legal ordeal — which she probably enjoyed — Madeleine learned that Minnoch had become engaged to another woman. Madeleine went south, and in 1861 married George Wardle, a member of the pre-Raphaelite group. She lived in Bloomsbury where she associated with William Morris and other prominent English socialists. After a separation from her husband she lived in Staffordshire, then emigrated to the USA at the age of seventy. She took a second husband, lived in New York, and died in 1928 at the age of ninety-three. Her gravestone is inscribed 'Lena Sheehy' and she died without giving away any significant secrets.

MARY SMITH

(19th century)

A FARMER'S WIFE, Mary Smith was well described by Sir Walter Scott who attended her trial on 19 February 1827 and recorded his impressions in his Journal: 'It was a face to do or die, or perhaps to do to die. Thin features, which had been handsome, a flashing eye, an acute and aquiline nose, lips much marked, as arguing a decision, and, I think, bad temper — they were thin, as one of a rather melancholy disposition.'

At his farm at West Denside, near Dundee, Mary's husband employed a farmgirl Margaret Warden. Mary was furious when she learned that Margaret had had an affair with her son. The girl was dismissed, which would have been the end of the affair had not Mary convinced herself that Margaret was pregnant. Mary was motivated by a narrow self-righteousness and a dread of her own family becoming involved in a sexual scandal.

Accordingly, Mary asked Margaret to return to the farm so that she could make sure there was no baby to burden her son. Before dealing with Margaret's problem, Mary went to Dr Dick of Dundee and bought an ounce and a half of arsenic, saying it was 'poison for rats'. In the presence of Jean Norrie, another farmgirl, Mary gave Margaret Warden 'something in a dram glass' that looked like cream of tartar. After taking this, Margaret was violently ill. A doctor was called in and he diagnosed cholera, then rampant in the area. Margaret, however, knew better. Her last words were, 'Ye ken what is the occasion o' me lyin' here . . . My mistress gave me ——', at which point she died.

Because of suspicions of foul play, Margaret's body was exhumed and examined. Arsenic was detected and Mary faced a charge of murder. She said that she had given Margaret a dose of castor-oil and nothing else.

Scott described the outcome of the trial. 'She is clearly guilty,' he wrote, 'but as one or two witnesses said the poor wench hinted an intention to poison herself, the jury gave that bastard verdict, *Not Proven.* I hate that Caledonian *medium quid.* One who is not *proven guilty* is innocent in the eye of the law . . . There was an awful crowd; but, sitting within the bar, I had the pleasure of seeing much at my ease; the constables knocking the other folks about, which was of course very entertaining.'

Lord Cockburn, who conducted the defence, said that Mary 'was like a vindictive masculine witch. I remember [Scott] sitting within the bar looking at her. As we were moving out, Sir Walter's remark upon the acquittal was, "Well, sirs, all I can say is that if that woman was my wife I should take care to be my own cook."'

WILHELM JOHANN KARL EDUARD STIEBER

1818-92

ONLY DAYS BEFORE the outbreak of the Franco-Prussian war, Bismarck underlined in his private book of devotion a sentence by Martin Luther: 'In this affair no sword can advise or help, God alone must create here, without human thought and action.' This sentiment, seemingly so pious and Germanic, is not strictly sincere. Bismarck had already used human thought and action to ensure the speedy triumph of Prussian military might against France and the creation of the German Empire. The far from divine agent employed in these affairs was his master-spy, Wilhelm Stieber.

Wilhelm was born on 3 May 1818 in the Prussian town of Merseburg. His parents wanted him to become a priest, but he became a lawyer. By 1850 he had a legal practice in Berlin and was renowned as a defence lawyer with an astounding reputation for getting his clients off. There was more to this than met the eye. On the face of it, he was a liberal barrister who protected criminals and stood up for the lower classes. In fact, he was a police spy and editor of the Berlin police gazette. As a source of information he was invaluable to the Berlin law enforcement officers. He was a master of double dealing, for he used the insights he gained from his tactics on behalf of the police to the advantage of his clients in court. His skill in demolishing police evidence and discrediting police witnesses contributed to his success as a defence lawyer. He kept in with

163

the authorities by exposing criminal and anti-social activities from time to time. The timely unmasking of radicals and revolutionaries demonstrated his worth to the establishment. In 1845 he denounced the uncle of his own wife. To him this was a small price to pay to keep his hand in with the establishment. At the same time he openly sympathised with radical agitators.

He openly appeared in the streets with the mobs in Potsdam which threatened the stability of public order in 1848. It is reported that on one occasion Stieber was present in a violent mob which surrounded King Frederick Wilhelm. He got close enough to whisper to the King that all was well, as he was Wilhelm Stieber, a loyal spy, and that he and his equally loyal agents were present in the mob to protect his majesty. His reward was to be made Commissioner of Police in 1850. He worked tirelessly to annihilate all elements of opposition to the monarchy. He was gradually working himself towards a position of immense and irreplaceable power. Unfortunately Frederick Wilhelm was declared insane in 1855 and his successor, King Wilhelm I, did not take very readily to Stieber's charms and tried his utmost to get rid of him. Stieber had naturally made many enemies by this time and they rejoiced in this heaven-sent opportunity to discredit him. Their aim was to get him dismissed from office and struck from the register of barristers. He was brought to trial on a long series of indictments, but the lessons Stieber had learned as a practising lawyer, and the knowledge of his enemies and of people in high places enabled him to outwit the legal bigwigs ranged against him. He claimed that he had committed no crimes, that everything he had done was done with royal authority. The late king was now under medical care, and proceedings could not be taken against Stieber without discrediting Frederick Wilhelm. Stieber was acquitted.

He then took a long holiday in Russia, where he cashed in on a useful contact he had made in Berlin. While he was Commissioner of Police, he had saved a Russian diplomat who had managed to get himself embroiled in an unfortunate scandal. The grateful Russian now repaid this debt, and Stieber was given the job of revitalising the Tsar's secret police. Stieber's genius was here very well employed, and the system was extended to include all those suspected political or criminal elements who sought safety outside Russia. This bureaucracy of international surveillance lasted until the Russian Revolution of 1917. The dreaded *Ochrana* was really the creation of Wilhelm Stieber.

At the same time that Stieber was working for the Russians, he was serving the Fatherland, spying on all that he found in Russia and sending back information about all the countries he visited while on the Tsar's business. In 1863 he was introduced to Otto von Bismarck, whom he was to serve for almost thirty years. The information Stieber could supply Bismarck was invaluable, and Stieber was rewarded with Bismarck's protection and his authorisation for his activities. From Bismarck's point of view Stieber was almost a gift from on high. The Iron Chancellor was determined that the might and security of his nation could be attained by destroying the power of Austria. The foundations of Bismarck's plan for the unification of Germany and the formation of the German Empire were largely the work of Stieber, the master-spy. Bismarck asked him to investigate Austria's military potential.

The task appealed to Wilhelm Stieber's sense of cunning. He travelled widely in Austria, disguised as an itinerant salesman with a cart. His goods were contained in two separate boxes. One box contained religious statuettes; the other held pornographic pictures. Stieber believed that the punter who rejected the one might go for the other. Thus he peddled his wares from place to place for several months and wherever he went he took down details of barracks, troop numbers, transport, weaponry and personnel deployment. The information that he collected was vast and detailed. When his reports were properly processed in Berlin Count Helmuth von Moltke, chief of the general staff, was able comprehensively to plan the campaign against Austria. A short while before the war with Austria broke out, Bismarck told the Austrian ambassador that the only two possibilities between Prussia and Austria were: 'Either a genuine alliance, or war to the knife.' Prussian confidence of victory in such a war was firmly based on Stieber's work as a salesman of religious trinkets, purveyor of pornography and the careful collation of military intelligence. AJP Taylor comments in *Bismarck: The Man and the Statesman* (London, 1961) that: 'All wars are a struggle for power, but a practical occasion for their outbreak is usually found. In 1866 there was no disguise; Austria fought for her primacy, Prussia for equality.' Stieber's work ensured that the struggle was not an equal one. The campaign lasted hardly two weeks, and the Austrian armies suffered a humiliating defeat at Sadova (Königgrätz) on 3 July 1866. Prussian losses totalled 10,000 and the Austrians lost 45,000 including 20,000 prisoners. Stieber's reports would have told the Prussian general staff that the Austrian armies were equipped with muzzle-loading muskets, based on a model some one-and-a-half centuries old. The Prussian army had a new breech-loading rifle, capable of rapid fire, accurate up to five hundred yards, which could be loaded while the infantryman was lying down. Information of this kind gave von Moltke and his fellow officers the basis on which decisions of strategy, tactics and timing could be made. Co-ordination and timing were marked features of the battle of Sadova.

Stieber was rewarded with even more important duties. He was now to organise the secret police in Berlin, a special unit raised for the purpose. Stieber's agents had two main duties: the protection of important persons, and the gathering of intelligence. Stieber's peculiar genius forged a huge network of organisations which soon embraced the survelliance of enemy intelligence services, the censorship of much internal and external mail and the distribution of 'disinformation' to demoralise potential enemies of the Prussian state. He was now restored to royal favour and Bismarck called him 'my king of sleuthhounds'. To his superiors he acted like a fawning servile spaniel. To his subordinates he was a tyrant.

The next stage of Bismarck's grand strategy to make Germany a united nation state was a successful war with France. Once again, the slimy skills of Stieber were invaluable. He and two assistants, Zernicki and Kaltenbach, spent a year-and-a-half in France, undercover, constructing a vast and detailed intelligence report of the French military capability, and assembling a directory of local agents who would be ready, willing and able to assist the advancing Prussian armies when the war began. There is something wholly

Germanic in the total thoroughness of Stieber's work. He compiled data not only on French military matters but on transport, communications, rivers and waterways, public morale, the location of fortifications and armament dumps, factories, depots and personnel. The paperwork filled three large trunks. His exertions paid off. The war was declared on 17 July 1870 and lasted six weeks. The French armies under Napoleon III were defeated by the Prussians at Sedan on 1 September. General Auguste Ducrot, with his back to the Belgian frontier, was faced by 200,000 troops under von Moltke on his southern, western and northern flanks. The French cavalry, attempting to break out, were repeatedly raked by merciless rifle fire from the Prussian infantry, and French positions were blasted by Prussian artillery numbering 426 guns. French losses were over 17,000. The Prussians lost 9,000. But these were not the only casualties of the war.

A new and modern quality had entered the field — a new kind of professional ruthlessness which brought the world nearer the concept of total war. Wilhelm Stieber pioneered a policy of utterly destroying the enemy's resistance, root and branch. He waged a war on civilian populations which paralleled the war fought between the opposing armies. French men and women who might have seen troop movements, passing trains, transport carrying artillery, were hanged or shot. His own agents were left to fend for themselves also, as Stieber's view was that an agent should look after himself. He had long previously discovered the power of sexuality to unlock secrets, while selling pornography before the Austrian war. By the time of the Franco-Prussian war human sexual appetites ranked among his favourite weapons. Many of his most valuable agents were handsome young women who were prepared to make certain transitory sacrifices for useful information. In Berlin he maintained the infamous *Grünes Haus* where he laid on a vast variety of activities to satisfy all sexual tastes, however unusual or bizarre. Here were 'entertained' numerous visiting notables, whose activities were dutifully catalogued and recorded. The information was then used by Stieber and his agents in extorting information useful to the political masters he served — by means of blackmail.

Wilhelm Stieber was decorated twenty-seven times by Bismarck and the Emperor of Germany for his services to the state. He died in 1892 and his funeral was attended by the leading political figures of the day from all over Europe. Stieber had caused many of them to live in fear, and they probably wanted to make sure that the king of sleuth-hounds was truly dead.

GEORGE STONER
1916-

ALMA CLARKE was an infant prodigy celebrated in her native Canada for her brilliant musicianship. At the age of seventeen she played with the Toronto Symphony Orchestra and performed a violin and a piano concerto in the same programme. Alma married Caledon Dolling in 1913. Three years later he was killed by a shell at Mametz Wood. Devastated by this loss, Alma threw herself into war work and joined the Scottish Women's Hospital at Royaumant. Twice wounded, she was awarded the Croix de Guerre for her bravery as a stretcher-bearer.

In 1921 Alma married Compton Pakenham and though she gave birth to a son, Christopher, the marriage was not a successful one and the couple separated. The next man in Alma's life was Francis Rattenbury, a successful architect who was married with children. Rattenbury divorced his wife and arranged for Alma's divorce from Compton Pakenham. When Alma married Rattenbury in 1925 he was fifty-eight and she was around twenty-eight (her year of birth has never been exactly established).

Alma and Francis left Canada and settled in Bournemouth where she began to write songs under the pseudonym 'Lozanne'. These songs were published and recorded and were enthusiastically received by the public who responded to the romantic mood of longing in them. *Dark-Haired Marie*, recorded by Peter Dawson, was characteristically hopeful about the triumph of true love:

> I shall come to claim you someday,
> In my arms at last you'll be,
> I shall kiss your lips and love you,
> Dark-Haired Marie.

In contrast to such lyrical affirmations of passion, Alma had some dark moments in her domestic life. Both she and Rattenbury were fond of a drink, she increasingly so. There were occasional quarrels and once Francis blacked her eye, whereupon she bit his arm. She was, most of the time, content with the company of her children, Christopher (by Pakenham) and John (by Rattenbury), but sometimes her romantic nature aspired to something more than the affection of a husband old enough to be her father.

In 1931 Alma hired Irene Riggs to help her in her house — the Villa Madeira, 5 Manor Road, Bournemouth — and in 1934 she advertised for a chauffeur and odd-job-man. She wanted, so the advertisement said, a scout-trained youth, between fourteen and eighteen. She got George Percy Stoner who said he was twenty-two but was, in fact, going on eighteen.

A bricklayer's son, Stoner was forward enough to establish good relations with both Rattenbury and Alma. After a few days he was smoking Rattenbury's cigars, within a month he was enjoying sexual relations with Rattenbury's wife. He moved into the Villa Madeira as Alma's lover, a situation that did not unduly distress Rattenbury, who had lost his sexual drive and told Alma she could do as she wished. Rattenbury's room was on the ground floor; Alma and Stoner each had a bedroom on the first floor. It was an arrangement that suited Stoner perfectly.

Stoner now became the dominant figure in the household and treated Alma as his personal property. He criticised her drinking and occasionally pushed her around. For his part, he took cocaine but would not tolerate any attempt by Alma to put a stop to this habit. Stoner turned out to be an expensive habit for Alma. On a trip to London, Alma and Stoner took separate rooms at the Royal Palace Hotel, Kensington, and she bought him silk pyjamas, shoes, shirts and a suit at Harrods. Alma and Stoner spent three days enjoying themselves in London and returned to Bournemouth on 22 March 1935.

On Saturday, 23 March, Alma played cards with Rattenbury, or 'Ratz' as she called him, in the evening. The next day he was depressed and rambled on about suicide. At 9.30 pm, that Sunday evening, Alma decided to go to bed and went upstairs, leaving her husband with his book in his favourite armchair in the drawing-room. Shortly after 10 pm Irene Riggs, Alma's home-help, came back to the house and went to her bedroom on the first floor, where Alma and Stoner also slept. When, some minutes later, she went to the lavatory she saw Stoner — in his pyjamas — leaning over the banister. 'What is the matter?' she asked him. 'Nothing,' he replied. 'I was looking to see if the lights were out.'

Irene went to bed but was visited, some ten minutes later, by Alma, who wanted a chat. She said that she and Ratz were planning to go to Bridport the next day to see Mr Jenks, one of Ratz's business associates. Alma left and Irene went to sleep — but not for long. She was wakened by the sound of screaming downstairs. Rushing down to the drawing-room, she saw Rattenbury, still in his armchair, with blood on his hair and a black eye. Alma told her: 'Someone has hurt Ratz! Telephone the doctor!' Irene made the phone call and tried to bathe Rattenbury's eye. The two women couldn't move Rattenbury but Stoner appeared and the three of them carried the dying man to his bedroom.

When the doctor came, Alma was hysterical and dosing herself with whisky. When the police came, Alma told them: 'I did it with a mallet.' Early the following morning, Alma was charged with the attempted murder of Francis Rattenbury. She replied, 'About 9 pm on Sunday, 24 March, 1935, I was playing cards with my husband when he dared me to kill him as he wanted to die. I picked up the mallet. He then said, "You have not got the guts to do it." I then hit him with the mallet. I hid the mallet outside the house. I would have shot him if I had had a gun.' At Bournemouth Police Station, Alma reiterated her guilt: 'That's right,' she declared, 'I did deliberately, and I'd do it again.' By the time Rattenbury died, on the morning of 28 March, Alma was in Holloway Prison, where she was charged with the murder of her husband. The case seemed, at that stage, clear enough: a mallet, with the blood and hairs of Rattenbury on it, had been found by the police in Alma's garden and the lady was adamant about her guilt.

Meanwhile, Stoner was telling Irene Riggs that he had collected the mallet from his grandparents' house on the Sunday evening Ratz was murdered. He further informed her that he, not Alma, had killed Rattenbury because he had seen him making love to his wife that Sunday afternoon. On Thursday, 28 March (the day Ratz died) Stoner went to London and, as he got off the train, was arrested on a charge of murder. Irene had passed her information, via a doctor, to the police. On the Friday, Stoner had confessed: 'When I did the job I believed he was asleep. I hit him, and then came upstairs and told Mrs Rattenbury. She rushed down then. You see, I watched through the french windows and saw her kiss him goodnight, then leave the room. I waited, and crept through the french window which was unlocked. I think he must have been asleep when I hit him, still, it ain't much use saying anything. I don't suppose they will let her out yet. You know there should be a doctor with her when they tell her I am arrested, because she will go out of her mind.'

On Tuesday, 2 April, Alma and Stoner appeared before the Bournemouth magistrates and were remanded until 11 April. Since both of them had confessed to the same murder, the Director of Public Prosecutions charged each of them individually though they were to be tried together at the Old Bailey. While she waited in Holloway, Alma composed a song expressing her love for Stoner:

> By some mistake my spirit held you dear,
> But now I wake in agony and fear
> To fading hopes and thought distressed and grey,
> With outstretched hand I put your face away.

> By some mistake you filled my empty days,
> But now I wake to face the parting ways,
> I see your smile, I hear the words you say,
> With no reply I hush your voice away.

> By some mistake, by some divine mistake,
> I dreamed awhile, but now I wake, I wake.
> Yet, dying, dream you kept my vision true,
> I seem to climb to heaven in loving you.

On 28 May 1935 Alma and Stoner went on trial and both pleaded not guilty on legal advice. In the course of the trial, however, it was evident that Stoner was the guilty party. Alma's initial confession, on the night of the attack on Rattenbury, was interpreted as irrational as she had made it under the influence of alcohol and morphia (given to her as a sedative). On the other hand, Stoner's claim to have acted under the influence of cocaine was unconvincing since during his time at Brixton Gaol he showed no signs of drug addiction and he was unclear as to the colour of cocaine (which he thought was brown with black flecks when it is sold as a white substance). When Alma went into the witness-box she explained that Stoner had attacked Rattenbury on his own and had then told her about it. She added that she had had no sexual relations with Rattenbury for about six years and that she was in love with Stoner. Though the public were outraged at Alma, as a woman who supposedly dominated a man around half her age, the jury realised that Stoner was the more assertive personality. On 31 May 1935 Alma was aquitted and Stoner was found guilty of the murder of Rattenbury.

Ironically enough it was Alma — not Stoner — who died as a result of the murder and the ordeal of the trial. Appalled at the thought of Stoner's execution, she went to a Nursing Home in London and studied, obsessively, the press reports of the trial. On 4 June she took the Bournemouth train from Waterloo Station and got off at Christchurch. At the Three Arches bend on the River Avon, she wrote a message on an envelope: 'Eight o'clock, and after so much walking I have got here. Oh, to see the swans and spring flowers, and to smell them . . . It is beautiful here. What a lovely world, really. It must be easier to be hanged than to do the job oneself, especially under these circumstances of being watched all the time. Pray God nothing stops me tonight . . . God bless my children and look after them.'

She took a knife from her handbag, stabbed herself six times in the chest, and fell into the water. At her inquest, the coroner read from a letter Alma had written on 3 June: 'If I only thought it would help Stoner I would stay on, but it has been pointed out to me only too vividly that I cannot help him — and that is my death sentence.'

Stoner broke down in tears when he heard, in Pentonville Prison, the news of Alma's death. More than 32,000 people petitioned for a reprieve for Stoner who, now that Alma was dead, suggested that she was reponsible for the attack on Rattenbury. It was a confused situation and, on 25 June, Stoner's death sentence was commuted to penal servitude for life. A model prisoner, he served only seven years of his sentence and was released, in 1942, at the age of twenty-six. He subsequently fought in World War Two, married and settled down.

Until the publication, in 1980, of *Tragedy in Three Voices: The Rattenbury Murder* — by Sir Michael Havers, Peter Shankland and Anthony Barrett — a clear motive was never established. Stoner could hardly have killed Rattenbury out of jealousy, since Rattenbury had ceased to have sexual relations with Alma. Moreover, Rattenbury was quite content to have Stoner in his home though he knew he was sleeping with Alma.

On the night he was attacked, Rattenbury had announced his plan to go, next day, to Bridport to see a Mr Jenks. Rattenbury was engaged on a plan for the construction of a block of flats and Jenks's support was essential for this project. Havers, Shankland and Barrett talked to Mrs Daphne Kingham, the sister of Alma's second husband. When Mrs Kingham went to Holloway prison to see Alma, 'she asked Alma why Stoner had done it, and she replied he was angry because he had overheard Rattenbury telling her to make up to the man — presumably Mr Jenks at Bridport — who could arrange the finance for the projected block of flats, even expecting her to have an affair with him if necessary.'

Havers, Shankland and Barrett draw the following conclusion: 'If Stoner believed, perhaps mistakenly from scraps of conversation imperfectly overheard, that Rattenbury intended to exploit Alma's well-known magnetic effect on men for commercial reasons, we can understand and sympathise with the desperate action he took to prevent her going to Bridport. At last; forty-five years after the trial and Alma's death, we have a motive in which we can believe.' In a fragment of song, composed by Alma a few days before her death, it is clear she felt responsible, in some way, for Stoner's guilt:

> We have lived together
>   We two;
> We have loved together
>   I and you;
> We'll together die
>   You and I —
> We'll swing together.

HARRY KENDALL THAW

1872-1947

HARRY THAW was the son of a very wealthy Pittsburgh family whose riches derived from cornering the coke market. He was well educated and rather spoiled by his mother. Signs of wildness in his behaviour showed themselves at an early stage in his life. He had a particularly violent temper and a tendency to daydream. In an attempt to tame his son, his father cut Harry's allowance to $2,000 a year. His loving mother made up for this by granting him an additional $80,000.

Harry was now in a position to live out some of his deeper urges and fantasies. He had his own apartment in a New York brothel. Posing as a showbusiness magnate he was able to entice star-struck young girls by the promise of a career before the footlights. He soon earned an unsavoury reputation, not only as a seducer and debaucher of youth, but as a sadist. One or two of his aspiring hopefuls were beaten senseless. These things got to the ears of the Madame who ran the house. Her evidence was later to be useful.

A young and beautiful girl, Evelyn Nesbit, came to New York from Pittsburgh. She had ambitions in show business. At the age of sixteen she was in the chorus for a New York show. She came to the attention of the celebrated American architect and rake, Stanford White. There were several splendid buildings in New York to tesify to his skill, and his reputation as a *roué* was constantly fanned by rumour. He had several love-nests in the city, including one in the tower at Madison Gardens, where he had a room equipped with a red velvet swing. Here the young girls he tempted to accompany him would swing to and fro while Stanford White drank champagne and ogled at them. When he was drunk enough, the serious business of the evening would be completed. He became obsessed with Evelyn Nesbit and enticed her to the room with the red velvet swing. There, after the usual routine had been gone through, he seduced her. White was a generous man and made her many gifts and presents of money. He was also bountiful to Evelyn's mother. Nevertheless, Evelyn left him and married Harry Thaw. He had even more money to spend on her than White seemed to have.

The marriage was scarcely blissful and Evelyn was soon acquainted with Harry's peculiar appetites. He was terribly jealous and convinced himself that she had been White's mistress. He beat the secret out of her while on an ocean liner, making the crossing to Europe. He insisted that whenever she referred to White she simply called him 'the Beast' or 'the Bastard'. Thaw had decided now to take his revenge and on the evening of 25 June 1906 Harry and Evelyn went to see the premier of the show *Mam'zelle Champagne*. At this social occasion, attended by New York's upper crust, Harry Thaw shot Stanford White at close range during one of the production numbers.

He was arrested for murder and while in custody awaiting trial he continued to play the stock market and eat superb meals sent in to him from the best restaurant in town, Delmonico's. His mother spent a fortune on his defence, employing one of the best lawyers from the Californian bar, Delphin Delmas. The District Attorney was determined to get a conviction. 'With all his millions, Thaw is a fiend!' he exclaimed. 'No matter how rich a man he is, he cannot get away with murder — not in New York County!'

The trial lasted seven months. The defence pleaded insanity, and Thaw tried to convince the court that voices told him to commit the crime: 'I never wanted to kill him . . . Providence took charge of the situation.'

Some of the testimony was even more peculiar. One of the medical witnesses called by the defence, Dr Carl Wickland, who attempted to support Thaw's claim of being controlled from outside by voices which he believed spoke to him and urged him to kill White, had a wife who was a medium. She claimed that a spirit had communicated to her that Thaw's plea was correct. The voice she heard from the great beyond was the voice of one who had urged him on to do the killing. Mrs Wickland testified that the voice had said to her during a seance: 'I killed Stanford White. He deserved death. He had trifled too long with our daughters.' She also claimed to have messages from Harry Thaw's dead father: 'He is sensitive to spirit influence and has been all his life. He was always erratic and so excitable that we were afraid to correct him for fear he would become insane. But I see our mistake now.' Harry's father was also aware, from his side of the great divide, that Harry had been 'a tool in the hands of earth-bound spirits, evil spirits that ordered death. He was obsessed by revengeful spirits when he killed Stanford White.'

The defence advanced the theory that Thaw was suffering from 'dementia Americana' — a neurosis found only among some North American males and showing itself in an obsessive belief that their wives were sacred. The jury brought in their verdict — Thaw was Not Guilty on the ground of his insanity at the time of the crime. Harry Thaw was sentenced to life in the New York Asylum for the Criminally Insane. Years passed and Harry's loving mother spent thousands of dollars trying to get him out. In 1913 he could wait no longer and he escaped. He was picked up in Canada and sent back. In the meantime Evelyn Nesbit had been earning her keep as a stage performer. The case had made her famous. A son born to her was claimed by its mother to be Harry Thaw's child, fathered during a visit to the asylum when a guard was bribed to leave the happy couple to themselves. Harry denied this, though Evelyn sued for financial support.

In 1915 Harry Thaw was finally diagnosed as sane by experts whose testimony was good enough for the New York courts. He divorced Evelyn and began again to live it up in his characteristic ways. Within four years he was in trouble with the law again, this time for whipping a young boy named Gump. He attempted to buy off the boy's family — the rumoured figure was half a million dollars. He was sent back to the asylum until 1922.

He was fifty years old when he was released and he roamed the world's pleasure spots, posing as a movie mogul and trying to pull young hopeful females. His behaviour was frequently bizarre and frightening. He died in 1947.

JOSEPH WEIL

1877-1937

PSYCHOLOGY AND SOCIOLOGY are often needed to explain the sometimes astonishing success of frauds and confidence tricksters. This is particularly well illustrated in the astonishing case of Joseph Weil, 'The Yellow Kid', who claimed when he retired in 1934, that he had 'earned' over eight million dollars. It is true that he was a very intelligent and cunning man, and that these intellectual gifts were matched by good looks and immense personal charm, set off with an immaculate dress sense. But Weil could only have triumphed in a society — such as the United States immediately after the First World War — which was conditioned to believe that luck was just around the corner; that technology could 'fix' anything; that fortunes were to be made by the quick and the smart; and that everything you read in the newspapers was true.

Joseph Weil was born in Chicago in 1877 at the time when that city was vigorously justifying its claim to be the leading industrial and commercial centre in the mid-west, having defeated St Louis, Missouri, in the race for that reputation. The essential basis of Weil's technique was the exploitation of cupidity and credulity. He once read in the paper of a man who had put his

money into a disused gold-mine which, it was claimed, was worked out. The lucky investor made a fortune, as there was still plenty of gold in the mine. Weil noticed how other readers were impressed with the tale of the smart-Alec who made a quick fortune. Weil had the story made up on newsprint with his own name and photograph and went on tour through the mid-west.

He would arrive in town and leave his personal tailor-made newspaper in the reading room at the local library. He would then sell shares in his gold mine. 'Of course it's true! Go and look it up in the newspapers!' Willing investors, convinced that they, too, could make a few bucks, happily parted with their dollars to buy shares in his lucky strike. He would then pack up and leave, never to be seen again.

In Detroit he managed to sell some pills to an automobile industrialist after asserting that these pills had the capacity scientifically to change water into gasolene. This raked in several thousand dollars. Another celebrated trick of his required suberb stage management: this was the great bank rip-off. He rented a disused building which had formerly housed a bank. He hired an entire cast including bank clerks, security staff, customers — all recruited from acquaintances in the criminal world. People came in and deposited funds to open accounts. Once the 'bank' had secured really worthwhile customers, relieving them of their thousands as a first deposit, his real ploy came into effect. Behind the scenes the entire act was dismantled and Weil paid off his cast and decamped with the takings.

His stock-in-trade was his own undoing. He traded on his good looks and impressive appearance. Personal publicity was of course his main weapon. But, by 1934 he had become so well known that he was liable to be arrested the minute he set foot in any town. So he hung up his hat for good. He'd made his pile anyway. His own view of his career and his customers was: 'They were never any good. They wanted something for nothing. I gave them nothing for nothing.'

174

STANLEY CLIFFORD WEYMAN

1891-1960

AS THE BARD said, one man in his time plays many parts. Stanley Weyman certainly did. He was variously diplomat, air force officer, physician, head of protocol at the US State Department, lawyer, journalist and press officer with the Thai delegation at the United Nations. The only blemish on this distinguished and truly varied career was that he was not properly qualified for any of these positions. He was, in fact, one of the greatest imposters of modern times.

He was born Stanley Weinberg, of poor parents in Brooklyn. He was a very bright boy and early in his life decided to use his quick wits to compensate for his lack of socio-economic advantage in the rat-race of modern life. When he was barely twenty he passed himself off as the Consul-Delegate to Morocco in New York. This was a role he exploited to the full and soon ran up bills in hotels, stores and restaurants. The court sent him to reform school. Here he played another role — that of the young offender anxious to reform. He was paroled and went on to his next act, that of an officer in the navy. He was put inside again. Then he tried another diplomatic position, the Romanian Consul-General. In New York he invited the officers of the United States vessel *Wyoming* to dine with him at the Astor Hotel. He was arrested. He then tried a military 'career' and, as a high ranking Army Air Corps officer, he inspected the armory in Brooklyn.

Tiring of uniformed roles he next tried the medical profession and did rather well as medical consultant to a large building firm in Peru. He longed to return to the USA so, when Princess Fatima of Afghanistan visited his home town he appeared as a Lieutenant Commander, the State Department's head of protocol. It was all so simple. He informed her royal highness that it was the done thing to reward all the various officials who organised her visit. He had the responsibility, he explained, of actually dishing out the money to these important cogs in the wheels of international diplomacy. She handed over ten thousand dollars. He was so successful in this part that he arranged a visit to the White House, where he posed with her and US President Warren Harding.

He next appeared as a hospital administrator whose task it was to receive the fees from patients who came to have operations from a celebrated Austrian surgeon. Then he did a short season in jail.

At the funeral of Rudolph Valentino he appeared as an old friend of the Great Lover. He thus broke into the world of showbusiness, and became personal physician to Pola Negri, star of *Madame du Barry*, *Forbidden Paradise* and *Hotel Imperial*. Other parts he tried for size, including an interesting spell as a lawyer and several academic posts, were stints in medical school and law school. The fear of the draft in the Second World War offered a new departure in his career, and he set up business as a consultant advising on various methods of keeping out of the armed forces. By popular request he reappeared in prison.

He then tried the media, to which his skills were singularly appropriate. Working at the United Nations as a correspondent for a news service, he was approached by the Thai delegation who wanted a press officer. He would then have been given full diplomatic accreditation. This prompted one of the few honest and straightforward acts of his life: he contacted the State Department to enquire if this would affect his US citizenship. His name was still on file and his reputation was by no means forgotten. He paid the price all stars pay for being famous — he was recognised. This door to his career in the diplomatic service was quietly closed in his face. He next tried an ordinary honest to goodness career. He got a job as night manager in a hotel in New York. The job killed him. He was shot dead while attempting to protect the hotel's safe from criminals.

JONATHAN WILD

1682-1725

THE CASE OF Jonathan Wild is one of the most brilliant success stories in English criminal history, and in many ways one of the most base. What makes his tale so black is not so much his offences against society's rules, as a strong revulsion from his appalling self-seeking motives, and his readiness to sacrifice colleagues on the altar of his ambitions. Yet in some ways he was a victim of his time and his social class. Living and working over a hundred years before the foundation of the first metropolitan police force, when law enforcement was left either to incompetent watchmen or taken into the individual's hands, Wild realised that a vast fortune was to be earned by rationalising crime as an industry — by organising gangs of thieves and systematising a method of receiving stolen property for the owners, on payment of a reasonable fee. Wild's achievement was to make his business concern an essential part of the infrastructure of the criminal economy of London. He acted as an agency servicing both the criminal underworld as well as the honest citizenry who simply wanted to get back their stolen property.

Wild was born in Wolverhampton, the son of a carpenter. He was the eldest son and his father intended he should follow his trade. For some reason, his father changed his mind, and apprenticed his son to a buckle-maker in Birmingham. Jonathan served his apprenticeship, married and seemed about to settle down. But he felt life had more to offer than the life of a journeyman buckle-maker, and suddenly he abandoned his wife and child and went to London. His appetites soon outstripped his income as a tradesman and he was imprisoned for debt. In Wood Street prison Wild served another apprenticeship — when he left he was a graduate of criminal arts seeking an opportunity to put theories into practice.

The *Newgate Calendar* details the curriculum he had been privileged to follow: 'During his residence . . . Wild assiduously cultivated the company of the criminals who were his fellow prisoners, and attended to their accounts of the exploits in which they had been engaged with singular satisfaction.' It was while attending these studies that he met the young woman who was to become his wife, Mary Milliner, a notorious pick-pocket and prostitute.

The happy couple set up house together and, by dutiful application of their various skills, they soon gathered enough capital to open a tavern in Cock-alley, by Cripplegate church. This became the meeting place of London's criminal fraternity, which Wild soon decided to organise. The idea was first prompted in his mind by his contemplation of one of the basic problems of the thieves' craft — disposing of stolen goods at a reasonable price. The seriousness of the crisis was increased by the fact that an Act had recently been passed making it an offence to handle stolen goods.

He called a mass meeting of all the brotherhood. Most pawnbrokers, he told them, would only advance about a quarter of the value of goods. Even the best professionals would starve on such returns for their efforts. The risks of disposing of stolen goods by selling them to those not personally known to the thieves were considerable and might lead to arrest and conviction. You did not know whom you could trust in London. They all agreed that since the new Act things had come to a pretty pass. Wild's answer was to rationalise the entire operation. The thieves would go on his books, and when they had stolen everything, they were to bring it to him. He would then contact the owners and offer to restore the item, for a fee: 'by which means greater sums would be raised than by depositing them with the pawnbrokers, while the thieves would be perfectly secure from detection.'

The scheme involved Jonathan Wild in some considerable role playing, as he had to present himself to persons who had been robbed as one who deeply sympathised with their plight, but that some suspected property had been stopped by a very honest man of his acquaintance, and that if, by a happy coincidence, their goods were among them then he'd return them to their rightful owners. The broker would, naturally, be expecting some slight

recognition for his trouble and honesty . . . At the same time Wild had to assure his gang of thieves that he was working on their behalf, and would strive to his utmost to see that the best possible price was paid for the goods they brought in to him. The system worked. The thieves made a living. Jonathan Wild made a fortune.

His name got around and people knew where to come to get their property back. To make transactions easier he even opened an office, which was frequented by multitudes of people in the hope of recovering property and effects. Each customer had to pay a crown in consideration of receiving his advice. He was most fastidious in his transactions, taking down the minutest details of missing items, names and addresses, the rewards to be offered and anything else which might make the business easier to function. Once he had found out the highest price a customer would go to in order to get an item back, he'd request them to call at his office for its delivery. Everyone was satisfied. One interesting development was the fact that his operations now put a price on items not for their intrinsic worth or for what they could be sold for in the market, as being gold, silver or antique in value etc. Items of *personal* value — pocket-books, watches, trinkets, books of accounts — now became the object of interest to thieves. They were the items that Jonathan Wild knew he could drive a good bargain on, because those who had lost them would be ready to pay a goodly price to get them back. And he drove a very hard bargain.

His business prospered and he sported the best clothes, the best lace and gold braid, and wore a sword. He looked after his thieves well, paid them reasonable sums for their efforts and always endeavoured to help them if they fell foul of the law. But if they betrayed him then he would not hesitate to betray them to the authorities. When he was asked how he could carry on a business with thieves and yet be able to deny that he was in league with robbers, he would always reply: 'My acquaintance among thieves is very extensive, and when I receive information of a robbery, I make enquiry after the suspected parties, and leave word at proper places, that if the goods are left where I appoint, the reward shall be paid, and no questions asked. Surely no imputation of guilt can fall upon me; for I hold no interviews with the robbers, nor are the goods given into my possession.'

A few examples will serve to show how proficient Wild's agency truly was. A wealthy lady once visited Piccadilly and her servants, being left in charge of her sedan chair, left it unattended to restore their energies in a public house. When they returned, it was missing. The two men then went to Jonathan Wild, and, having detailed the loss and a fee being mutually negotiated, they were told to return to his office in two days' time. The men came back and Wild then demanded a considerable reward. This was typical of his method — raising hopes, and then cranking up the price as high as he thought it would go. He then told them to go to the chapel in Lincoln's-Inn-Fields the next morning during prayers. The two chairmen went as directed and there, under the piazzas of the chapel, was the missing sedan chair, containing, as promised, the velvet seat, curtains and all other furniture.

Another great source of income for Wild was claiming the rewards for the apprehension of particular criminals. Being so well acquainted with the underworld for professional purposes, he could usually cause wanted offenders to be turned in, and seemed to suffer little in the way of conscience when sending colleagues to the gallows. Wild was obviously personally responsible for the planning and execution of numerous crimes, including immensely profitable robberies and a few murders. In the end his very success destroyed him.

He began to be faced with a very serious problem, that of disposing of stolen property which was not claimed by its owners. So much of it was accumulated by his trusty gang of efficient confederates that he simply lacked the warehouse space to store it. He conceived the idea of shipping it to the continent and selling it off. He bought a sloop and put this enterprise into the hands of one Roger Johnson, who was to be in control of Jonathan Wild's enterprises in such places as Bruges, Ghent, Brussels, Amsterdam, Ostend. Things went quite well but then Johnson fell out with some of his crew who impeached him. Wild saved him on this occasion, but Johnson also quarrelled with a certain Thomas Edwards, who kept a house of resort for thieves in Long Lane. Both charged the other with felony and were apprehended. Wild bailed Johnson but Edwards was not prosecuted. As soon as Thomas Edwards was released he gave information against Wild.

Jonathan Wild's premises and warehouse were now searched by the authorities and much stolen property was recognised. Wild caused the arrest of Edwards, by insinuating he was Johnston and claiming that the goods belonged to him. But Edwards/'Johnson' got bailed out, tracked the real Johnson down and handed him over to a peace-officer. Wild managed to rescue Johnson by provoking a riot in the ale-house where he was being detained, but was himself arrested by the high constable of Holborn division on 15 February 1725.

Although he was charged under no less than nine counts, including consorting with thieves, forming a corporation of thieves, running a gang of thieves, associating with known felons and those who returned from transportation before their time was due, supporting felons with money, receiving stolen goods, selling stolen property abroad and procuring false evidence for blood money, convicting him did not prove an easy matter. He was finally indicted under an Act passed in the fourth year of the reign of George I, which was read in court:

> And whereas there are divers persons who have secret acquaintance with felons, and who make it their business to help persons to their stolen goods, and by that means gain money from them, which is divided between them and the felons, whereby they greatly encourage such offenders. Be it enacted . . . that whenever any person taketh money or reward, directly or indirectly, under pretence, or upon account of helping any person or persons to any stolen goods or chattels, every such person do apprehend, or cause to be apprehended, such felon who stole the same, and give evidence against him shall be guilty of felony, according to the nature of the felony committed in stealing such goods, and in such and the same manner as if such offender had stolen such goods and chattels, in the manner, and with such circumstances, as the same were stolen.

If it could be proved that Jonathan Wild was an accessory to felony, then he would stand as liable to be found guilty himself of such felony as if he himself had committed it. He was found so guilty, on Monday, 24 May 1725.

He hoped daily for royal mercy to grant him reprieve as he had been so instrumental in getting goods returned to so many grateful owners. He feared to attend chapel for devotions, saying that there were so many who were exasperated with him that his devotions might be disturbed by their insulting behaviour. He exhibited other signs of agitation and infirmity.

He tried to poison himself with laudanum and was taken in the cart to Tyburn in a state of near insensibility, followed by a howling mob who pelted him with stones and dirt and execrated him as the most dreadful villain that ever disgraced human nature. He still seemed stunned when the cart arrived at the scaffold. The executioner was prepared to give him time properly to recover himself and make himself ready for the awful process the law required. The crowd became enraged and threatened the executioner with his own life if he delayed matters any further.

Thus ended the career of Jonathan Wild. His body was buried in St Pancras churchyard, but a few nights afterwards was taken up for the use of surgeons. At midnight a hearse and six horses was waiting at the end of Fig Lane. The next day the coffin was found empty. The receiver of these stolen goods was never apprehended, nor were the goods ever discovered.

THOMAS JAMES WISE

1859-1937

WITH A GENUINE passion for books and a good working knowledge of bibliography, Thomas J Wise built up the Ashley Library, an important collection he later sold to the British Museum. On the basis of this and his uncanny ability to satisfy the needs of the American book market, Wise became a greatly respected figure who was friendly with the likes of Edmund Gosse. In 1913 Gosse wrote to Wise: 'I love to be associated with you in your beautiful and disinterested labours.' Gosse also predicted that he and Wise would 'go down in posterity, hand in hand, as two entirely conscientious bibliographers'. In fact Gosse's association with Wise has done his reputation no good at all. Wise himself is regarded as the most audacious literary forger of his time.

As a young man, Wise worked as a clerk in the City and his proximity to so much money may have encouraged him to enrich himself by exploiting his knowledge of the book trade. For Wise was a clerk with a difference: he wrote poems and published *Verses* in 1882; he also produced facsimiles for the Shelley Society.

Wise realised that collectors would pay a lot of money for rare items and so set about the creation of spurious first editions. What he did was so simple, yet effective. He would take a text from a published book and reprint it as a pamphlet with an earlier, and bogus, date. Thus, from the 1850 edition of Elizabeth Barrett Browning's *Poems* he lifted the sequence 'Sonnets from the Portuguese' and had it printed as a pamphlet, *Sonnets* by E B B , with the date 1847. According to Wise this pamphlet had been printed at Reading under the supervision of Mary Russell Mitford, a friend of the poet's. Wise's story was believed and *Sonnets* circulated as a valuable first edition. In 1901 a copy was sold for $440 in New York; in 1930 a copy went for $1,250.

In his bibliography of Swinburne, Wise wrote: 'easy as it appears to be to fabricate reprints of rare books, it is in actual practice absolutely impossible to do so in such a manner that detection cannot follow the result'. Wise escaped detection until late in his life. In October 1933 John Carter and Graham Pollard, two scholars, approached Wise and informed him that they planned to publish a book implying that he had knowingly sold forged first editions. Wise described Carter and Pollard as 'sewer rats' and refused to co-operate with them. However, he was worried and summoned one Herbert Gorfin to his presence.

Gorfin had worked for Wise first as an office-boy then as his agent. When Wise retired from the business of forging first editions, he sold the main bulk of his stocks to Gorfin. Now that Carter and Pollard were closing in on him, Wise wanted to destroy the incriminating evidence. He offered Gorfin £25 for the return of the bogus pamphlets. When Gorfin did not immediately accept, Wise increased the offer to £400. Gorfin took the money and returned the pamphlets, which were burned in the presence of Wise's lawyer.

Carter and Pollard published *An Enquiry into the Nature of Certain*

Nineteenth Century Pamphlets (1934) and though they did not directly accuse Wise of fraud, they condemned him for being involved in the distribution of the so-called first editions: 'Mr Wise, by his credulity, by his vanity in his own possessions, by his dogmatism, by abuse of his eminence in the bibliographical world, has dealt a blow to the prestige of an honourable science, the repercussions of which will be long and widely felt.' By studying the paper and typography in Wise's pamphlets, Carter and Pollard established the element of fakery. For example, Wise used paper containing esparto, a material introduced to paper-making in the 1860s. By using this paper in editions claiming to predate the 1860s Wise was clearly guilty of fraud.

In his *Books and Book Collectors* (London, 1956) Carter describes Wise as a man motivated by vanity and greed: 'What put Wise head and shoulders above any other recorded practitioner in fraudulent printing was his early realisation (after a few experiments) that *imitations* of books are always discovered: that you must *invent* an edition if you are to avoid the untimely fatal comparison with a genuine original. If he could then get his product on to the right shelves and into the right reference books, it was possible, as Wise proved in spite of mistakes, to get away with murder. His wide-ranging operations were finally unmasked only by the application to each pamphlet of such technical tests of its type-design and paper-content as were hardly to be anticipated in the 1890's, the decade of his main activity as a forger.'

When Wise died he was a discredited man, destined to fall even further from scholarly favour. Even his Ashley Library had its faults. It transpired that when pages were missing from a book owned by Wise, he went to the British Museum and stole the relevant pages which were then inserted in his own copy. Edmund Gosse, who was duped by Wise and unwittingly assisted him by praising the forged first editions, said: 'I am sure that on the Day of Judgement Wise will tell the good Lord that Genesis is not the true first edition.'

WILLIAM CHARLES YELVERTON, 4th VISCOUNT AVONMORE

1824-83

WILLIAM CHARLES YELVERTON was born into a distinguished Anglo-Irish family with legal and military connections. His grandfather was Barry Yelverton, first Baron Avonmore, who had been Attorney General and Chief Baron of the Court of Exchequer, a Viscount of the Irish peerage and Baron of the United Kingdom. William Charles was born in Woolwich, and entered the Royal Artillery, soon becoming a captain and a major during his service in the Crimean War, 1854-56. His name became a household word as the result of his association with Maria Theresa Longworth (1832-81) with whom he passed through a form of marriage ceremony in 1857.

This marriage was the subject of much dispute and litigation, the several trials which it caused making Yelverton notorious. Maria Theresa was brought up a strict Roman Catholic and Yelverton was a Protestant. He claimed that a marriage to Maria would ruin him, and that, for this reason, and this alone, the ceremony had to be secret. It was inferred in later legal proceedings that he promised Maria he would marry her with the full knowledge and support of his family at a later date, but that he regarded the marriage in 1857 as just as legal and binding as any marriage could be. The couple were married by a priest at the Roman Catholic chapel, Restrevor, Ireland. The priest was aware, and later admitted in court that he was aware, that it was a felony to join a Protestant and a Roman Catholic in holy matrimony.

Yelverton and Maria consummated the marriage and lived as man and wife, though they were frequently separated. In 1858 he married the widow of Edward Forbes, Professor of Natural History at the University of Edinburgh (who had died in 1854). Yelverton repudiated his marriage to Maria Theresa Longworth. In 1861, the validity of this first marriage was established in the Irish court in a sensational trial, but annulled in the Scottish court, in 1862. The Scottish judgement was confirmed by the House of Lords in 1864. Nevertheless, Yelverton emerges with little credit from this affair, and it is pretty clear that he had been deeply attracted to a very beautiful young woman whom he deceived, enjoyed and then abandoned when something else turned up. He knew that his family would disapprove of his association with a young Roman Catholic woman and therefore kept his liaison secret from them. He was able to persuade Maria to go through with it, although she was obviously not happy about the arrangements, by saying it had to be clandestine for the time being, but that he would go through 'another' service of marriage with her in due course, when the time was right for him to approach his family. He was hissed in court and witnesses were openly barracked. He was suspended from military duties in 1861. Maria published several novels and *The Yelverton Correspondence* in 1863.

Yelverton's motives were openly admitted even by his defence counsel, Abraham Brewster, who suggested on the one hand that Maria was very taken with Yelverton and resolved to pursue him — having her mind clouded with Sir Walter Scott and French novels and romances — and that she hoped to compel him ultimately to lead her honourably to the altar; but that on the other hand, Yelverton was infatuated with such a charming young creature and resolved to enjoy her. 'The view I take of the case is this,' Brewster said:

> The lady believed what was her heart's desire; but although she worked with energy and determination to get married to him, he had no intention in his mind at all. I repeat that I do not seek to justify Yelverton in the slightest degree for his violation either of the moral or of any other law; all I say is that it must be perfectly plain to any one who read the correspondence that Yelverton had in his mind all through a thorough determination not to marry her. That he was enthralled by her notwithstanding, there is no doubt, and very probably he did think that they might live together and enjoy each other's society, he remaining free. To be sure, it is a dreadful thing to conceive such a thing for the woman. Every one must know the dangers which a woman, living in this state, was exposed to, although it is not uncommon that such concoctions, after a long term, were merged into the sacred relations of lawful married life. The lady's case is that, during all the time covered by this extraordinary correspondence, she was engaged to be married. Nowhere in these letters is the word marriage mentioned . . .

The verdict of the trial in Dublin went in favour of Maria Theresa, and disgraced Yelverton. It was received with great public rejoicing. A contemporary account records:

> One of the greatest demonstrations of popular enthusiasm that perhaps ever was witnessed in Dublin, took place as the Honourable Mrs Yelverton proceeded from the Four Courts to the Gresham Hotel . . . Over fifty thousand people frantic with joy proceeded to bid her welcome as she issued from the hall . . . From an early hour in evening thousands flocked in from every quarter of the city, and waited in feverish anxiety the result of the deliberations of the jury . . . When it was known that the jury had retired to consider their verdict . . . the crowds became feverish with excitement . . . Shortly after six o'clock, the cheering in the interior of the court was taken up outside, and when it was known that the Hon Mrs Yelverton had triumphed, one loud cheer burst from every mouth, and was again and again repeated. Hats were thrown into the air, and every external demonstration of delight was evidenced by all present. Men shook hands with people they did not know, save by the fact that they looked as glad as themselves . . .

Although subsequent proceedings were to give the verdict to Yelverton and his marriage to Maria was legally annulled, public sympathy remained very much with her. It could not better have been articulated than it was by her counsel, Edward Sullivan. Describing her just before her 'marriage' to Yelverton, Sullivan said in court:

> She was then a lovely and accomplished girl. I believe as lovely a woman as ever breathed the breath of life. You should not expect to see her so now. She has changed. Her cheek is paler and thinner than it should be for one so young. She has gone through years of suffering which a soul of heroism alone could endure. When you have heard her story from herself, you will ask yourselves how great must have been her mind, how fresh the sense of her own character, to enable her to bear up against the infamous treatment to which she has been subjected . . .

Yelverton's counsel, Mr Brewster, paid lavish praise to her charms and asserted that the best thing that could happen to her would be that she was severed from Major Yelverton, so that she could make a handsome match somewhere else:

> Of course, gentlemen, everybody must see that she is a woman of most extraordinary talents — perhaps of greater talent than you ever had an opportunity of seeing before. For my part, I never saw her like. But she is more than a woman of talent — she is a woman who has had that talent cultivated to the highest possible pitch . . . I presume from the noises that I heard from time to time during the progress of this trial, and from none more than my young friends behind me (the junior bar) that if she should be disappointed on this occasion she will not be disappointed long; for, if I don't mistake, no person since the beginning of time has ever enlisted a greater number of ardent sympathisers and admirers . . .

Major Yelverton did not make such a good impression. The court reporter describes him as being of medium height and rather slenderly built:

> His erect bearing indicated the soldier, and his manners and demeanour were those of a polished man of the world. His features are by no means striking, with the exception of the eyes, which are deeply set and penetrating in their gaze. His forehead is not large, but is well formed, and shows the marks of mental cultivation. His mouth is well shaped and rather voluptuous, clearly evincing those strong passions which, by his own confession, form so prominent a portion of his character. His hair is of a light brown colour, and rather thin on the crown of his head. He wears large sandy whiskers and moustache. Nothing could surpass the self-possession, coolness, and deliberation with which he gave his evidence, even those portions of it which, by the revolting cynicism of their avowals, caused a thrill of horror to run through the crowded court . . .

The pathetic figure cut by Maria, the caddishness of Yelverton, and the high drama of the trial in Dublin really caught the public imagination and prompted much street literature and balladry. One example, *The Lady Beat the Soldier* makes comic play of the fact that counsel had the title 'serjeant' and puts forward the idea of the bold captain being thoroughly drilled by Maria's advocate, Serjeant Sullivan:

185

YOU are all aware as well as me,
   There has been great consternation,
In Dublin has a trial been
   Which excited all the nation;
There was a blooming lady, who
   Did wed a soldier laddie,
And he was afraid of his mamma,
   And he dare not tell his daddy.
The lady licked the soldier well,
   Cause he refused to take her,
And the Irish lads were all so glad,
   To see her beat the Major.

He is the son of a great lord,
   Stand at ease, and order;
He took a bonny, blooming maid
   Over the Scottish border;
He told her pretty tales of love,
   Embraced her round the middle,
And when they were at Gretna Green
   The Major caught the fiddle.

He took then to Paddy's land,
   So gentle, meek, and clever,
He disgraced the Holy Church of Rome,
   He did, the naughty fellow;
He vowed that she was not his wife,
   And caused a pretty bother,
He clapped his knapsack on his back,
   Then went and married another.

Brave Serjeant Sullivan was the man,
   No lawyer could be bolder,
With gallant Whiteside went to work,
   And fired away at the soldier;
While every upright person there
   The lady pitied, who was round her,
The sheepish Major droop'd his head,
   And pop went the powder.

He was a Major, a Lord's son,
   As evil as a monkey,
All the religion that he cared about,
   Was who had got most money;
The fool was of no creed at all,
   The Church of Rome defied a sad way,
He could swear a lie thro' a nine inch wall,
   And cover his nob with pipeclay.

Now like a brick the soldier's licked,
    And his coronet is troubling,
She shamed him in the Four Courts,
    In the good old town of Dublin;
They made the naughty soldier jump,
    If the ladies could have caught him,
They would have ducked him underneath the pump,
    And better manners taught him.

He drove the lady round and round,
    While riches she had any;
To Waterford and to Belfast,
    To Bantry and Kilkenny;
He disgraced the Holy Church of Rome,
    The naughty soldier laddy,
And all because he was afraid
    Of a flogging from his daddy.

He had made a pretty kettle of fish,
    He has lost his wife and baby,
The Dublin lasses shout huzza!
    May Heaven bless the lady;
She like a brick the Major licked,
    The naughty wicked soldier,
He bolted out of Dublin town,
    With his firelock on his shoulder.

If to Gretna Green he goes again,
    To play his hey down diddle,
Let the ladies pray both night and day,
    That he may get the fiddle!
And then go mad to Ballinafad,
    Where they will stand no parley,
So cut your stick, your Irish licked,
    And a regular guy is Charlie.

He married a wife and then made strife,
    Such terrible tales he told her,
It was such sport in the Dublin court,
    To see Sullivan drill the soldier.